the Unofficial Guide™ to Study Abroad

Ann M. Moore, Ph.D.

IDG Books Worldwide, Inc.
An International Data Group Company
Foster City, CA • Chicago, IL • Indianapolis, IN
• New York, NY

1st Edition

IDG Books Worldwide, Inc.
An International Data Group Company
919 E. Hillsdale Boulevard
Suite 400
Foster City, CA 94404

An ARCO Book

For general information on IDG Books Worldwide's books in the U.S., please call our Consumer Customer Service department at 800-762-2974. For reseller information, including discounts and premium sales, please call our Reseller Customer Service department at 800-434-3422.

Library of Congress information available upon request

ISBN: 0-02-863700-3

Manufactured in the United States of America

10 9 8 7 6 5 4 3 2 1

For all the world travelers in my family: my mother and brother, my husband, my children and grandchildren, and for the cats who stay at home and wait for us.

Acknowledgments

Many people offered to provide information for this project and directed me to the wealth of materials available about work, study, and travel abroad on the Internet, and in numerous handbooks and publications, so that the resources could appear in this guide. Among the many who offered assistance are the staff of the American Council for Teachers of Russian office in Washington, D.C., for advice about obtaining a visa for study abroad in Russia; Cindy Chalou, who created a Web site of ideas from Michigan State students for financing study abroad; Stephanie Clements, for information about independent lending sources for study abroad; Todd Davis, for permission to use data from the edition of *Open Doors* that will appear in print early in 2000; Norma Day-Vines, a visionary program director who identified key objectives for study abroad programs; Angela DeGruccio, who compiled a list of Web sites of pre-departure orientation information; Andy Dusenbery, who suggested books to help get students and teachers started on keeping journals and writing about the study abroad experience; and Ronald Hallett, an experienced resident director, who gave valuable suggestions about host family etiquette, safety precautions, and visiting Paris.

Assistance was also offered by David Larsen for clarifying the role of several international education organizations in the compilation of the health and safety guidelines; Robert McLaughlin, who suggested ways of evaluating international airline safety; William Nolting for his words of encouragement and permission to use information from the University of Michigan Web site on study abroad; Alison Noyes of Smith College for information about graduate examination sites abroad; Poul Olson for permission to quote from his article; Mitchell Reiss, my boss, for allowing me the vacation time to complete the book and for providing abundant encouragement; Kathleen Sideli, who signaled the impending publication of useful materials on financial aid, work abroad, the history of study abroad, and a number of other topics so that the titles could appear in the bibliography; Members of the national team of SECUSSA, the study abroad arm of NAFSA (Association of International Educators) who answered important questions; Roxane Stanfield, my editor, who had the original idea for the book and provided tactful and supportive editing and encouragement throughout the project; countless William and Mary students who wrote articulate reports and comments about their study abroad experiences and presented excellent orientations for the next generation of study abroad students; and my neighbors, colleagues, and technical supporters, Gary Balogh and Charles Green, who kept my computers and e-mail working throughout the project.

Lastly, for all their love and encouragement, my mother, Eric and Adele, Phoebe and Grace, Anthony and Lydia, and—most of all—my husband, Thomas, who said the right thing at the right time.

About the Author

Ann M. Moore, Ph.D., has personally helped more than 2,000 students successfully study and work abroad. As head of Programs Abroad at the College of William and Mary, she has first-hand experience working, studying, and traveling all over the world and has managed and evaluated study abroad programs for American universities for the last 19 years. She presently represents study abroad professionals in the Mid-Atlantic region on the national team of NAFSA (National Association of Foreign Studies Advisors), the world's largest organization of international education professionals.

Ann began venturing abroad by living with a family in Nantes, France. She later returned to France as a Fulbright Scholar. After university, she traveled to Chongqinq, China, to teach English for a year at the Sichuan Institute of Foreign Languages. She has been a French and Spanish professor for more than 20 years and has coauthored "A Vous La France," a French text-workbook to accompany a BBC video.

Ann Moore has taken groups to Paris and Beijing and traveled and inspected study abroad programs all over the world, including France, Germany, Spain, Italy, Switzerland, Belgium, Great Britain, Ireland, China, Japan, the Phillipines, Thailand, Mexico, the Dominican Republic, Argentina, and Canada.

Contents

Why Study Abroad?

I f you are considering study abroad, be prepared to join thousands of students, from all over the world, in the adventure of a lifetime.

Study abroad has never been as popular among people of all ages as it is today. The trend is not limited to Americans. Everywhere on the planet, people are more eager than ever before to acquire at least a portion of their university education in another country. They are not just touring, but traveling to other countries with the purpose of earning credit and acquiring important skills. Some are working abroad or participating in internships, earning money to cover part of their expenses while getting valuable training. Study abroad can be a short- or long-term experience. Programs to suit the needs of many different people are available.

From the beginnings of history, people have journeyed in search of knowledge and training. Experiences in other countries have transformed lives and sent people into entirely new careers. In the 16th century, for example, a disabled veteran from Spain went to study in Paris, where he made friends with another Spanish student at the

University of Paris. Together, these two study abroad students went on to found a worldwide teaching organization. Their names were Francis Xavier and Ignatious Loyola, and the organization they founded was the Society of Jesus. The value of study abroad has become part of our literature and our legends. From *Hamlet* to *Star Wars*, fictional characters go to strange new lands in quest of insights and skills.

Here are just a few examples of famous people who studied abroad and what they later accomplished:

Bodhidharma	Monk who brought Buddhism to China
William J. Clinton	U.S. president
Alrecht Dürer	Renaissance painter
Mahandas Gandhi	Leader of India's independence movement
Jacqueline Bouvier Kennedy Onassis	First lady, editor
Franklin D. Roosevelt	Longest serving U.S. president
Sun Yat-sen	Founder of the Republic of China
Gloria Steinem	Writer, women's rights leader
Paul of Tarsus	Religious leader

Go to the Web site of the Institute for International Education (www.iie.org), seek out its most recent data on study abroad, and you will discover that more than 113,000 American students studied in other countries in 1997–1998, a whopping 14.6 percent increase over the previous year! In fact, the IIE reports that the movement of U.S. students around the world to study and learn from other peoples has been steadily increasing since the early 1950s and shows no signs of tapering off. But this is only part of the picture. Students from many other countries are also going abroad to learn. In 1997–1998, the IIE reports, more than 481,000 students came to study in the United States, and some European countries record even larger numbers on international students enrolling in universities there.

To stay current with this global movement, increasing numbers of Americans of every age are looking for opportunities to go abroad.

I believe that every American can benefit from the opportunity to see how people live in other countries and how they solve life's daily problems. Further, I believe that students who encounter other cultures discover much greater possibilities in themselves. Recognizing the opportunities that internatioal experiences offer, I began to think about writing an impartial book that would take students and their families through the entire process from beginning to end.

Why Unofficial?

As the market for information increases, the volume of material covering every step in the process is exploding as well. Some companies attempt to capitalize on the growing demand by advertising services you might not need. There are also pitfalls—unnecessary expenses, unreliable sources of information, choices that would not result in transferable credit, and health and safety problems for the unprepared. The difficulty for you is to know how to sift through all the information and find out what you really need to know before you enroll in a program that could be unsuitable for you.

Finding the Program That Is Right for You

Busy study abroad offices are willing to provide information, but some might not have enough time or staff to review and provide access to large numbers of programs. They might prefer to focus on a select group of programs that meet institutional goals. Depending on institutional priorities, some offices might have to concentrate on selecting and preparing students only for a particular group of programs. The flow in interested students is so great that advisors might not have enough time with each individual to cover all the available choices. Thus, you might not get the chance to find out about programs appropriate to your skill level or to the part of the world in which you are interested, unless you know where to search out the information for yourself.

The Unofficial Guide to Study Abroad is a practical guide for you, the student, as well as for your family. It explains each stage of the process, from the first preparations through the actual study abroad experience and beyond. The chapters lead you through the various steps and help you take care of any practical details that a program leaves you to handle by yourself. With plenty of time to plan for the experience, you have energy left to get the most out of the actual experience of living and learning in another culture.

Special Features

To help you get the most out of this book quickly and easily, the text is enhanced with the following special sidebars:

1. "A Student Speaks Up"—Advice from students who have returned from their study abroad experiences

2. "Quote"—Statements from professionals that can give you valuable insights

3. "Timesaver"—Tips and shortcuts that save you time

4. "Moneysaver"—Tips and shortcuts that save you money

5. "Watch Out!"—Cautions and warnings about pitfalls to avoid

6. "Bright Idea"—Strategies that offer an easier or smarter way to do something

7. "Unofficially..."—An insider's fact

How This Book Was Written

The book constitutes a combination of accumulated experience, information from returning students, and data that study abroad professionals collect and publish. The chapters take you through the complete sequence of all aspects of study abroad, from the preliminary planning to the financing, the actual experience, and how to benefit from your experience. You can find out how to have a smooth and rewarding experience, spend your money wisely, and apply credit earned abroad to your U.S. degree. It explains how to get information about health and safety and suggests measures to take to ensure your safety when you are on your own. You will learn to avoid pitfalls.

Advice from students who recently studied abroad provides a combination of accumulated experience, information that returning students offer to the next outgoing group.

The book helps you take advantage of the expertise that professional organizations provide to their members through publications, Web sites, and e-mail newsletters. It could not exist without the resources provided by the professional associations of international educators. A vast amount of information is available in publications and on the World Wide Web. Teams of professionals in the field of international education have spent years developing detailed guidelines. This book tells you when to look for this material and where to find it and helps you sort through the information and use it well. Another goal in writing this book is to dispel some of the myths that might prevent you from studying abroad by showing you the variety of opportunities that exist to accommodate virtually every time framework, academic program, need, and budget.

This is an overview of the field, without partiality to the agenda of any particular organization, institution, or study abroad program. The book is organized to help you get access to information and find the program that is right for you. It does not contain a list of "the best" programs. What is best for one person might not be appropriate for another person. You and your parents, in consultation with the instructors and advisors who know you, are the ones who should make an informed decision about the program that will help you meet your goals.

One of the greatest benefits of learning abroad is that it broadens your perspective on everything you do. You acquire the ability to look at any source of information, situation, or problem from many different points of view.

Although the information provided is as current as possible, many new information sources appear all the time. New publications might appear before the *Unofficial Guide* reaches the stores. This is why the book provides many Web sites where there are constant updates to information. Check regularly for new ideas.

Enjoy your journey, and consider this the start of the greatest adventure of your life.

Investigating Study Abroad Options

GET THE SCOOP ON...
The rapidly expanding world of international
exchange ▪ The educational benefits of study
abroad ▪ The career benefits of study abroad
▪ The personal benefits ▪ The importance of
international exchanges

PART I

Why Go Abroad

Recently in Ghana, a group of future high school counselors participating in a study abroad program stood on the parapet of Elmina Castle, one of the former slave fortresses along the coast of Ghana. Study abroad opportunities such as this have the special purpose of introducing students to the process of crossing cultures. They help students acquire the skills they need in order to be comfortable crossing cultural boundaries in the future. Frequently, students must observe and record what they experience. This will prepare them, professors believe, to advise and counsel many who are adjusting to a global society, moving rapidly from one country and culture to another. International firms increasingly send new employees abroad in the first few years of employment. They recognize the need for people who are already comfortable functioning at the international level. Students who gain that experience through study abroad will be ready for the opportunities that lie ahead.

Chapter 1

❝

For almost an hour, I listened to a 28-year-old Ghanaian . . . skycap share his life experiences and most intimate hopes and dreams. . . . At that moment, I looked at the world with a new awareness of my humanity. . . . At the core, we are all, as the Ghanaians say, brothers.
—Poul Olson, *William and Mary News,* August 19, 1999

❞

In the last two decades, the economic ties between the countries of Europe have gradually strengthened and the development of a single currency, the Euro, is one of the final steps in their economic unification. In the meantime, the North American Free Trade Agreement (NAFTA) has tightened the economic ties between the United States and its North American neighbors. Multinational corporations are multiplying rapidly, and transportation and communications technologies have increased the pace of global communication. The amount of international exchange activity has never been greater, and opportunities for careers in international fields have never been better. With all this expansion in international enterprises, opportunities for young people to become involved in international exchanges are multiplying rapidly.

In response to these events, business schools all over the world are developing exchanges for their students. In the U.K., Norway, Austria, Costa Rica, France, and many other places, MBA candidates at prestigious business schools are spending one semester abroad out of the precious four that they invest in earning their degree; often, they exchange places with students in the United States. Thus, young managers in all of these countries are learning to work with each other as students, laying the groundwork for future partnerships, and applying their skills to situations that may arise in their dealings with each other's countries during their careers. As the international language of commerce, English is the language the faculty and students use in many programs, regardless of their location.

Administrators of schools of business recognize the critical need to prepare their graduates for a world of international marketing, information technology, commerce, and management. Undergraduate business programs, too, are encouraging students to go abroad in order to familiarize themselves with the global economy. Approximately 600 different undergraduate study abroad opportunities in business appear in the current study abroad catalogs.

Scientific research is another area in which scholars are moving back and forth across the world's boundaries to share their findings and their expertise. Applied science centers in many parts of the world are setting up short-term research exchanges, allowing their students to trade places and collaborate upon research in more than one country. In some parts of Europe, the science classes are conducted in English, partly because the professors are moving freely from one European Union (EU) country to another and from one language group to another to lecture and carry out research. The EU students are moving too, crossing the old national boundaries with the help of scholarships in order to spend one or more semesters at other EU universities.

In the EU, the development of the ERASMUS program, which now carries the name SOCRATES, allows students to spend semesters in different countries as a part of their education. As an example, one cooperative master's degree program in urban studies through a consortium of universities in the EU features opportunities to live and study in four different countries in the process of completing the degree.

A new approach to curriculum design, exemplified by the curriculum structure at the Shonan Fujisawa campus of Keio University, reflects another trend in the increasing amount of global

Unofficially...
A research physicist explored ancestral connections while doing atmospheric research in the North Atlantic. The research team took atmospheric samples over the British Isles last summer. "One evening at dinner [in Ireland], we found three of us had fathers or grandfathers in the coal mining business, and mine had been in the iron mining business. Small world."

A Student Speaks Up
Our class used live Internet connections for research. We watched live lectures from the United States, worked in pairs with American students, and gave presentations in real time via the Internet. The more we worked together, the more we wanted to meet face to face. I made three trips to the United States to set up the next class.

information exchange. This branch of Keio, which specializes in information technology, groups faculty and students into problem-solving teams instead of the usual disciplinary units. The problems they address have a broad focus, affecting several nations or regions. Upstairs in a laboratory, a professor of economics from Belgium and another from Japan review their years of combined work on environmental problems. They arrange to put videotapes of all their lectures and disk files of all their papers onto the World Wide Web to make the information available to policymakers in many countries. One team of students and faculty might consider a problem such as the desertification of grazing land in Mongolia. One professor on the team might have a background in Spanish language, and another a Ph.D. in math. The team members combine the skills from their various backgrounds to work on a problem.

At the same university, students prepare to spend a month in the United States studying American English and multicultural studies by participating in real-time question-and-answer sessions with their American instructors. Via e-mail, the instructors send study questions, and then they appear via the Internet's video-conferencing capabilities, asking questions and encouraging the group to discuss their answers. By the time the students arrive in the United States, they are not only familiar with the issues they will study, but they also feel more comfortable with American English.

These examples from one university illustrate new trends in international education that will affect study abroad in the future. The Internet accelerates the rate of movement by preparing students to work together around the world, using a combination of skills and information technology to address the problems we share.

In many parts of the world during the 1990s, conflicts have flared up as old empires such as the former Soviet Union collapse and the struggle for new boundaries begins. These conflicts have created work for relief programs, for trained negotiators who know the cultural issues to be resolved, and for planners. People-to-people planning projects, intended to help a society rebuild in the aftermath of conflict, are another valuable form of international exchange. Projects of this kind have multiplied rapidly in the last decade.

Another major development of the 1990s is the rapid advance in information technology that permits almost instantaneous transmission of duplicated material from country to country. This development has created issues of intellectual property rights and has led to the need for legal institutions to resolve these new boundary disputes. Study abroad programs in international law offer opportunities for young lawyers to visit other countries and work in partnership with other attorneys. Americans travel to the EU, and lawyers from Eastern Europe come to the United States. All of them are seeking the training they need to address increasingly important international legal issues.

Educational Benefits of Study Abroad

Many students say that the academic education they receive on a study abroad program does not compare in rigor to the one they have at home. Sometimes, they complain about intensive language courses because the native speaking teachers set much higher standards than they are used to. In

Bright Idea
My international relations class discussed development in Palestine after the peace accord and proposed investment models and projects for schools and community groups. I proposed re-establishing Rotary clubs, which formerly existed in Palestine. I got a scholarship to work on the project. These new Rotary clubs now serve as community centers from which humanitarian projects, such as English or public health classes, can evolve.

other classes, however, they might not feel that the instructors are demanding as much of them as their American teachers do. To some degree, the educational structure in other cultures puts the burden on the student, not on the faculty. Therefore, the faculty might not require students to take frequent quizzes or turn in short papers just to show that they are grasping the material. All the emphasis is placed upon final examinations and lengthy written projects that students submit at the end of the semester. Some Americans, accustomed to frequent assignments and feedback on their performance, undervalue a system that requires students to prepare independently for a single final examination. Good students quickly adjust to the new time frame and work diligently to prepare for the lengthy final examinations.

Here are some of the changes educators say that they notice in students after they have been overseas:

- Comfort with complexity and ability to cope with ambiguous information
- Willingness to challenge answers that seem too simplistic or formulaic
- The ability to see more than one side to a question
- Tolerance for the opinions of others
- Flexibility, the ability to expect the unexpected
- Willingness to understand differences and to try to understand different cultural perspectives
- Confidence in their own opinions, coupled with willingness to justify their position

A Student Speaks Up
It's hard to say I'm more interested in the subject, but I'm more competent. I was interested from Day 1! My host family helped me improve my Spanish. Having time to travel on weekends and participate in cultural activities provided my most important lessons. The Spanish culture/civilization class was perfect and prompted a lot of discussions with my host family.

- Creativity in looking "outside the box" for solutions to problems
- Willingness to research a question thoroughly before offering a solution

Career Benefits of Study Abroad

Some fields in which international experience pays off and international job opportunities exist are journalism, law, diplomacy, the fine arts, music, theater, education, environmental studies, commerce, counseling, finance, fashion, architecture, information technology, counseling, engineering, geology, health services, extractive industries, economic development, relief services, energy, agriculture, resource management, computer graphics, and more.

However, even in fields that do not seem to require overseas experience, the fact that you have studied abroad is of interest to employers. They recognize the skills you acquire through learning other languages and adjusting to other cultures, and they see ways to use them. Study abroad marks you as a person with an open and inquiring mind who is creative, self-confident, and well informed—someone who is able to learn new skills and adapt quickly to new situations.

There are many trouble spots around the world where expert help is needed. Changes brought about by the collapse of the Soviet Union, coupled with regional crises in many parts of the world, are creating the need for negotiators trained in the languages, cultures, and histories of whole new regions of the globe. Rebuilding countries in the aftermath of these crises creates many opportunities for people

Unofficially...
As director of a large research library, my boss places great importance on international experience in hiring. When he starts reviewing applications for any opening at the library, he puts all the ones with international experience on top of the pile and looks at them first.

in service careers: teachers, medical professionals, and relief and development workers. All the changes are rapidly creating new employment opportunities in the U.S. as well as overseas.

Immigration attorneys present the cases for refugees seeking asylum. Other attorneys specialize in representing international clients before the Food and Drug Administration, the Department of Commerce, the Federal Trade Commission, and other government agencies that examine and approve their products and license or approve the activities of multinational corporations in the United States. Study abroad programs in international law help prepare attorneys to deal with all of the international facets of the profession and open career pathways to them.

The recent establishment of the International Criminal Court provides an institution through which the world can hold war criminals accountable for their actions. It also creates the need for experts to prepare and review the cases. As the world creates more transnational institutions of this type, there will be an ever-growing need for professionals with the expertise to administer them and carry out their functions.

Experts in international relations find employment with the World Bank, with international investment corporations, or with associations of businesses seeking to establish joint ventures in the part of the world with which they are familiar.

An October 1998 *National Geographic* article examined global migration patterns and studied their effects upon the world of the 1990s. While thousands of people move to escape natural disasters, war, or failing economies in their home countries, many professionals respond to changing job

"
I studied in France as an international relations development concentrator and wrote a paper on Hungary's recent economic development. Now, I work for an investment firm where this type of analysis is useful. The most rewarding aspect of my experience was experiencing another culture, but I also benefited from personal growth and increased confidence.
"

opportunities around the world. Trade associations need skilled administrators with appropriate experience. This experience comes from studying in the region, language training, and related coursework that will help administrators handle necessary cross-cultural communication. Such associations hire young people with international study experience. Students today have the opportunity to study abroad as undergraduates, to teach English overseas after graduation from college, and to work as translators, tour guides, or interpreters. A steady accumulation of international experience as an undergraduate and early in your career can open the door to one interesting employment opportunity after another.

The need for exchanges of business and management trainees is growing as well. The International Association of Students in Economics and Business Management (IASEC) is a worldwide student organization that offers more than 5,000 internships in over 80 countries, according to the University of Michigan's Work Abroad Web site directory. This staggering number reflects a worldwide need for skilled workers and management personnel with recent training as well as a multinational perspective on the world of international commerce.

Some interns might conduct conversation classes in their native language for employees. Others translate or edit translations of a variety of publications, including training materials, owner manuals, company newsletters, and publicity brochures. Still others might compile statistics, conduct training classes, or learn the workings of a new product in order to write a training manual. Proficiency in more than one language is essential in

66

I spent the summer as an intern for an international photographic supply company, living in the company dormitory, wearing the company uniform, eating in the company cafeteria, and working out in its recreation center. I edited translations of training materials to train repair staff and taught English conversation classes to Japanese coworkers. I made friends and got constant practice in Japanese.

99

A Student Speaks Up

I'm interviewing for jobs, and everyone asks me to discuss my semester abroad. The classes offered helpful direct contact with the languages and cultures. We learned more because we had to interact with the people for our assignments, which required us to interview our house families and the local people.

international commerce as well as in communication between the various branches of multinational corporations. The availability of so many internships demonstrates the importance of current training and international experience in the world's business workforce.

In addition, there are many internships available for students in technical fields. AIPT (Association for International Practical Training)/IAESTE (International Association for the Exchange of Students for Technical Experience, www.aipt.org/programs.html) offers several different programs. Among these, one of the most important for students in engineering and science is IAESTE, www.aipt.org/iaeste.html. This initiative offers internships in more than 60 countries.

In addition to these opportunities, the University of Michigan's Web page on work abroad (www.umich.edu/~icenter/overseas/work/index.html) identifies information sources leading to literally thousands of additional internships around the world. The tremendous growth in such internships proves there is a mushrooming need for business trainees, managers, technicians, scientists, and others in professional training programs who can cross national boundaries to provide these services. Here are just a few of the highly specialized fields of study for which international training programs are now available:

- More than 20 countries host study abroad programs in accounting.
- Advertising programs recruit students to study abroad in 15 programs from Argentina to the United Arab Emirates.

- Programs in agriculture, aquaculture, agronomy (including four programs in soil and pasture management), agribusiness, and agricultural economics take students to South Africa, Costa Rica, Ghana, India, and many places in Western Europe to compare techniques and review the challenges of development.

- Hundreds of programs in computer science and computer graphics are available. Scientific research programs draw students of chemistry, physics, biology, marine science, and geology.

- Even such specialized areas as entomology, anatomy, botany, or biomedical sciences offer a number of study abroad programs in each category.

There are training programs in specialized fields for every letter of the alphabet, starting with actuarial science and including broadcasting, catering, dentistry, editing, family services, glassmaking, human resources, international shipping, jewelry-making, laser technology, mining, neurology, pharmacology, robotics, screenwriting, textiles, urban planning, virology, winemaking, and zoology.

Interdisciplinary programs in fields such as environmental studies are booming as the world takes a close look at its resources and nations recognize the need to work together to protect and sustain them.

Personal Benefits of Study Abroad

Confidence and Self-Awareness

Getting away from your usual surroundings and friends helps you to understand yourself better. Looking at your own talents and potential through

A Student Speaks Up
Some of the benefits are knowing that you can survive in another language, . . . being completely independent, having to start over in a new country, knowing no one, and building an amazing life that I didn't want to leave. My enhanced confidence and skill level make me comfortable with talking and making mistakes.

the eyes of a completely different culture makes you aware of your innate strengths and aptitudes and allows you to cultivate what is unique in you. You might live in an environment where the standard of living is lower than what you are used to. This experience can help you discover your own resourcefulness, flexibility, and endurance. You will become aware of your fundamental needs and learn which aspects of life at home are most important to you.

Many students speak of the confidence in their inner resources that study abroad gives them. In addition, they gain confidence as they build their language skills or carry out the professional training for which they went abroad. Students on internships become familiar with corporate culture. Many of them spend at least part of their time drilling management trainees in proper English usage. From this experience, they acquire first-hand experience with the requirements of management training programs. Students who do research in laboratories in other countries acquire a different cultural perspective on what it means to work in science and come back with greater confidence in their own ability to carry out research projects.

The opportunity to travel independently and to manage your own affairs is another aspect of life in a different country that gives you confidence in your abilities. Many students say that it allows them to face life after graduation with a newfound confidence.

Many people become more creative. Living in another culture and seeing things from the perspective of other peoples helps you look for fresh perspectives and think "outside the box."

A Student Speaks Up
I was under pressure to be like my friends before I left. This year in another country has given me the opportunity to try being someone new who isn't like everybody else and to grow strong. When I go back to start medical school, I hope to remain the new, stronger person that I have become.

Long-Term Friendships

One of the most informative parts of a study abroad experience is learning how much friendships mean to people in many other cultures. In public, you might find many of the people of different cultures brusque and businesslike, especially those doing business in crowded cities. The French, in particular, have a reputation among Americans for being brusque in public, primarily because they value their language and prefer to speak it rather than English. Put yourself in their position and imagine how you would feel if visitors came into your store all day demanding that you speak their language in your country! This might help you understand how they feel. In fact, the French unfairly get all the blame, for you will find the same reserved public behavior in many other parts of Europe. The truth is that you might experience the same thing in almost any city in the world if you are there long enough to explore on your own, whether you are in Hong Kong, Buenos Aires, or Dublin.

However, the same people who are standoffish in public and with strangers might be ready to make friends with people to whom they are formally introduced. Once you have made friends with people, expect those relationships to be close and possibly to last for many years. People might feel hurt if you first appear eager to make friends and later seem to lose interest in carrying the friendship to a more enduring level.

Different approaches to making friends come from different living styles. Traditionally, families in most parts of the world live in the same community and keep the same friends for a lifetime. Life in Europe these days is changing rapidly with the

Unofficially...
It's an interesting cultural exercise to observe how Europeans handle themselves in public. People don't smile as much or look one another in the eye. An easy friendliness is often met with suspicion; a non-motivated smile can mean that you want something or are being hypocritical.
—A faculty resident director

A Student Speaks Up
I made tons of lifelong friends, both Danish and American, and got to see the world and many other cultures. The most rewarding part of my experience abroad was really feeling that I became a part of [the country's] culture and knowing that I always have a home [there]. The friends I made were wonderful and my host family played a very important role in my happiness.

increasing expansion of businesses across national borders, and many careers require people to relocate to new cities or even to different countries. Nonetheless, Europeans still place a high value on spending their free time with their family and the same group of close friends they have known for many years. If a strong friendship forms, you might remain in contact with a host family or a classmate for a lifetime.

As a student, you will not only meet the people of the country, but will also make friends with other international students who, like you, have come to perfect their language skills or learn more about the country. You will find that people who go out of their way to live in another country can be rewarding to get to know, and of course, they are likely to find you the same. If these friendships develop fully, you may very well continue to stay in touch for many years.

Professionals from the United States who studied in Europe in the 1960s and 1970s, when study abroad opportunities began to be widely offered at American universities, still return to Europe to visit the families they lived with as students as much as 30 years before. Each time they visit the country over the years, they stop in to see the hosts who offered them a home away from home.

A 20-year-old student at the Institut Polytechnique might write to the American woman who stayed with his grandparents 25 years before. The American might continue to correspond with the student's mother and visit occasionally. The student can spend the summer with the American family. Later, the American family might help the student gain admission to an American graduate program.

The friendship and exchange between families can extend over three generations. The second and third generation of a family might exchange places, improving their language skills and making contacts that benefit them in their studies and professional lives.

Ability to Contribute to Social Programs

In some countries, you might see people living in conditions that make you want to do something about the suffering and starvation around the world. Such experiences can be disturbing and difficult, but with some preparation, they might reveal things that you can do to help.

Some students recommend that you look for a cultural and practical life, not academic learning experience. They say that it will be incredible. They advise you to keep an open mind.

Some study abroad programs are at universities that offer community outreach and social programs. Visiting students can volunteer to help with these projects after class. The director of a relief effort in the Dominican Republic arranges for students to visit the camps of Haitian refugees after classes at the university in Santiago. They study there under the auspices of the Council for International Educational Exchange (CIEE). As a participant, you might visit rice fields where refugees have found work. You will meet people who develop social programs for the workers and move them toward economic independence.

Volunteers might have the opportunity to help teach refugees to read and write their language or to learn a widely used language that will enable them to become self-sufficient by moving into the wider work world. Student volunteers help with the

A Student Speaks Up
I enjoyed the pleasure of exploring Greece on my own at times. I loved the natural beauty and felt the spirituality of the ancient sites. [As a math major] I chose this program because I am just interested in learning other things, not to earn credit for my degree program. My future actually looks clearer to me now than before I came.

A Student Speaks Up

The living conditions age people prematurely. The refugees live in a huddle of dark, windowless huts. They grow a few vegetables for sale and live on the earnings of prostitutes and field workers. Cooking water comes from the drainage ditch. An old, bent woman grinned from a doorway, her smile wide but toothless. Through an interpreter, I learned that she was 39.

classes and with efforts to improve the workers' living conditions.

The Partnership for Service Learning is another program offering educational opportunities to assist with relief and educational projects. Experts in worldwide learning who design and administer such programs feel visits to such locations might be difficult for students to handle without some advance preparation.

Before you volunteer to help in poverty-stricken areas where you will see examples of so much suffering, experts recommend that you get some preparation from instructors and program administrators, as well as returning students. After the visit, get some advice on ways in which you can help. With the help of knowledgeable advisors, these deeply disturbing encounters often become transforming experiences for young Americans who visit refugee camps. For example, American doctors and other healthcare professionals join volunteer groups and donate vacation time to providing free medical care to poor Haitians. A recent graduate of Georgetown University's language program served as an interpreter in Spanish and French for the UN peace-keeping force that went to Cuba in 1994 to return Haiti's President Aristide from exile.

For some students, volunteer work abroad might lead to a career in a relief organization, a stint as a Peace Corps worker, or a return to a country or region as teachers, health workers, or technical experts. Others may become involved with a church group or volunteer organization through which their community in the United States provides assistance to communities at risk in other countries.

Each year, Transitions Abroad publishes an issue on responsible travel and programs with articles, advertisements, and program listings for opportunities to teach or engage in service activities all over the world. Many of the participants write about the career opportunities that opened for them after study abroad experiences.

Just the Facts

- Exchanges are booming in business, public policy, the sciences, and information technology.

- Creative curriculum designs emphasize how exchange programs can address world issues.

- Rapidly changing situations in the developing world call for people-to-people planning projects, relief efforts, and development expertise.

- Third-world service work requires preparedness, hard work, and international experience.

- Learning abroad increases language skills, builds confidence, provides valuable training, and develops leadership skills.

GET THE SCOOP ON...
American organizations and institutions
▪ Organizations and institutions in other countries ▪ Island programs ▪ Language programs

A Quick Guide to Types of Study Abroad Programs

Chapter 2

All study abroad programs fall into one of two general categories, depending on who serves as the sponsor—that is, who offers the program and makes the arrangements for you. The sponsor could be an American organization or university or an institution in the country where you are going. You can further group programs into two basic categories describing the program of study: university enrollment or island programs. A simple "four-leaf clover" design illustrates these program types.

In the following figure, Leaf Number One represents programs that American organizations, colleges, and universities organize to help American students make smooth arrangements to enroll directly in university classes in another country. Leaf Number Two represents host universities that encourage American students to apply directly to

Figure 2.1

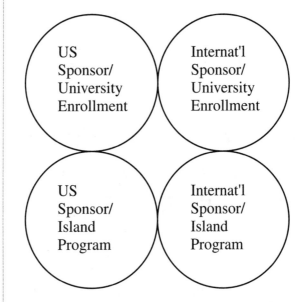

Timesaver
You can quickly
review concise
descriptions of
almost 2,700
semester or year-
long programs
for American
students in
*Academic Year
Abroad,* which
the Institute for
International
Education pub-
lishes annually
(New York).
Available in
most libraries
and on the Web
at www.iie.org.
(See Appendix B,
"Directory of
Online
Resources.")

them, and the foreign university makes all the arrangements for the students. Leaf Number Three stands for programs that American institutions and organizations arrange especially for American students, creating the curriculum and making all the arrangements for them. Leaf Number Four stands for programs that institutions overseas arrange, either just for Americans or just for international students.

Before you begin to review program descriptions and choose a program, it is helpful to understand the differences between these four basic types of programs. Then you can decide which type is best for you.

University Enrollment Programs Through U.S. Organizations and Institutions

A U.S. sponsor can help you enroll in a university in another country where you can choose from a broad selection of courses. Most of your classmates (except for a few others participating in the same program) will be regular degree-seeking students at the university, and the professors will be the regular university professors. You will fulfill the same requirements for a grade as the regular students do, and (in theory) you will not receive any special consideration because you are an international student. In practice, your program sponsor will probably provide advice and other assistance.

Naturally, this arrangement requires you to understand lectures in the language of the host country and to use that language for most of your reading as well as for the tests (some of which might be oral examinations) and the papers you write. This is not always the case, for there is wide use of English in university classes in some countries even when it is not the official language. Read more about English-language programs all over the world in Chapter 3, "Other Types of Programs."

The sponsor usually provides a comprehensive catalog or handbook of information to help you find your way around the university you will be attending and any course information that is available before you leave. A pre-departure orientation meeting might take place to introduce you to other students on the same program and to prepare you for the experience. The fee for this type of program almost always includes group international transportation and transfer to the program site. In addition, an on-site resident director or coordinator is usually available throughout the year to provide an initial orientation, oversee registration, and attend to the needs of the American group. One of the most important functions of the resident program coordinator is to help students gain a better appreciation and understanding of the culture and intervene if any cultural adjustment problems occur. At the end of the year, the sponsoring American college or university will usually issue its own transcript reporting the grades and credit in accordance with the American system.

Where can you find a U.S.-sponsored program? The first place you should check is your home institution. Programs that your college or university sponsors are among your best options. With your home university, you have the best chance of qualifying for financial aid, scholarships, or any discount in the program price. Credit arrangements will probably be compatible with your degree program, and it will be easy to maintain connections while you are away.

If your university has these arrangements, faculty and advisors at your home university might encourage you to arrange for such an experience. Your campus advisors will determine whether you have the language proficiency and whether you are prepared for the cultural differences you will encounter. They will advise you in the selection of your courses, help you arrange for credit when you return, and put you in contact with the faculty and administrators at the host university who will help you when you arrive. With this type of support structure in place, you might be able to arrange for a successful semester or year abroad at a distinguished university in the country. Inquire early about application procedures and deadlines, information sessions, and pre-departure orientations.

Some universities design special, money-saving direct enrollment programs for their own students. These programs, called tuition exchanges, offer students the opportunity to pay their regular tuition to their home university and to enroll directly at a partner university in another country. If you are attending a state university and paying in-state tuition, you can save quite a bit by choosing this option. In-state tuition can often be thousands of dollars less than the normal international tuition that a university charges visiting students. Be sure that your home university, or the host university or exchange partner, offers plenty of information about the university you will be attending and provides an orientation and assistance with course enrollment, housing, and other services to make your study abroad program go smoothly. If the host university does not recognize how much assistance an international student requires, you might consider your first few weeks difficult as you find your way around.

If your home university does not have an approved direct enrollment program at the university you are considering, the next step is to search for another American university that sponsors a program there. You can use the sources outlined in this guide to search for a U.S. college or university that sponsors a program at the destination you prefer. The nearest college or university study abroad office or library is likely to have copies of the IIE catalog as well as *Peterson's Guide to Study Abroad*. If you do not have access to a college or university reference center, check for these books in the reference section of your public library. You can purchase either one, but they are expensive items for students.

Many universities accept applicants from other American institutions on their programs. Beaver College and Butler University have established a reputation for reliability and efficiency in making such arrangements for American students. Many other American universities offer enrollment in regular university courses in countries where English is not the language of instruction. In Madrid, for example, eight American universities recruit students for programs offering enrollment in Spanish-language courses at Spanish universities. Students attend classes with Spanish students or with Spanish and other international students. The universities are Arizona State, Boston, St. Louis, Tufts, Tulane, and Indiana University in cooperation with Purdue University and the University of Wisconsin. (See Appendix B for addresses and Web sites.)

You might have to spend some time carefully examining large program catalogs to find direct enrollment programs in the location you want. Your study abroad advisor can save you some time by directing you toward programs he or she knows.

If you are on your own, you can easily tell from the catalog descriptions whether you will be attending regular university classes, special classes for international students, or courses for American students in a format already familiar to you. Each program summary indicates the language of instruction and tells who the other students in your classes will be. If you find phrases such as "mostly host country," you will know that the program offers direct enrollment in regular university courses. "Mostly international" suggests that the curriculum consists at least in part of intensive language and culture courses for students from around the world. If you see "mostly U.S.," you can expect large numbers of U.S. students in the classes and what we refer to as an island program.

If you and your advisor cannot find a sponsor, it could mean that the university you were considering does not have trained staff available to assist international students and will not be able to give you much help when you arrive. See Table 2.2 at the end of this chapter.

University Enrollment Through a Foreign Sponsor

Many prestigious universities in other countries encourage Americans to apply directly to them. The range of their curriculum and the reputation of these universities are strong attractions for students and their families. They encourage American students to work directly with them and enroll directly in their courses without going through a sponsoring American institution. If you are considering such an option, it is essential to consult the study abroad advisor at your home institution well in advance!

This direct plan has advantages. Some American professors strongly recommend it, believing that students with a strong academic background do not need the assistance of an American sponsor to have a successful study abroad experience. Sometimes the plan can save you money because the host university usually charges all students the same reasonable tuition it charges citizens of the country. (In Germany, tuition is almost nothing.) If your language skills are good enough, you can enroll in classes with host country students, an option discussed later in this chapter. Direct enrollment offers you the best opportunity to make friends and learn about the host country from the perspective of typical university students there.

Direct enrollment works out best for you when the host university has a well-trained staff that is serious about helping you find your way in your new cultural surroundings as much as the academic ones. They know that you will encounter great

Watch Out!
If you choose a direct enrollment program primarily because of the name and reputation of the university you plan to attend abroad, you should know that you will probably receive the transcript from the American university sponsor. Instead of bearing the seal of "Big Famous University in Famous City, Overseas," the transcript will be issued by "Reliable American University in Anytown, USA."

differences between the teaching styles, course format, and university organization you know and those of the universities you will find in other countries. They want to help make that adjustment smooth.

If you have heard of a university in another country and think you would like to enroll there, ask your study abroad advisor whether it has an international office that makes frequent contact with American universities. Ask whether they visit the campuses regularly and participate in professional meetings of international educators. These are good indications of an overseas university's commitment to providing you with a good introduction and assistance while you are studying there. Some examples of universities that are strongly committed to this process are the London School of Economics General Course (Junior Year Abroad), University of Lancaster, University of St. Andrews, Trinity College in Dublin, and University of Adelaide in Australia.

The Pitfalls

If the host university is not ready to provide assistance to visiting international students, you could find direct enrollment frustrating. You might have to arrive in a strange country by yourself, find your way to the university, and learn your way around the institution by trial and error. You will have to adjust to a different teaching style, different expectations, a different credit system, and a different culture without any support from the international office staff. There is more about these differences in a later chapter.

Some universities in other countries like the idea of enrolling visiting American students but do not recognize the dimensions of the adjustment they have to make and the amount of service they need to provide for you. This is why it is critical to consult your study abroad advisor about your plans. Not only do you need to decide whether you are ready to study at the university you have in mind, but you also must determine whether *it* is ready for *you!* See Table 2.2 at the end of this chapter.

American Universities in Other Countries: A Special Kind of Direct Enrollment

Some American educators and foundations have incorporated universities in other countries in order to offer overseas students an American liberal arts curriculum with instruction in English. A number of these institutions have U.S. accreditation, often emphasizing international affairs, business, and other subjects that appeal to students whose goal is advanced study in the U.S. or an international career where American English will be an asset. Some overseas American universities have junior year abroad programs for Americans featuring courses in the language and culture of the host country (taught in the language) as well as courses in English where American and host country students can interact. Many of these universities have trained staffs to assist Americans with cultural adjustments, and some even offer the opportunity to live with local families. (Read more about home stays in Chapter 10, "Registering for the Program," and Chapter 17, "First Things First: Getting Settled.")

A disadvantage for some American students could be the tuition charged by some American universities abroad. Another is that those wanting to learn the host country's language might not get to use it much because the host country students are eager to improve their English proficiency. Finally, most American universities are too small to offer the

Watch Out!
In some countries, universities charge visiting students tuition as high as that of many private American colleges. Therefore, direct enrollment might be even more expensive than working through an American sponsor.

laboratory science, graduate programs, and other courses that a larger university could provide. Because American universities are a good option for some students but not the best option for others, you should discuss the option thoroughly with your study abroad advisor.

The following accredited international American universities have programs for U.S. study abroad students: Franklin College in Switzerland, The Center for International Studies in Madrid, The American University in Paris, The Hebrew University of Jerusalem, The American University in Bulgaria, and Richmond College in London. Many have U.S. recruitment offices (see Appendix B).

American-Sponsored Island Programs

In many countries, regular universities do not have the staff to provide assistance or to arrange special language courses for international students who want to take courses there for just a semester or a year. In these cases, American universities or organizations sponsor programs especially for visiting American students. These are called island programs because you enroll in classes designed for Americans and have virtually no classroom contact with students from the host country. You enter a special center, perhaps under the auspices of a host country university that offers a program of courses you can use to meet degree requirements back home or courses of particular interest to international students. There are usually introductory courses on the history, literature, and culture of the country.

More specialized programs focus on business, law, engineering, fashion design, or an undergraduate degree program such as sociology, biology, or environmental studies. Some of the biggest American universities enroll large numbers of students and offer a broad spectrum of courses from their regular catalogs, taught in English. The purpose of these large overseas centers is to encourage as many students as possible to experience life in an overseas setting while earning credit applicable to their majors. Examples are programs that the University of Pennsylvania, New York University, the University of Rochester, and Syracuse University offer.

Whatever the course selection may be, your classmates in an island program will either be Americans or other international students. Your professors might be specialists in teaching language and culture, professors from the sponsoring American university, or special guest lecturers. If you want such a program, you can take classes overseas that have a familiar format and requirements similar to those at your home institution.

The objective of an island program is to introduce you to a country and its culture through an appropriate selection of courses without interrupting your progress toward an American university degree. An additional advantage of an island program is that the program fee almost always includes international airfare, transfers from the airport to the program center, and the services of a resident director and, sometimes, additional staff. Excursions are always provided. In many cases, family home stays provide an opportunity for immersion in the culture. Students frequently consider their home stay the most valuable part of their study abroad experience.

Another advantage of island programs is that they offer a curriculum and services that students could not find in the regular universities of the country. The School for International Training, for example, offers college semester abroad programs that emphasize what Richard Wood of Yale University has called "creating cultural empathy." The Center for Global Education states on its Web site: "The Center for Global Education, nationally recognized for its work on experiential education in the Two-Thirds World, was founded in 1982 to help North Americans think more critically about global issues so they might work toward a more just and sustainable world."

In these programs, students can learn about other cultures through a combination of language study, where appropriate, and core courses offering analytical tools for the study of cultures and peoples. Core courses in some programs might consider development, gender, or environmental issues. Many times, students live with host country families.

The obvious disadvantage of some American programs is that you could spend too much time with students from your own culture, speaking your own language, in a setting where you were hoping to acquire some understanding of a new country. On one hand, the group might not be big enough to offer sufficient opportunities for making friends and expressing yourself. On the other hand, planned activities with the group might take up the time you would need to interact with, and make friends in, the community. Make sure the size of the program is right for you and check into its arrangements to help you meet people your own age. It is also wise to consider whether the program takes place in a large city where many international tourists gather or in a setting more typical of the host country. The fewer Americans and English speakers you have around you, the more progress you are likely to make in getting to know people from the country and in improving your language skills (if that is one of your reasons for going abroad). See Table 2.3 at the end of this chapter to compare university enrollment and island programs.

Island Programs Operated by an International Sponsor

The fourth type of program is the island program organized by a university or institute in the host country. Although universities in other countries encourage international students to enroll directly in regular university courses, they often provide one-month to six-week intensive orientations before regular classes begin. These meetings help new international students adjust to the university system and acquire some basic information about the culture that will be useful in their courses. For students whose language skills are not adequate for regular enrollment, there might be a separate language center available, offering intensive language instruction throughout the academic year.

Some excellent examples of island programs are administered entirely by the host country with courses in English. Danish International Studies, established by the Danish government, offers courses in business, the social sciences, and the humanities, taught in English but with the opportunity to learn Danish. Courses address the future of Europe and the Baltic region in the aftermath of the disintegration of the former Soviet Union.

Advanced Studies in England offers courses in a range of subject areas related to English literature, history, and culture. The program takes place in

A Student Speaks Up
Find something to do that gives you a chance to meet people who have nothing to do with the university or your program. In Santander, I signed up for a class in Tae Kwon Do and made some friends who were completely different from the university types.

Watch Out!
When you choose
a program
through a spon-
soring organiza-
tion that is not a
degree-granting
college or uni-
versity, make
sure that a
degree-granting
university will
issue the tran-
script. Otherwise,
credit probably
will not transfer
to your home
institution. Ask
your study
abroad advisor
about this
potential
problem.

Bath with field trips to Oxford and Stratford and with instruction by Oxford University instructors.

A number of organizations specialize in offering study abroad programs. They make it possible for you to choose a program with all the advantages of a sponsor, even if your home university does not offer a program in the location you want. Examples of sponsoring organizations are The American Institute for Foreign Study (AIFS), The Council on International Educational Exchange (CIEE), and The Institute for the International Education of Students (IES).

This is not an exhaustive list. Be sure to check Appendix B and ask your study abroad office for other addresses.

Your institution might belong to a regional consortium of institutions offering programs for students of the member institutions. Ask your study abroad office whether your institution offers programs through such a consortium. Here are some examples of consortia from around the country: Associated Colleges of the Midwest (ACM), College Consortium for International Studies (CCIS), The Great Lakes Colleges Association (GLCA), The Virginia Council for International Education (VaCIE), University Studies Abroad Consortium, and the Oregon University System (OUS).

Intensive Language Programs

There are so many hundreds of language programs that it is worthwhile to put them in a separate category. Although language programs fall into all four of the basic categories, depending on the sponsor and the scope of the program, we usually call them intensive language programs. In intensive language programs, you undergo a placement test when you arrive to determine your level of proficiency in the language. Then, you enroll in classes at the appropriate level for you. Here are some of the variations to look for, depending on who sponsors the program and who your classmates are.

American sponsors offer hundreds of summer, semester, and year-long programs for American university students. The programs are usually at an intermediate level requiring two years of prior study of the language. You will study the language and take associated courses such as literature, art history, music, or theater, usually with some related social science topics. Often, the program requires all the students to enroll in a "core course." This course is interdisciplinary, usually with a strong social sciences focus that looks at a culture from several different perspectives, such as anthropology, history, art history, or sociology.

Intensive language programs take place either at host universities or at special language institutes. Your teachers will have special training to teach the subjects in the language you are studying and in a manner that is not too difficult for you to understand with two or more years of language study. The American sponsor might work closely with the host university to select the teachers and plan the curriculum to meet your needs.

If you are an *advanced* language student, you might enroll in an American university program offering complete immersion in the language for a full year. This is an excellent way to make friends with whom you can practice the language. The American university will arrange a one-month intensive language program for you in the fall, before the regular students return to the university. After you bring your language skills up to the level you need

A Student Speaks Up
My host family was awesome. They really helped me to learn Italian. I couldn't believe the summer was over so quickly. I called my university as soon as I got home to find out about another program in Florence so I can go back for a longer stay.

for direct enrollment, you sign up for regular courses at the university and attend classes with the students of the country. Your resident director might recommend a special selection of classes that are an especially good fit with your skill level and your home university's requirements. You will probably continue to take some advanced language courses during the year. A good program has people to advise you and assist you in making the adjustment to the teaching style and requirements of the host university.

Universities in other countries might organize their own semester or year-long direct enrollment language programs for international students. The students expect to spend most of their time studying the language. They take related courses, all in the language of the host country, but again with some adaptation to accommodate the language level of the students. Once again, when you consider direct enrollment at a host university, you should investigate carefully and consult with your study abroad advisor. Make sure that the university provides advising services and assistance when you arrive, an intensive "refresher" language program at the beginning of the year to bring your language skills up to speed, and someone to advise and assist you in adapting to cultural differences.

If you want to perfect your Spanish, German, or French, you can choose from many language institutes in Europe and in Latin America, particularly in Mexico, offering short-term intensive summer language programs. In the best of these centers, the staff is particularly effective in assessing the students' proficiency and placing them at a level of instruction that enables them to make rapid and continuous progress. Some institutes offer short

Watch Out!
In many parts of the world, students begin the study of second and third languages earlier than in the United States, so they are more advanced when they go to the host country to study. Expect the pace of the classes to be more advanced when international students from many countries enroll in the program.

courses throughout the year so that students can enroll at any time during the year to take intensive language courses. In Germany, the best known of these institutes are under the direction of the Goethe Institute, which has centers in cities around the world. Similarly, French speakers can enroll in courses at worldwide Alliance Francaise centers. However, there are many other institutes in France and Germany, as well as in other German- and French-speaking countries, and the choices in Italy and the Spanish-speaking world are also wide.

There are two things to consider if you are interested in a short-term language program at a language institute. First, in view of the large number you have to choose from and the great variation in quality, you should do everything possible to find out about the quality of the institute. Consult with your language instructors and your study abroad advisor. Find out whether any American universities regularly arrange for their students to study at the center. This arrangement is a good indication of quality. Obtain references or review evaluations of the center with the help of your advisor. Make sure that you can obtain good information about health and safety issues in the program location. If your study abroad advisor cannot assist you in assessing the possible risks you might encounter at the location, you should probably reconsider your choice. Further information about health and safety is provided in later chapters.

Second, remember that you probably will not be able to transfer credit from a language institute unless a degree-granting institution oversees the program and issues the transcript. This is why it is wise to select an institute that is under the auspices of a university in the host country or enroll in the

A Student Speaks Up
I spent a lot of money to spend my first year of graduate study at {famous international art school}. I found very complete facilities there, but the graduate students spend most of their time working on their individual projects. There are no classes, and there is very little feedback or direction from professors. I came expecting close attention and a lot of advice and instruction.

institute through an American university program that offers academic credit.

You might find that enrolling at a language institute is less expensive than enrolling through an American university sponsor. Chapter 7, "Figuring Out the Cost of Programs and How to Finance Them," will help you decide whether this option is really a bargain or whether there are hidden costs.

A good question to ask is, "If things do not go as I expected, where do I turn?" If an American university is willing to sponsor the program and be accountable for its quality, you can be reasonably sure that the program will make every effort to provide what it advertises. Additional assurance is a strong recommendation from somebody reliable who has attended the institute or has recommended it to students in the past.

If you are interested in a short-term language program, the IIE has a shorter version of its comprehensive catalog *Vacation Study Abroad*, which lists 2,200 summer, winter-block, and other short-term programs. Your study abroad advisor might be able to assist you in searching this list by using the Web version that is available to member institutions. Two other useful Web-based program listings are Studyabroad.com and Transabroad.com. Because there is no charge for listing programs in these databases, you will find a large selection. Again, you should review your choices carefully with your study abroad advisor. Language institutes offer short-term programs that can really improve your language skills, but you might not be able to get credit for them unless an accredited university sponsors the program and issues the transcript.

Just the Facts

- American sponsors offer numerous programs abroad, providing support services and helping students fulfill degree requirements in many different fields.

- Host country universities might offer programs of high academic quality and an opportunity to learn from the host culture and take a different approach to the subjects.

- Island programs offer a curriculum designed for international students but do not provide contact with students from the country.

- Studio and language programs might offer many benefits even without academic credit.

- You need to research choices carefully when selecting an intensive language program.

TABLE 2.1 STUDY ABROAD DESTINATIONS BY 15 LEADING DESTINATIONS

Destination	1996/97	1997/98	1997/98 Percent Change	Percent of of all Study Abroad
United Kingdom	22,787	25,900	13.7	22.7
Spain	8,840	10,393	17.6	9.1
Italy	9,074	10,142	11.8	8.9
France	8,362	9,776	16.9	8.6
Mexico	6,865	7,574	10.3	6.6
Australia	3,870	4,355	12.5	3.8
Germany	3,815	4,146	8.7	3.6
Costa Rica	2,609	2,973	14.0	2.6
Ireland	1,926	2,522	30.9	2.2
Japan	2,018	2,285	13.2	2.0
China	1,627	2,116	30.1	1.9
Israel	1,718	1,988	15.7	1.7
Austria	1,621	1,609	−0.7	1.4
Ecuador	1,122	1,229	9.5	1.1
Russia	1,205	1,145	−5.0	1.0
Total	**99,448**	**113,959**	**14.6**	

Davis, T. (1999). *Open Doors 1998/99: Report on International Educational Exchange.* New York: Institute of International Education.

TABLE 2.2   ENROLLMENT IN A HOST COUNTRY UNIVERSITY: COMPARISON OF SPONSORSHIP AND SERVICES

	International Sponsor	U.S. Sponsor
Recruitment	Host university recruits students	U.S. university or organization recruits students and sponsors program
Summary of Level of Services	Degree of assistance varies	U.S. institution usually offers high level of assistance
Financial Arrangements	Participant usually pays host university	Participant pays fee to U.S. sponsor tuition
Cost Comparison	Might be lower but varies	Might be higher but varies
Travel		
International travel	Usually not included	Usually included
Airport-to-university transfer	Usually not provided	Often included
Local transportation to classes	Usually not provided	Often included
Housing	Assistance may be offered	Guaranteed
Choice of housing	May be offered	May be offered
Home stay	May be offered	May be offered
Meals	May be included	Most meals included
Resident Director or Coordinator	Rare (possible faculty advisor)	Almost always available
Cultural Orientation		
Pre-departure	Not included	Often included
On site	Often included	Always included
Assistance with cultural adjustment during year	May be available, depending on culture	Always available
Excursions	Rare	Almost always provided
Academic Advising		
Course information	Often not available until arrival	Often provided before departure
Help with course selection	Available on site	Available on site

(continues)

	International Sponsor	U.S. Sponsor
Academic Advising (cont.)		
Range of courses available	Usually full university curriculum	May be very wide
Other students in classes	Host university students	Host university students and some international students
Instructors	Host university instructors	Primarily host university instructors
Teaching style and expectations	Consistent with host culture (no allowances made for international students)	Some courses might be especially designed for, and geared to, international students
Special assistance with differences in academic expectations	Might be provided	Always provided
Academic Reputation	Desirability of program depends on high institutional reputation and/or cultural location	Sponsor selects for quality, safety, cultural features, and convenience
Language of Instruction	Host country language	Usually host country language
Transcripts	Issued by host university	Usually issued by U.S. university (if sponsor is not a university, special arrangements must be made)
Credits	Might be host country system; might require interpretation by home university	Converted to U.S. system
Health and Safety		
Healthcare	University or local clinic	Clinic instructions or assistance provided
Health insurance	Possibly required, depends on country	Usually require U.S. plans; offer enrollment options and information
Safety/risk factors	Participant must assess	Sponsor assesses— usually safe

	International Sponsor	U.S. Sponsor
Examinations	All students take regular host university examinations at end of term or year	Usually host university examinations, but sponsor might arrange special examinations to adjust to U.S. calendar
Academic Calendar	Often differs from U.S. models: Fully year enrollment might be required First semester may end in late Jan. Terms might yield one-third of U.S. semester credit South of equator, year might begin in Jan.	Sponsor might offer options to adjust calendar to U.S. model when feasible

TABLE 2.3 ISLAND PROGRAMS AND LANGUAGE PROGRAMS

	Island Program	University Enrollment
Recruitment	U.S. university or organization usually organizes program and recruits students (with a few exceptions*)	U.S. or host country sponsor may offer program and recruit students
Summary of Level of Services	High level of assistance provided	High level of assistance
Financial Arrangements	Participant pays program sponsor	Participant pays program sponsor
Cost comparison	Often corresponds to private U.S. university tuition	Fee often corresponds to private U.S. university institution
Travel		
International travel	Almost always included	Almost always included
Airport-to-university transfer	Almost always provided	Almost always included
Local transportation to classes	May be included	Often included
Housing	Guaranteed	Guaranteed
Choice of housing	May be offered	May be offered
Home stay	May be offered	May be offered
Meals	Most meals included	Most meals included
Resident Director or Coordinator	Always provided	Always provided (might be host country academic director or professor)
Cultural Orientation		
Pre-departure	Often included	Often included
On site	Always included	Always included
Assistance with cultural adjustment during year	Always available	Almost always provided
Excursions	Always available	Almost always provided

	Island Program	University Enrollment
Academic Advising		
Course information	Detailed and available in advance	Detailed and available in advance
Help with course selection	Available on site and in advance	Available on site and in advance
Range of courses available	Narrow range of courses	Focus on language and culture
Other students in classes	American students	International students
Instructors	American or specially selected host country instructors	Specially selected host country instructors
Teaching style and expectations	Geared to Americans	Geared to international students
Special assistance with differences in academic expectations	Always provided if needed	Always provided
Academic Reputation	Based on that of sponsoring university	Based on host and/or sponsor
Language of Instruction	English or English plus second language country language	Primarily or entirely host
Transcripts	Issued by sponsor	Usually issued by U.S. university (if sponsor is not a university, special arrangements must be made).
Credits	American credits	Usually converted to U.S. system
Health and Safety		
Healthcare	University or local clinic	University or local clinic
Health insurance	U.S. insurance usually required	U.S. insurance usually required
Safety/risk factors	Carefully monitored by program sponsor	Carefully monitored by program sponsor

(continues)

	Island Program	University Enrollment
Examinations (cont.)	Geared to American expectations with frequent assessment, term papers, midterms, and finals	Adjusted to American and other international student expectations
Academic Calendar	Usually American-style semesters: Aug. to Dec., Jan. to May, Summer	Usually American-style semesters: Aug. to Dec., Jan. to May, Summer

*Example of exceptions: Danish International Studies, organized by the Danish government, offers an island program to American students under the auspices of the University of Copenhagen. Advanced Studies in England, entirely operated by Brits, offers a program of study for Americans under the auspices of University College, Oxford.

Other Types of Programs

Chapter 3

A growing number of people want to do something out of the ordinary. They recognize that the training and experience they acquire in other countries will pay off regardless of whether they bring back credit to apply to an American university degree. Opportunities for professional and artistic training have always been available around the world. Today, it is easier than ever before to get information and to arrange for international training. You can set things up yourself or take advantage of expert organizations to help you with the arrangements. Furthermore, there is a world of opportunities beyond the traditional locations in Europe. You do not have to be proficient in another language to expand your horizons beyond the ordinary, although you will soon see how the possibilities increase for you if you add other languages to your skills. If you were able to circle the earth on a satellite, you would find cities and university communities everywhere on the globe where students, scholars, merchants, and diplomats exchange ideas in English. Not only can you take courses in English in many locations, while beginning or improving additional language skills, but you will find exciting and unusual study abroad programs as well. You will find many ways of acquiring global expertise and addressing issues confronting all of the world's people.

Studio Programs

If you want to study music, the fine arts, or theater, you can find stimulating opportunities in many European countries. However, you should give serious consideration to whether you want to earn credit for the experience or simply to practice and develop your skills. Most European countries separate the performance and studio arts from other academic fields. Courses in art history, aesthetic theory, and related theoretical subjects are offered at European universities. Advanced professional study in performance or in studio art generally takes place at conservatories and institutes where you can devote all your time to trying out ideas and honing your skills. Along with that opportunity come stimulating chances to exchange ideas with other students. Don't expect to find the American university model of credit-bearing programs that combine artistic training with a foundation in the liberal arts.

If you are an advanced student in the visual arts, expect to spend a great deal of your time working independently. In many European countries, training in the arts is a full-time course of professional training that begins as soon as a student completes secondary school. Rather than enrolling in a broad program of study in the liberal arts at a university, the artistically motivated student enters a conservatory program in which all the training focuses on developing the person's artistic talents. A musician, for example, receives rigorous training in theory and composition as well as in performing the instrument he or she has chosen. Each year, juries examine the students and hear them perform until they are judged worthy of a first prize.

If you want to take music or painting lessons as a sideline or hobby, you can arrange to take private lessons from one of the many instructors who have earned diplomas at the conservatories of art or music. Ask for assistance in selecting an instructor as soon as you arrive in the host country. Lists of certified instructors are usually available in local newspapers and telephone directories. As in the United States, the best way to find a good teacher is usually by word of mouth. If you are interested in music as an outside interest, rather than as a degree program, some universities might have performance centers where you can join musical ensembles and participate in organizing and presenting concerts. The University of St. Andrews in Scotland, for example, has a music center.

In the visual arts, students enroll in a conservatory. As they progress in their field, they might sign up for space in a workshop or studio where they can exchange ideas with other artists, but where they can perfect their skills in pursuit of one or more techniques or approaches that interest them.

As a visiting student, you might have the opportunity to enroll in art or music classes for credit through an American sponsor. On the other hand, many advanced students of the arts, particularly those over the age of 21, simply arrange to sign up for work in a studio (sometimes called an atelier), or they arrange to study privately with a celebrated

Unofficially...
At 22, I was too old to enroll in the Paris Conservatory of Music, so I studied privately, using my savings and a bank loan. I gave recitals and organized concerts, met artists and musicians from all over the world, and made a lot of contacts. I still send my students to study with people I met when I was a student.

artist or performer. Through interaction with other artists at a students' and artists' association, or through residence in an international student center in one of the world capitals, they can exchange new ideas about their work and take advantage of facilities where they can present recitals or exhibit their work.

Today, students interested in going to Paris, Florence, London, or Glasgow enroll in formal study abroad programs for Americans at one of the conservatories or schools of design or at international artistic centers. They can choose to live in one of the international student centers established by private foundations to serve young students and artists, or they can live in housing provided by an American sponsor.

If you want to earn credit for the experience, be sure to check with your home institution study abroad office about the procedure. If you select an art school that is not affiliated with a degree-granting university, many American institutions will not accept the credit. They require you to enroll through a degree-granting sponsoring institution in order to receive credit.

In Florence, students can earn transferable credit by enrolling at the Lorenzo de Medici Institute through half a dozen American universities, including the University of North Carolina at Chapel Hill, Fairfield University, Drake University, and others. Studio Art Centers International (SACI) also has American sponsors, including Bowling Green State University, which offers an M.A. in art history in cooperation with SACI. The American Institute for Foreign Study (AIFS) offers credit through Richmond College in London for study in Florence.

In the U.K., Beaver College sponsors a program at the Glasgow College of Art and AIFS sponsors programs at the Royal College of Art. Students can also enroll for art programs at Goldsmith College of the University of London. Consider your options carefully and ask your study abroad office for assistance as you review the catalogs and weigh your options.

Outside of Europe, you might have an opportunity to study the art, distinctive musical instruments, and dance traditions of many cultures. The catalogs mentioned earlier are well indexed to help you find this information. For instance, both Tufts and the School for International Training offer programs in Ghana that include studio art and music. In Indonesia, programs in the performing and fine arts of Bali and Java are available. Numerous other opportunities can be found in all parts of the world.

Non-Credit Programs

In addition to study abroad programs that provide credit, there are numerous opportunities to go abroad for practical experience without earning credit, or opportunities that combine credit with experiential learning. If the opportunity to gain practical experience and to develop skills is more important to you than transferring credit back to an American university or college, you might be interested in some of these choices. In other chapters of the guide, you will find lists of programs and places to get information about non-credit programs.

Summer Home Stays

You can spend your summer or spring vacation with a host family and learn about a culture without having to worry about attending classes and earning credit. Coordinators arrange groups of similar ages and interests. There are opportunities for high school, college-age, or adult participants. A popular summer home-stay option for high school students is offered by the Experiment in International Living (www.worldlearning.org). The Experiment is one of the oldest and best established international programs. Participants in its programs have a unique opportunity for total linguistic and cultural immersion. They spend one month in a family, sharing all the family's activities and chores, as well as any outings or festivities that happen to take place while they are there.

Participants in the Experiment are carefully screened to make sure that they are ready for complete immersion in a home stay during which they might not often see other program participants or the group leader. Before joining their host families, they undergo a thorough orientation to the culture they will encounter. Program staff encourage them to expect the unexpected and to try to understand any striking cultural differences through the eyes of the host culture. After a month family stay, members of the host families and of the American groups travel together and a big city stay is often a part of the experience.

Although the Experiment is one well-known example of this type of experiential learning (learning through practical experience rather than through formal classroom instruction), there are other home-stay programs.

A Student Speaks Up
While I was in high school, my teacher arranged for me to spend a month with a family in the Loire Valley. We had weekend outings to several of the chateaux, but on ordinary days I just helped with the chores—great for my French!

Study Tours

Museums and alumni associations organize many study tours featuring lectures and guided visits to locations of historical or natural interest. The Center for Global Education is just one of the organizations offering informative, non-credit vacation travel programs for adults.

The Council for International Education offers faculty development seminars through which university professionals can study the contemporary situation in critical locations around the world, especially those undergoing rapid transitions.

If you are interested in a study tour program, consult the pages at the front of the section for each region of the world and each country in the study abroad catalogs. There, you will find programs that visit more than one country or more than one city.

Some experts in the field of international study feel that a study tour allows too brief a stay in each location along the way. For those who are looking for an opportunity to immerse themselves in a language and culture, a study tour is not the best choice. A student of art or architecture, on the other hand, might benefit from the chance to compare city plans, monumental architecture, and museum collections in several locations. Consider your goals carefully as you review your options.

Internships

Internship is one of the fastest growing areas of international education. Although many study abroad programs offer internships as part of an academic program, you can find internship programs that just provide practical experience without the credit. Strongly recommended by William Nolting of the University of Michigan, who is a nationally recognized expert on disseminating information on work abroad opportunities for students, two excellent books provide internship information: the IIE catalogs mentioned earlier and the *Directory of*

A Student Speaks Up
Our study tour preceded three terms of intensive language study. We climbed holy mountains, visited universities, toured ancient Xi'an, and ate spicy Sichuan food with students. Nonetheless, it was too structured; we would have liked more time to explore on our own. Now, we are deep in our books and too busy to get out!

International Internships published by Michigan State University.

Send a payment of $25 to:

    Michigan State University
    Career Services and Placement
    113 Student Services Building
    East Lansing, MI 48824
    Phone: 517-355-9510
    Fax: 517-353-2957
    www.isp.msu.edu/InternationalInternships

The International Association for the Exchange of Students for Technical Experience, or IASTE (www.aipt.org/ iaeste), a division of the Association of International Practical Training, or AIPT (www. aipt.org/programs), offers internships all over the world for students with technical training. The University of Michigan's comprehensive Web site for work abroad opportunities provides 19 pages of annotated addresses for many other organizations offering internships and work experience (www.umich.edu/~icenter/overseas/work/ workabroad1.html).

The Commonwealth of Virginia has a semester-long internship program for Virginia students with placements in a variety of locations worldwide under the auspices of James Madison University. Summer internships are also available. Information is available from:

    Judy K. Cohen, Director of International
    Internships
    Office of International Education
    Hillcrest House, 2nd floor, MSC 1503
    James Madison University
    Harrisonburg, VA 22807
    Phone: 540-568-6979
    www.jmu.edu/intl-ed/internships/

Many programs combine some academic credit with an internship opportunity.

Internships to combine Chinese language learning with business or work experience in China are available through Ohio State University:

304 Ohio Legal Center
33 W. 11th Ave.
Columbus, OH 43201
Phone: 614-688-8425
Fax: 614-688-5583
E-mail: shepherd.37@osu.edu
www.cohums.ohio-state.edu/flc/
  US_CHINA_LINKS/

Among the many other widely used study abroad programs that provide internships are programs offered by:

Boston University
www.bu.edu/

The University of Rochester
www.rochester.edu/College/
  study-abroad/index.html

The Institute for the International Education of Students
www.iesabroad.org

There are many others. For more assistance in finding the program that is right for you and that combines credit with an internship, consult with the study abroad advisor at your home institution, with study abroad catalogs and the study abroad information sources mentioned here.

Volunteer Programs

Volunteer programs are reasonably priced chances to live simply while participating in an archaeology

Watch Out!
If you want to earn credit for an internship, check with your study abroad advisor before enrolling in a program. Some institutions have special procedures or restrictions governing internship credit.

project, trail restoration, or some other worthwhile and useful activity, during which you'll learn a lot and make some valuable friends. The University of Michigan Web site can get you started with a list of useful Web sites for students interested in programs with a service orientation. In addition, *Transitions Abroad* magazine (www.transabroad.com) publishes an issue each year with many useful articles by experienced volunteers, detailed lists of opportunities, and helpful ads. The experience you gain through participation in a volunteer program might help you qualify later for a prestigious scholarship or grant such as the Rhodes, Marshall, Rotary, or Fulbright scholarships.

A new edition of a popular directory of volunteer programs has just appeared: Filomena Geise, ed. with Marilyn Borchardt and Martha Fernandez, *Alternatives to the Peace Corps: A Directory of Third World and U.S. Volunteer Opportunities.* 8th ed. Food First (1999).

To order a copy from Food First, send $13.95 (each additional book $10.95) to:

> Subterranean Company
> Box 160
> 265 South 5th St.
> Monroe, OR 97456
> Phone: 800-274-7826
> Fax: 541-847-6018
> www.foodfirst.org

See also: "Responsible Travel: The Key Resources," a selected list of organizations and publications dedicated to the promotion of responsible and volunteer travel. The first list, compiled by Deborah McClaren, appears in *Transitions Abroad,* Nov./Dec. 1996. Watch for program ads and updates to the guide in subsequent issues of *Transitions* devoted to responsible travel.

You can order the issue for $6.95 from:

Back Issues
P.O. Box 1300
Amherst, MA 01004
Phone: 800-293-0373
E-mail: Trabroad@aol.com

Service Learning Programs

If you want, you can combine credit with a significant service-learning opportunity. The International Partnership for Service Learning (www.studyabroad.com/psl/) is one of the leaders in organizing semester-long study abroad in non-traditional destinations such as the Czech Republic or Ecuador and centering the experience on a service opportunity. The University of Minnesota Web site has further information about volunteer programs or study abroad with a service focus (www.istc.umn.edu/work/volunteer-search).

Short-Term Work Abroad

Recover some of your expenses while learning about the job market in another country. Council Work Abroad (www.ciee.org) and British Universities North America Club (BUNAC, www.bunac.org) offer assistance with your visa application and useful guidelines for locating a job. Short-term work visas are available for work in France, Ireland, Canada, Germany, New Zealand, Costa Rica, the U.K., and Australia. Abundant opportunities for short-term work are available. See Appendix C, "International Careers" for publications and other resources to get you started.

> **"**
> A student on the Partnership for Service Learning in the Czech Republic earned an award for her commitment to combating illiteracy by collecting books in the United States to send to areas in transition. She collected a huge supply of texts to send to Africa.
> **"**

Unofficially...
The British government now allows visiting students who are enrolled for more than six months to work in Britain. Spring enrollment at some universities technically is valid through August, so American students can work in the U.K. during the summer months after their classes end.

The most comprehensive guide to short-term paid work abroad appears on the University of Michigan Web page created and regularly updated by William Nolting (www.umich.edu/~icenter/overseas/work/shortterm1.html).

Additional information about short-term work abroad is available at www.studyabroad.com and at www.transabroad.com. You might also want to consult issues of *Transitions Abroad* that focus on short-term work abroad experiences.

Teaching Abroad

Many services offer assistance in placing teachers overseas. In the past, many emerging countries hired recent college graduates with good academic backgrounds but little formal training. These young teachers learned on the job, often went on to obtain further training, and made teaching their careers. Today, it is becoming more important to have appropriate training and qualifications in order to accept an extended contract to teach abroad. Nonetheless, introductory opportunities for recent college graduates are still available. The number of apprenticeship or training opportunities is increasing. There are many resources available for teachers of English and other subjects.

The University of Michigan Web site, once again, is one you must consult. *Transitions Abroad* offers an issue each year on teaching abroad, with a wealth of helpful articles on the challenges and rewards of teaching overseas. Each issue contains practical tips for finding suitable positions and getting the training you need for an extended career in the field. Numerous teacher placement services place ads in *Transitions*.

If you decide to make a career of teaching English as a second language, further training is necessary. For information about graduate training programs in Teaching English as a Second Language (TESL), consult the annual membership directory of the Modern Language Association, which you can find in most college and university libraries. For additional assistance, contact the NAFSA home page (www.nafsa.org) and check the ATESL section for the names and addresses of experts in the field.

Expanding Your Horizons

Before you submit program applications, stop to think about parts of the world you would enjoy exploring. Don't assume that you must be proficient in the host country's language in order to travel outside the United States or even outside the British Isles. In many countries, courses are available in English through the host universities or through American program sponsors. You can begin your study of the language of the host country or converse with citizens of a country where English is the official language and who therefore are proficient in your own language. You can even study a specialized field, such as law or business, side by side with citizens of the country who want to perfect their skills in English by taking their courses in that language.

Exciting programs taught in English await you in countries you might not be considering. The following list is intended to give you an idea of all the possibilities from which you can choose. It is not intended to be an exhaustive list or to exclude any programs not mentioned here, but it will give you

66
Even with no experience, I found a teaching position in Japan. I later became a corporate trainer and learned to manage people, give seminars, and have confidence in my abilities. Now that I have returned, I use all of these skills in my present job and use the teaching skills I learned to help immigrants in my community learn English.
99

an idea about the global reach of the English language and the availability of programs for the student who does not feel ready to take all his or her classes in a second language. Further details about contacting these programs are provided in Appendix B:

- Danish International Studies offers a stimulating collection of options for business, engineering, marine biology and ecology, international studies, and architecture, sponsored by the Danish government. Courses are taught in English with the opportunity to learn Danish and live with a Danish family.

66

As an Indian American returning from Prague, I wrote about the deeply troubling mistreatment and discrimination that gypsies face in the Czech Republic. Eastern Europe is going through difficult changes and the future is unclear.

99

- The University of Economics in Prague features programs sponsored by the American Institute for Foreign Study.

- A Central and East European Studies Program is taught in English with opportunities for studying German and Czech. Courses offer a balance of topics in the social sciences and humanities, well suited to an interdisciplinary major such as international studies.

- The School for Field Studies offers environmental studies in a variety of locations such as the British West Indies, Canada (British Columbia), Australia (a rainforest study center in Queensland), Costa Rica, Kenya, and Mexico. For example, the Center for Wildlife Management Studies in Kenya invites students to explore human and wildlife management issues through the eyes of local ranchers and native communities, to live close to the wildlife on an experimental ranch, and to explore parts of the country not open to tourists. (Visit the site www.fieldstudies.org/pages/programs/kenya.html.)

- The School for International Training offers a range of interdisciplinary semester programs in the regions mentioned earlier and in addition has programs available in Asia and Oceania. Among the opportunities described in more detail in its program brochures and on its Web site are two semester programs in India, one on arts and culture and the other in gender studies. A program on the unique cultural heritage of Bali considers Bali's anomalous role in predominantly Muslim Indonesia. Among the other programs in this one region of the world are studies of the natural and human environment in Nepal and Pacific Islands studies in Samoa. (Visit www.worldlearning.org/sit.html.)

- Environmental Studies in Australia are offered through AustraLearn, a program coordinated by the Australian government. You can find the university in Australia that has an academic program and setting most closely linked with your own interests. Whether the academic focus of your studies is in psychology, public health, or environmental science, you can find a university offering courses appropriate for the pursuit of your goals. (See www.australearn.org/.)

- Business programs in many countries offer advanced training in English to their own students. Americans who have studied the major European languages have additional opportunities to study international business and improve their language skills at centers such as the Norwegian School of Business and Economics, INCAE (in Costa Rica), the University of Business and Economics in Vienna, and other locations. MBA students and undergraduate business students interested in such exchanges can get further information from their home institutions, or they can contact an American university such as the University of Rochester, Bentley College, or Boston University for information about programs open to students from other institutions.

- Kansai Gaidai University in Japan offers an Asian Studies program in English. Previous study of Japanese is strongly recommended, and Japanese language courses are an important part of the curriculum. Nonetheless, students can choose from a range of courses, including business, economics, history, literature, studio art, religion, philosophy, and anthropology. All the courses offer an opportunity to learn more about Japanese and Asian cultures while increasing your proficiency in Japanese. (See www.kansai-gaidai-u.ac.jp/bekka/asian/index.html.)

In short, just about any program of study that interests you is probably available in an English-language curriculum in a part of the world you might not have previously considered. Regard this list as an introduction to the possibilities available to you. Consult your study abroad advisor and the catalogs of programs. Review general Web sites such as Transabroad.com and StudyAbroad.com, and keep your mind open to the rich variety of programs available.

Even in countries where English is not the official language or where it is only one of the languages spoken, there are study abroad programs in English. The universities offering them encourage Americans to learn more about the history and culture of the country, as well as explore development issues and take courses in business, economics, environmental studies, and a range of other subjects.

Some Other Locations You Might Consider

- **Scandinavia:** Numerous programs in each of the Scandinavian countries offer academic programs in English. Science students might find the offerings of particular interest, but there is a wide range of programs through American sponsors and through direct enrollment.

- **Belize:** Biology and environmental studies are available in English.

- **New Zealand:** Several universities offer direct enrollment.

- **Kenya, Ghana, and South Africa:** American university sponsors offer programs in East, West, or South Africa.

- **The Netherlands:** Courses in English are available at the Universities of Leichen, Amsterdam, and elsewhere.

Considering the Road Less Traveled

In addition to considering formal programs in unusual parts of the world, you might be interested in putting together your own program of study or research. Ask whether your college offers fellowships that help students to create and implement their own short-term projects such as volunteer, service, or research projects.

Recently, faculty at one of the historically black colleges and universities (also known informally as HBCUs) responded to an initiative begun by the governor of its state. Several faculty members went to Guyana and Brazil to explore study abroad program development for their students. Other institutions are forming partnerships so that they will have a combined group of students large enough to offer programs in unusual locations. These collaborative arrangements make it possible to offer programs in locations as unusual as Azerbiajan, Belgium, Venezuela, Jamaica, Malta, Kyrgyzstan, and Vietnam. Writing in the Nov./Dec. 1996 issue of *Transitions Abroad,* Janet Park points out that interested volunteers can help with natural history studies at the Howler Monkey Research Project in Belize, sponsored by the Oceanic Research Society. The phone number is 800-326-7491.

Older travelers can participate through the Elderhostel Service Project in Belize. A catalog of other service projects is available from the Elderhostel Boston Office if you call 617-426-8056.

Those interested in combining service with academic credit might be interested in Duke University's summer archaeology program in Galilee, Israel:

> Office of Foreign Academic Programs, Inc.
> Duke University
> 121 Allen Bldg.
> Box 90057
> Durham, NC 27708-0057
> Phone: 919-684-2174
> Fax: 919-684-3083

Michigan State University offers an exciting but economical semester program in Nepal, with courses that consider global diversity and management of subtropical natural resources. An added feature of the program, hiking in the Himalayas, takes you to some of the least traveled roads in the world of study abroad:

Office of Study Abroad
Phone: 517-353-8920
E-mail: Ovr05@msu.edu
www.study-abroad.msu.edu

Just the Facts

- Consider your credit options carefully.

- Look for performance and studio art programs outside the regular university environment.

- Explore the expanding world of international internship opportunities.

- Consider teaching abroad as a career or as a prelude to other work opportunities.

- Explore a wealth of volunteer opportunities around the world.

- Be open to unusual destinations and activities.

GET THE SCOOP ON...
Finding accessible programs ▪ Selecting
programs for mature students ▪ Choosing
options for busy parents ▪ Finding good,
reliable programs for teens

Choosing Study Abroad Programs for Non-Traditional or Special Needs Students

Chapter 4

I t is probably safe to say that there are few, if any, study abroad programs that are accessible to every disabled student who enrolls at an American university. Each person's needs are unique and the degree to which any program can meet them will vary. The process of choosing a program is time-consuming and some students will inevitably decide not to go abroad. However, the good news is that the number of services is increasing and more opportunities are becoming available.

Little by little, awareness of the needs of travelers with special interests and needs is growing. Numerous shorter programs work for people with families or for working students. Some summer programs are ideal for older travelers wanting a stimulating and informative experience abroad.

67

Teenagers, too, are finding an increasing number of opportunities especially for them.

The leading authority on the issue of accessibility in worldwide study and travel is Susan Sygall, Director of Mobility International USA (MIUSA). MIUSA is a nonprofit organization providing resources to persons with disabilities seeking ways to travel alone or with groups:

> P.O. Box 10767
> Eugene, OR 97440
> Phone: 541-343-1284 (voice and TDD)
> Fax: 541-343-6812
> E-mail: miusa@igc.apc.org

Sygall has written numerous articles and given presentations at international education conferences and other meetings on positive approaches to travel and study abroad for travelers with disabilities. She stated recently that choice is important because obstacles exist and vary with each individual (see *Transitions Abroad,* Jul./Aug. 1999, 68). Materials and information from Sygall and MIUSA can help you select a program:

- "A World Awaits You (AWAY)"
- *Looking Back, Looking Forward,* a 17-minute video
- "Home Is in the Heart: Accommodating People with Disabilities in the Homestay Experience"
- "A World of Options: A Guide to International Educational Exchange, Community Service, and Travel for Persons with Disabilities" (on the Web at www.transabroad.com)
- *Building Bridges: A Manual on Including People with Disabilities in International Exchange Programs*

- Equal Opportunities in the U.S. and New Independent States (NIS)

- *Over the Rainbow,* MIUSA's quarterly newsletter

Sygall contributed much of the material in "Disability Travel," an entire section of *Transitions Abroad,* Jul./Aug. 1999. This issue, or any other issue of the magazine, is available for $5.00 from *Transitions Abroad.* The Jul./Aug. 1999 issue lists 14 organizations whose function is to assist world travelers with disabilities. They offer vacation travel packages, information about facilities, lists of hospitals and physicians in certain locations, and a free clearinghouse of information to help people with disabilities find a full range of international exchange opportunities. In addition, the Jul./Aug. issue identifies 19 publications with information about accessibility issues and 17 disability tour programs. The issue lists 11 Web sites providing information to assist travelers with disabilities and three groups of programs that describe themselves as "disability friendly." Finally, two articles by Sygall offer practical tips for travelers with disabilities and an overview of the current state of services around the world.

> If we are truly traveling to create a better and more just world, then let's be sure that we are including all of its citizens.
> —Susan Sygall, *Transitions Abroad,* Jul./Aug. 1999, p. 68.

What Questions to Ask

Regardless of the special assistance you receive at your home institution, or the arrangements you make in your life to accommodate even the most common of medical or therapeutic needs, you must ask detailed questions about services at host institutions and in host countries abroad. Many developed countries provide ample services, from contact lenses and asthma inhalers to wheelchairs and the parts needed to repair or maintain them. However, you cannot assume that *any* specific product, accommodation, treatment, or service that you require in the United States is available in exactly the same form in another country. Although some individuals will be able to substitute another, locally available product or service, you cannot assume that this will work for you. If you are thinking of going abroad, follow these guidelines:

- Ask suppliers about the availability in the country and city you are considering of any product you regularly use.

- If you have a learning disability requiring special assistance, such as extra time for taking an examination, ask about the accommodation that the host university provides.

- Ask specific questions about accommodations for mobility. Ask in particular about the design of public toilets in the country you are going to.

- Ask about the availability of elevators in the classroom buildings and in public transportation centers, such as bus and train stations. Ask about curb cuts and other means of aiding mobility in the city that interests you.

- Ask about the assistance available for students with hearing or vision impairment and the arrangements for compensating those who provide the assistance.

- Just keep asking questions until you have all the information you need to make your decision!

Who Makes the Decision About Your Participation

You should be the one to decide. Some program administrators might assume that there is no way to accommodate your needs and prefer to reject your application rather than feel obligated to provide services that would be difficult to provide.

"Many exchange advisors assume that accommodating people with disabilities in their programs will be prohibitively expensive," states the MIUSA Web site, A World Awaits You (AWAY). "In fact, many accommodations are cost-free or quite inexpensive. The key to finding low-cost solutions is to foster open communication with the exchange participant and to think broadly about the possibilities and resources available to the organization and the student (www.miusa.org/awaylowcost.htm)."

You are the one who knows exactly what limitations you live with, and you have the responsibility to find out what accommodations can be made for you in different locations. You should make the decision about whether the program is accessible for you. By working closely with program administrators about the accessibility and services you need, you should be able to make an informed decision about whether any given program can accommodate you. With information available from a wide range of programs and services, you can look forward to finding a program. You might need to be flexible about location and academic setting. If it does not look as if one city, country, or program will work out for you, you have a good chance of finding an alternative.

"My study abroad advisor encouraged me to apply to two programs in the U.K. offering courses in my major. We chose the two that seemed most accessible for me. Because I get around on crutches, we pretty much ruled out London because of the traffic. After I was accepted to both programs, I contacted them by e-mail to get further information about services.

After several e-mail messages, one university advised me that it would not be able to accommodate me, but the second program really wanted me to come to the city of Avon. I learned that program participants travel about the city on foot and by public bus. I would have to manage steep climbs on and off the bus and up and down the streets in some hilly sections of the city. To help with this, the program offered me a ground floor room close to the administrative and classroom building. I requested privacy and they gave me a single room. The study abroad advisor had visited the program and asked about some other things. For instance, students get into the buildings by punching a security code on keypads by the doors. We made sure I could reach all of those.

Things seemed to be going well until I asked about meals. Students on the program have to shop and fix their own meals. I asked whether there were any funds to pay for eating in restaurants because I don't cook. The study abroad advisor found out from the Dean of Students Office that the college provides funds to help students with academic needs, but the choice of meal plans was optional, so they could not help me with money to eat in restaurants. When I heard this, I decided to learn to cook.

I went to the U.K. and attended all program events. I went everywhere on my own and had a great time. My housemates and I divided up the tasks, so I had no problem doing my share of the work. I had a great semester". The account above is based on the experience of a real student who achieved the goal of study abroad by gathering a lot

Watch Out!
I chose a summer program in France because program administrators told me I wouldn't have any problems. However, I discovered that most of the public toilets in Western France are Turkish toilets. You have to squat to use them. My knee joint is stiff and I can't stoop down. I couldn't go to the bathroom!

of information and planning everything carefully ahead of time.

Your Rights Under the Americans with Disabilities Act

Find out about your rights under the Americans with Disabilities Act. Next, research the institutional policies concerning access to study abroad programs. Institutions interpret the law in various ways. For example, some colleges and universities might take the position that the ADA obliges them to provide only academic assistance and only that which the student requires for academic work on the home campus. Some institutions state that they do not provide assistance in obtaining optional services, such as food and housing. Some institutions regard study abroad programs as optional and do not assist the student with access to any programs. Others might provide assistance only with access to the academic components of the institution's approved programs. Although you might expect an institution to provide access if study abroad is required of all students, you should check to be sure.

To find your rights under the Americans with Disabilities Act, visit a variety of Web sites to help understand the implications of the law and how to use it:

Disability Related Resource Menu:
www.icdi.wvu.edu/others.htm

A Compliance Guide to the ADA:
www.thompson.com/tpg/person/able/
  able.html

Mid-Atlantic Region Guide:
www.adainfo.org/

The U.S. Department of Justice home page
on the ADA:

www.usdoj.gov/crt/ada/adahom1.htm

Disability Rights Activist, a publication for
showing people with disabilities how to
obtain the services they should receive under
the law:

www.teleport.com/~abarhydt/

Other information about the law, activism,
and your rights:

consumerlawpage.com/brochure/disab.shtml

To order publications on the Americans with
Disabilities Act, see the MISUA Web site. For a free
brochure, "Rights and Responsibilities: A Guide to
the Americans with Disabilities Act (ADA) for
International Organizations and Participants,"
send your name and address to MIUSA via regular
mail or e-mail. Check with MIUSA about any
regulations in other countries that help ensure
access.

What You Should Know About Limitations on Services in Other Countries

Although many excellent products and services are
available in other countries, some of which might
seem superior to those you can find in the States,
you should never assume that any services will be the
same. For students on any prescription medication:
Be sure to take with you a complete supply of your
medication. Label it clearly and keep it in the containers in which it was dispensed so that you will not
run into any difficulties in a customs inspection. You
need to take enough for the entire time you
are away. For example, Ritallin, which many
American students take, is not available in many

other countries. It is not recognized as a necessary medication in Great Britain, for instance.

Even if you are taking classes through an American university, you should make sure you can make the same arrangements that you do at home for taking an examination. Special accommodation might be different for students requiring extra time, a reader, or other special services while taking examinations. For example, although a British university might allow extra time, it may be more limited than the time offered at an American university.

Take a complete supply of any healthcare products such as contact lenses. In addition, you might have to leave instructions behind to have replacements of other supplies shipped or express-mailed to you if needed. Find out whether you can make substitutions for any over-the-counter preparations that you use regularly. Specific brands of American-made healthcare products, such as contact lens solutions, might not be available. If you do find them, they might be much more expensive. However, in some cases, local brands offered in the pharmacies can be much cheaper and just as effective.

Many locations, including the western part of France, still have so-called Turkish toilets in public restrooms. Except in hotels and restaurants catering to foreign visitors, restrooms in China, Thailand, Japan, and other countries have toilets that require users to squat. Alternatives might not be available at some of the scheduled excursion stops. If a crouching or squatting position is difficult or impossible for you, please alert program administrators and ask about restrooms in areas you will be touring. If you are visiting older buildings and monuments, or the older sections of cities, do not expect access for persons with disabilities such as ramps and elevators. Curb cuts are rare in other parts of the world.

Unofficially...
Our faculty director in Italy has used a wheelchair for several years. She gets around the cities by cab and there is an elevator in the apartment building where she stays. However, the wear and tear on her wheelchair is terrific because it has to handle the old stone streets and plazas. The cost of repairs after each trip is around $350.

Be prepared for different levels of acceptance, ranging from indifference to curiosity. Culturally, many countries do not have the same attitude as North Americans toward people with disabilities. In China, people stare without any embarrassment at persons in wheelchairs or people displaying other unusual features. Some Europeans might regard signing in public as amusing, a source of entertainment. Take advantage of the material available from MIUSA and other organizations and ask questions about *everything* you might encounter.

Finding and Choosing Programs for Retirees, Parents, Teachers, and Other Non-Traditional Students

Summer Language Programs

Summer language programs are a popular option for adults seeking study abroad opportunities. Here are some of the advantages of signing up for a program through an American college or university. First of all, you can work on your language skills, if you'd like to brush up on a language you've studied or start a new one. Secondly, you can take advantage of a well-organized program, including travel, hotel arrangements, excursions, and housing. If you want to visit an unusual destination, you will be able to take advantage of pre-departure orientations, recommended readings, and guided visits during the program.

Knowledgeable faculty might be able to arrange guest lectures or provide opportunities to interview well-known public leaders, artists, or other important personalities from the country. They might be able to get students into locations where commercial guided tours do not have permission to go. You will have the pleasure of associating with a lively group of college students from the United States and, depending on the program you select, a group of interesting international students who have chosen the same destination. Finally, you might find the group leader, and the leaders of other groups at the same destination, to be interesting colleagues and companions. Your spouse or friend might want to join you at the end of the program for some leisure travel.

Vacation Study Abroad, edited by the Institute for International Education, offers more than 2,200 short-term study abroad programs ranging in duration from two weeks to an entire summer term. As the title indicates, the program listings are not just for summer. Many universities arrange short-term sojourns abroad for December through January vacation periods or during spring break. With some universities beginning their summer break as early as May and others extending theirs until late in September, a great many different schedules are available. Programs are grouped by region of the world, country, and city. Cross-references group programs by subjects, length of program, and cost. Each listing includes the person to contact for an application and more information. Most programs include their fax number, e-mail, and Web URL. The new catalogs appear early in March and provide information for short-term programs during any vacation period in the following academic year.

What to Ask When You Contact the Program

Ask whether any of the activities planned would be difficult for a spouse or for yourself if you aren't as physically active as the rest of the group. Bear in mind that a college program might expect you to walk long distances and perhaps use subways and

Unofficially...
At 70 years old, Richard was a great addition to our group. He turned out to be a gourmet cook and fixed us a special French meal. He went everywhere with us and even went back the following summer for more French language practice.

stairways. Summer programs are likely to include beach outings, visits to parks and other natural settings, and even hiking, boating, or other sports. Students usually have to carry their own luggage at some point. On the other hand, with advance notice, programs should be able to accommodate a person who isn't able to carry luggage or walk long distances. If you alert the program to any difficulties, you and the program administrator can determine together whether special arrangements are possible. If one program cannot make adjustments, it might be wiser to select another program.

Similarly, you should make note in your application of any vision or hearing loss, diet restrictions, or other limitations that might require special accommodation. There are so many programs available that you can find one to work with any special needs you have. (Refer to the information about MIUSA at the beginning of this chapter.)

Non-Credit Language Programs

If you are not interested in earning credit for the program, you might prefer to enroll directly in a summer language institute in another country. If you select that option, you have to make your own arrangements for getting to the program site. Arranging housing and meals might require time and effort as well. Finally, you might not have as many choices of excursions as you would with a sponsored American university program.

On the other hand, you might be able to save money on your travel, arrange housing that suits your personal preferences, and have more flexibility in choosing your return date and scheduling travel after the program ends. You'll also have more

flexibility in taking family or friends along and
arranging to spend free time with them. Here are
some language institutes that you can contact
directly:

- **Italian:** Linguaviva, accredited by the Italian
  government and one of the oldest and
  biggest language institutes in Italy with
  centers in Florence, Milan, and Lignano
  (www.linguaviva.it/).

- **Alliance Française:** The leading worldwide
  organization for the dissemination of French
  language and culture, with centers around the
  world. Find centers in France by city on the
  Alliance Web page (www.best.com/~afsf/
  sites.html New UPV Web page).

- **Goethe Institutes:** The official German center
  for teaching German language and culture
  with centers worldwide, including 17 in
  Germany. The addresses are available on the
  Goethe Institute Web site:

  Berlin

  Neue Schönhauser Str. 20

  10178 Berlin

  Director: Franz Xaver Augustin

  Phone: 030-25906-3

  Fax: 030-25906-400

  E-mail: berlin@goethe.de

  www.goethe.de/p/depadr2.htm

- **Spanish-Latin American culture:** A number of
  American universities prefer the Centro
  Mexicano Internacional for teaching Spanish
  and Latin American culture because of its
  good facilities, services, and location:

Fray Antonio de San Miguel 173

Morelia, Michoacan 58000

Mexico

Phone: 800-835-8863

Fax: 011-524-313-9898

E-mail: cmi@morelia.podernet.com.mx

www.spanish-language.com/

Special Interest Exchanges

If you are interested in an exchange that does not involve credit but emphasizes making contact with families and communities abroad, there are numerous exchange programs for adults. *Transitions Abroad,* which specializes in non-traditional experiences abroad, offers numerous possibilities at its Web site: www.transabroad.com. See the actual Web site for many choices.

Here are some great examples:

- **Elderhostel:** Educational adventures for adults over 55. Sponsors more than 2,000 nonprofit, short-term programs in 70 countries:

    75 Federal St.

    Boston, MA 02110

    Phone: 617-426-7788

    www.elderhostel.org

- **Eldertreks:** "Exotic adventures for travelers 50 and over"

    597 Markham St.

    Toronto, Ontario,

    Canada M6G 2L7

    Phone: 800-741-7956

    Fax: 416-588-9839

    E-mail: passages@inforamp.net

    www.eldertreks.com

- **Women Welcome Women:** This organization promotes exchanges between women around the world:

    88 Easton St., High Wycombe

    Buckinghamshire

    HP11 1LT, UK

    or

    2 Michallan Court

    Donvale 3111

    Australia

- **WWOOF** (Willing Workers on Organic Farms) An international volunteer program:

    3231 Hillside Rd.

    Deming, WA 98244

    (Other offices in Australia, Germany, Ireland, and the UK)

Short-Term Programs for Students with Families

Whether you intend to go abroad for a short period yourself or take your whole family with you, a lot of choices fit your interest and schedule. Some exchanges require only a membership fee or service charge for families who want to save money by swapping homes for a short period of time. Others allow you and your family to live with a family in another country and invite them to your home later, so that you can get to know one another. Still others are not exchanges, but simply an opportunity to stay for a while as a paying guest in a family atmosphere.

Exchanges for the Whole Family

Once again, *Transitions Abroad* provides a large menu of resources about family exchanges and home stays. The Web site features a comprehensive list of books and organizations to tempt you with home stays for families and young people. The following extract from the Web site is only a small piece of what is available in exchange living for adults around the world:

- **FAMILYHOSTEL:** 10-day learning and travel programs in foreign countries for families, including parents, grandparents, and school children:

  6 Garrison Ave.

  Durham, NH 03824

  Phone: 800-733-9753

  www.learn.unh.edu/INTERHOSTEL/IH_FH.html

- **Friends in France:** French families offer hospitality and local expertise to paying guests in their Paris apartments, chateaux, villas, or farmhouses:

  40 E. 19th St.

  New York, NY 10003-1303

  Phone: 212-260-9820

  Fax: 212-228-0576

  E-mail: stay@friends-in-france.com

- **Friends Overseas:** Provides lists of people who want to meet Americans in several countries, including Scandinavia (especially Finland), Australia, Japan, Mexico, and Russia:

  68-04 Dartmouth St.

  Forest Hills, NY 11375

- **Friendship Force:** An international friendship organization founded by Jimmy Carter:

  75 Forsyth St., NW Suite 900

  Atlanta, GA 30303

  Phone: 404-522-9490 or 800-688-6777

  Fax: 404-688-6148

  www.friendship-force.org

For a Single Family Member

If you are interested in a short-term program for yourself but want to limit your time away from your job and family, many references can help you find a program to suit your schedule. *Vacation Study Abroad,* an annual publication of the Institute for International Education, offers more than 2,200 short-term study abroad programs ranging in duration from two weeks to an entire term. With some universities beginning their summer terms early in May and others extending their summer terms until September, many different schedules are available. Many universities arrange short-term trips abroad for December through January vacation periods or during spring break. This guide has a superior format, presenting program information in a succinct manner that makes it easy to compare dates, prices, and subject areas. Remember that the prices include only the program fees. You might have to add on the cost of international transportation, meals not included in the fee, and other costs (see Chapter 7, "Figuring Out the Cost of Programs and How to Finance Them").

On the Web, consult transabroad.com or studyabroad.com for an overview of short-term study abroad programs.

Field Trips

Short-term field trips offer one of the best ways for an adult to have an international experience without sacrificing too much time from work, family obligations, or regular studies on campus. University summer study abroad programs can help a teacher earn additional credit toward certification.

Many programs cut costs and time by combining an introductory period of study on an American

Moneysaver
At the end of two weeks of local study with experts, we had learned a lot of observation and identification techniques. After our examination, we headed for the airport. With our professor, we spent two weeks in Costa Rica, observing and identifying tropical birds. My school paid the tuition because it was additional training for my certification as a high school biology teacher.

university campus with a short-term field study in another country. This setup controls the costs of the program and allows adult students to live at home and continue with their regular routines while learning the basic research techniques and concepts to be used in the field study. The instructors can take full advantage of all the laboratories and other facilities available on their home campus while they introduce the students to the basic "building blocks" of the course. Then, at the end of the course, the students and faculty member go abroad to apply the research methods to the subject in the host country. Teachers can earn credit for an archeological field study in the Caribbean, a tropical botany program in Central America, a primatology field study in Tanzania, or any other course that combines an introduction to research methods with actual hands-on experience in another country.

For further information about field study programs of this kind, consult the index of *Vacation Study Abroad*. Request further information from faculty members in the fields that interest you. Ask whether a short-term field study trip is being planned by any of the faculty on your own campus or whether any of them are teaching a vacation period field study course through another university. In certain fields of research, the professional journals list short-term field study programs that are available for the following summer.

The Virginia Council for International Education (VaCIE) is one state-wide organization that coordinates short-term summer programs for students on a tight budget or a tight schedule. For additional information, contact your local community college to see whether it offers any short-term programs.

Be sure to contact the study abroad advisor at your home institution. Through professional networks, your advisor might be able to find additional short-term study abroad opportunities that combine with pre-departure or follow-up classes in the United States.

Study Abroad Opportunities for High School Students

Research shows that many students first consider study abroad while they are in high school. Some of you start looking for opportunities to study or travel abroad as soon as you can. However, unless your teacher or your school is currently organizing a trip or exchange, it might seem difficult to find good, reliable programs. If you are a teenager looking for a chance to live or study in another country, we have good news for you. The number of opportunities is increasing rapidly, and you can find a great deal of information once you know where to look.

Information Sources for High School Students

The first place to start arranging for a study abroad or exchange program is at your school or through a community organization. Here is how high school exchanges work: A teacher, administrator, or official in your community arranges for a group of students from another country to visit your town, usually for about one month. The families of students at your school invite the students to stay with them. The community plans social events for them and organizes outings to show them the attractions of your area. If the visit takes place during the school year, students might attend classes at your high school. Some time later, perhaps the following summer, students from your school have a chance to visit the town from which your guests came and stay with their families. Some longer programs arrange for a student to spend a semester or an entire year in another country.

You and your parents will look for someone reliable who can recommend a program of high quality. Begin with the closest source of information; ask your teachers. If your school already offers an exchange program, you can be reasonably sure of the quality of the program. Several professional organizations promote international exchanges and monitor the quality of programs offered for high school students.

Ask your teachers whether a program is already available in your school district or state. Most language teachers belong to the professional associations for their particular language and many belong to the American Council of Foreign Language Teachers. Reliable programs publicize their exchanges through these organizations. Your state's language teachers organization probably knows good summer exchange or language study programs, available through regional coordinators right in your area. If your town has a sister city program, your school might arrange its own exchange with one or more sister cities. If your school does not offer a program, you, your teacher, and your family might want to get a program started.

"VIVE (Virginia International Vendôme Exchange) is the best high school study abroad program I know," says Tyla Matteson, a French teacher at Hampton High School in Virginia. "We set it up ourselves with the help of the French consular official in our area. She had relatives in the Vendôme, south of Paris in the valley of the Loire River. Our city had historic connections with the area because of the French soldiers who came to help win the

American Revolution. Every other spring, a group of students goes to stay with French families. The school board gives each program the same careful scrutiny that it did the first year to ensure that the high quality of the program continues."

Another good resource to consult in your search for a reliable, rewarding program is the principal of your school. He or she probably belongs to national organizations that review and approve exchange programs and help promote exchange partnerships between secondary institutions around the world. School Partnerships International is administered by the National Association of Secondary School Principals:

> 1904 Association Dr.
> Dept. CS
> Reston, VA 20191-1537
> Phone: 703-860-0200
> Fax: 703-476-9319
> E-mail: jacksonr@nassp.org

Council on Standards for International Education Travel (CSIET) is a nonprofit organization that sets standards for the quality and safety of high school exchanges and monitors programs to ensure their compliance. You and your parents might want to contact them to request their publication: *Advisory List of International Educational Travel & Exchange Programs* (published annually, $15 post-paid in the United States). Consult with your local teachers and administrators to see whether they are willing to help you, and your family, organize a program for your area:

> 212 S Henry St.
> Alexandria, VA 22314
> Phone: 703-739-9050
> Fax: 703-739-9035

Several civic groups participate in exchange programs. Kiwanis International offers an exchange program through Rotary International. Find out whether your community has a Kiwanis or Rotary Club that would like to help organize an exchange.

Your parents might want to propose an exchange program to the members of their church or civic group (such as the Elks, Lions, Shriners, or Chamber of Commerce). One of these groups might like to contact an exchange organization to start a program for your community.

Descriptions of Some Great Programs

Some reputable institutions and organizations put together groups of applicants from all over the country, rather than from a single community.

The Experiment in International Living, from the World Learning Center in Brattleboro, Vermont, is one of the best known programs for cross-cultural understanding:

A Program of World Learning
Kilpling Road
P.O. Box 676
Brattleboro, Vermont 05302-0676
Phone: 802-257-77511 or 800-345-2929
Fax: 802-258-3428
E-mail: eil@worldlearning.org
www.worldlearning.org/ip/summer.html

Founded in 1932, the Experiment has offered summer home-stay programs for high school students for longer than half a century. Now expanded into the World Learning Center, which includes a complete degree-granting university, the center is among the leaders in developing educational programs with an emphasis on building cultural understanding.

A number of high school study abroad programs are listed on the comprehensive study abroad Web site administered by Marc Landon: www.studyabroad.com. Together with the program listings, which include a separate group for high school programs, is the helpful and thorough general guide, the *studyabroad.com Handbook* by William Hoffa. The Web site offers links to the following programs especially for teenagers. In addition to the World Learning Center, other colleges and universities sponsoring programs especially for high school students include:

> University of New Orleans
> Division of International Education
> www.uno.edu~inst/programs.html

> Pennsylvania State University Summer Study
> at the American University in Paris
> www.summerstudy.com

> Youth for Understanding (summer, semester, and year abroad programs)
> Phone: 800-TEENAGE
> www.youthforunderstanding.com

Language programs are available in France, Italy, Spain, and Argentina. Other programs include Switzerland, Norway, Ecuador, Brazil, the Czech Republic, Hungary, Russia, Latvia, and Estonia.

AYUSA International, based in San Francisco, is a highly recommended high school exchange organization offering semester or year abroad programs:

> AYUSA International
> One Post St., 7th Floor
> San Francisco, CA 94104
> Phone: 888-55-AYUSA

Kiwanis International offers an exchange program through AYUSA.

Other programs for high school students include the American Council for International Studies (ACIS):

> AIFS College Summer Division, Attn: Beth Avitabile
> 102 Greenwich Ave.
> Greenwich, CT 06830
> E-mail: bavitabi@acis.com
> www.acis.com

Its high school program offerings include three, six-, and nine-week programs for high school students in London. You can also choose from a four-, six-, and eight-week French language program in Cannes or Paris and a five-week program in St. Petersburg, Russia. There is also a four- or six-week program in Salamanca, Spain. In addition, the Web site offers a brief but useful set of guidelines to help high school students prepare for study abroad.

The *Transitions Abroad* Web site offers a special selection of study and travel abroad programs for teenagers (www.transabroad.com/frames/trstudy. htm).

The Jul./Aug. 1999 issue of *Transitions Abroad* offers five extensive pages of organizations, programs, and resources for teens, including:

- EF Foundation for Foreign Study (known internationally as EF High School Year) is a non-profit organization that organizes cultural exchanges. As listed on www.transabroad.com, the program has arranged more than 40,000 exchange placements:

  > 1 Education St.
  > Cambridge, MA 02141

Phone: 617-619-1400
Fax: 617-619-1001
www.ef.com

- AmeriSpan Unlimited offers family, teen, senior, and adult language programs in 12 Spanish-language countries. Destinations include Mexico, Spain, and Central and South America. Housing is with host families. A display ad is listed on the home page of www.transabroad.com:

   P.O. Box 40007
   Philadelphia, PA 19106
   Phone: 800-879-6640
   E-mail: info@AmeriSpan.com
   www.amerispan.com

- Alliance for International Educational and Cultural Exchange (AIECE) lists high school and college exchange organizations and others involved in international exchange at all levels. AIECE publishes a useful guidebook: *International Exchange Locator: A Guide to U.S. Organizations, Federal Agencies, and Congressional Committees Active in International Exchange.* This annual publication costs $29.95 plus $4 for shipping:

   1776 Massachusetts Ave.
   Suite 620
   Washington, DC 20036
   Phone: 202-293-6141
   Fax: 202-293-6144

Pitfalls in Choosing Programs Designed for Older Students

Parents often ask about enrolling their son or daughter in college-level study abroad programs.

High school students often do well in college-level classes they take at universities and colleges in their local communities. There are many college-level study abroad programs available, so parents often contact program directors to see whether a high school student is eligible to participate.

The main thing to remember about study abroad programs is that they are not organized around classroom activities alone. The group of students travels together and spends most of their time together during the program. All the social life as well as the classes center on activities appropriate for the college crowd. There might not be so much difference between the two age groups in class, but socially, they will feel quite distinct. As a teenager on a college program, you might feel left out of many activities.

Here are some of the facts to consider before you and your parents inquire about college programs. In most of the world, there is no minimum drinking age, or the minimum age is 18 or lower. All college students in a study abroad program will probably be the legal drinking age for the country and many will drink. Ask whether the program will have something for you to do when older students decide to go to a bar or disco.

College-level study abroad programs do not structure the free time of participants as much as high school programs do. Various optional recreational activities are available, but you have the freedom to organize your free time around recreation or study. The social activities are probably those that college-age students enjoy. Many college programs allow participants free weekends to travel on their own. Students might also be free to travel before the program begins or after it ends. Although the program might ask you to leave your travel plans with an administrator, it is not responsible for you while you are traveling on your own. Ask your parents whether they want you to travel on your own or remain in town while the older students leave.

As in a graduate or upper-class residence hall at a university, supervision in residence halls does not focus on controlling the behavior of the residents but on building maintenance and security against intruders. Students might be free to go out in the evenings to eat, attend films, or pursue other entertainment and might have keys or a security system allowing them to return late, or in some instances, at any time of the night. In many cities around the world, public transportation stops around midnight or 1 a.m. If you remain out after that time, you have to walk home or take a taxi.

Host university instructors might be used to giving fewer assignments than American professors. They might not give any exams or quizzes until the end of the course. There is much less day-to-day supervision of student work, so you do not get as much information about how you are doing in the class. This arrangement might be difficult for you to adjust to if you are used to daily assignments and regular quizzes.

There are so many excellent study, travel, and home-stay programs designed around the interests and needs of teens that it is really not necessary to apply to college-level programs to find one in the country that interests you.

Just the Facts

- Finding an accessible program involves gathering as much information as possible and making the final decision yourself.

- Older students can choose between stimulating credit-based programs and a wide range of informative travel options.
- Busy families can go on exchanges together or find a short-term program for a family member who wants to study abroad without being absent too long.
- Many exciting options are designed especially for teenagers.

GET THE SCOOP ON...
Using publications to find the best program
▪ Getting updates, valuable resources, and tips
from the Internet ▪ Consulting the experts on
your campus ▪ Getting the real story from
returning students

The Smart Way to Use Information and Evaluate Programs

Chapter 5

No matter who you are and what type of program you are looking for, the most reliable information is the closest. Nothing compares with the detailed, up-to-the-minute advice you can get from study abroad advisors, teachers, and returning students on your campus. For additional information, the best source depends on the type of program you want.

For college and university academic programs, the best and fastest way to get basic information and to compare study abroad program options is to consult comprehensive catalogs that give you an overview of many programs in one compact volume. The Internet is the quickest route to information about alternative programs, scholarships, work abroad, study abroad for high school students, and volunteer experiences. For everyone, the Internet adds a whole new dimension of up-to-date supplementary information about practical matters: the best airfares, packing, and special services to make working out the details faster and more convenient. The key to success in using the available information is to combine all the resources.

Meeting with Study Abroad Advisors and Faculty Members

Faculty and study abroad advisors are your best source of information about the academic quality of programs and the relationship between your studies abroad and your U.S. program of study. If you want a good language program, they can tell you how much progress in the language you can make and how much credit you will be able to earn. Faculty and study abroad advisors know which programs offer you the best chance of earning credit that you can apply to concentration requirements or degree requirements in various fields. They can give you an overview of programs that provide good advising and assistance with placement in courses. This topic is discussed more fully in Chapter 8, "Making Your Home University Your Study Abroad Ally."

Study abroad advisors can also provide you the program's extended history of service to students at your institution, going back several years to see whether any program participants have had difficulties with housing, financial arrangements, safety issues, or other concerns. Faculty can tell you about the program's academic reputation among experts in your field of study. They can help you find the best universities in the country that interest you for political science, engineering, laboratory science, mathematics, and other areas.

If you are a high school student, you and your parents want a program that is supervised and approved by your school and well organized to provide you with cultural benefits and language skills. Your teachers and school administrators are the best information sources about reliable opportunities that your school district approves and arranges. When you choose programs operated by your school, you can take full advantage of pre-departure orientations and follow-up activities after you return home.

Getting the Inside Story from Former Program Participants

Former program participants are the best resource for how the program works, overall enjoyment, feasibility, comfort, entertainment, and a way to tell what you will get out of the experience. No matter how many facts you assemble, a student who tells you about his or her experience will pull it all together for you and help you decide whether the program is right for you.

You can learn more about the country you are interested in by obtaining names of students from the host country who are on your campus. Ask the study abroad office for names and e-mail addresses of program participants currently studying abroad. Attend information sessions on your campus. Ask for a schedule of meetings and workshops on study abroad at various locations and plan to attend so that you can meet students with first-hand experience. Call returning students and ask them as many questions as you can. Your parents might even want to talk to the parents of students who have returned. If you are an older student, ask for the names of older program participants, including people with families or jobs, and contact them to ask about their experiences. Students who have disabilities might want to discuss accessibility at specific program sites

Bright Idea
Your campus organization can schedule a social event or meeting and invite students returning from study abroad to tell you about the programs they attended. Ask how they financed it, how financial aid worked, and how they arranged for credit.

with others whom they can contact through Mobility International.

Traditional Sources: Catalogs, Brochures, and Advertisements

Using Catalogs of College and University Programs

College and university students: This section applies mainly to you.

Three catalogs available in your study abroad office or in the library are still among the best resources you can use to get detailed information about academic programs in a convenient, systematic way. The catalogs that can help you the best and save you the most time are:

> *Academic Year Abroad,* published annually by the Institute for International Education (IIE).

> *Vacation Study Abroad,* published annually by the IIE. Information about summer study abroad and programs offered during other vacation periods (www.iie.org).

> *Peterson's Guide to Study Abroad Programs,* published annually by Peterson's (www.petersons.com/stdyabrd/us.html).

Looking at these reference books is the fastest way to get a complete picture of all the programs that are available. You can zero in on the country and city that interest you and see all the options. Do you need a special combination of courses? An index quickly identifies the countries and programs offering the subjects you want. Concerned about the program starting and ending dates? There is no faster way to scan all the summer or academic year programs to find any that fit your special calendar. Do you want to make sure the program fits your

Watch Out!
Although you can order them from the Web, the catalogs are expensive. Check your local library collection for copies, and ask at the study abroad office and college library. Recent copies are usually available to you somewhere.

budget? For all of these questions, the catalog has quick and easy answers.

The concise format enables you to make an efficient comparison of program elements so that you can find the combination most suitable to your needs and preferences. The following information appears in most catalogs:

- Geographical location: region, country, and city

- Prices: program fees and other costs

- Program starting and ending dates

- Course offerings: an essential factor in your choice of program

- Housing options: lets you compare programs to find your preferred options quickly

- Primary language of instruction: lets you distinguish between programs offering beginning and intermediate language instruction, those with courses in English, and advanced language programs with a range of courses taught in the language

- Where the students are from: host country students, all Americans, or a mix of international students

- Who teaches on the program: U.S. faculty, host university faculty, or instructors recruited especially for the program

If your advisor suggests that you look for economical, high-quality programs offered by state universities, you can skim the pages and jot down the programs fitting that description. For the student who is looking for something different, such as a science program in Spain, a business program in France, or a program combining math and

Watch Out!
Check calendars carefully. Fall semester examinations sometimes run through January. It is difficult for professors to give you an early examination to get you home in time for spring semester classes. On the other hand, spring semester exams might conflict with summer work schedules.

A Student Speaks Up
To get the same basic information from the Internet for each program I was interested in, I had to keep backing in and out of program descriptions and printing out many pages of information. The Internet saves me time for some kinds of information, but the catalogs were a great way to start organizing my search.

secondary education, the catalogs are more efficient than any other source of information. All the material is cross-indexed to allow you to search by subject area, location, sponsor, or calendar. Currently, no Web site provides as comprehensive a comparison in the same amount of time and in such a compact location.

If your parents are asking tough questions about a program that interests you and trying to make sure that you've done your homework by considering all the options, the catalogs provide quick answers to their questions. They help you use the same criteria with each program you consider. Setting aside the attractive photos and glossy formatting of some brochures, you can study the fundamental components of each program in the same, objective way, looking only at the essentials.

Peterson's takes a slightly different approach by asking some good questions about each program and by attempting to estimate each program's total cost, including elements that are included in the program fee and those you have to pay for separately.

You can order the IIE catalogs online or use them in study abroad libraries or public libraries. IIE has launched a new Web site that study abroad advisors are currently evaluating. The *Peterson's* guide is available in college libraries and bookstores and directly from *Peterson's* Web site as well.

When you begin to narrow down your search, the contacts for further information are available in the catalogs. In addition to toll-free numbers and fax numbers, you can also find the e-mail addresses and the URLs you need to request or download more detailed information. Course descriptions, comments from students, and detailed information about excursions and housing are all easy to obtain after you select the programs that appeal to you.

Brochures and Posters

Until recently, brochures and flyers mailed to your study abroad office were the main sources of detailed program information. Students could find information in catalogs. Then, they wrote, called, or faxed for brochures, applications, and additional information if their college did not already have them on file.

Some universities and sponsors list their programs in a comprehensive catalog showing all the programs offered by that institution. Others prepare program-by-program or country-by-country brochures. Some do both.

Some programs invest in campus-wide poster campaigns to encourage students to make further inquiries in the study abroad office and call for information. Exercise some healthy skepticism when you look at a program brochure. The glossy format and beautiful pictures are costly to produce. This conveys the message that the program is well established and that the sponsoring institution strongly supports the program. However, beautiful brochures say nothing about the academic quality of the program. They are expensive to produce and part of your program fee might go to support that expense. Slick brochures also signal that a large number of students must enroll to support publicity costs. Students pick up huge numbers of brochures every year, glance at them, and discard them. A great expense on any given campus yields a relatively small number of applications. After seeing a poster, you still have to request additional material from the program in the form of application and

Timesaver
Save time! Go to your study abroad office first. Even if you send for information about a program whose poster you have seen on display around campus, you will soon find out that you need to go into the study abroad office to get your application approved. After you learn more, 70 percent of you will end up choosing a program that your own institution sponsors.

❝

I signed up for an intensive French language program with a home stay, offered by an American university. My wife came with me and signed up for a cooking class offered in the city where the program took place. We both enjoyed the students, the classes, and our host family.

❞

registration materials, course descriptions, and the like.

Many programs are putting material from their brochures on their Web sites so that you can gain access to it more quickly and save paper. You can read the material online and print only what you need.

Magazines

Seniors, volunteers, students with disabilities, and everyone who wants something just a little unique and personal: This section is for you.

Many publications can answer your questions or provide information about special interests. One of the most important sources of information for everyone who seeks a special, personal answer for travel abroad is the magazine *Transitions Abroad,* www.transabroad.com. Each year, *Transitions* offers issues on special topics, including work abroad and responsible programs. Responsible programs include service, volunteer, earth-friendly, and socially responsible programs.

You can order past issues for $6.25 each. Other magazines published by travel services include the AAA newsletters, publications of timeshare exchange networks, and other travel magazines with ads about travel related to the readers' interests. For other interest-related tours, consult issues of *Audubon* for information about bird-watching tours, *Natural History* for cultural tours, and *Sierra* for hiking, back-packing and other outdoor tours. College alumni magazines often advertise informative alumni association trips featuring lectures by professors from the institution. Ask friends for copies of their alumni magazines for more choices.

Food First, a nonprofit organization, offers *Alternatives to the Peace Corps: A Directory of Third*

World and U.S. Volunteer Organizations. Filomena Geise, Ed. with Marilyn Borchardt and Martha Fernandez. 8th ed. $9.95 plus $4.00 shipping for first book, $1.00 for each additional book. Order from:

> Subterranean Company
> Box 260
> 265 South 5th St.
> Monroe, OR 97456
> Phone: 800-274-7826
> Fax: 541-847-6018
> www.foodfirst.org

A Student Speaks Up
To get the most current materials, check your local college or university study abroad office, get the Web sites of program sponsors, and ask for information about additional programs in new locations.

Guidebooks and Other Publications

For detailed information about places to visit in the country where you plan to study, guidebooks are an excellent resource. Like the catalogs, they offer you an overview of the cities and regions you want to visit. They provide convenient ways to keep a great deal of information in one spot and to compare it quickly. To plan travel and prepare a budget for your entire trip, there is no better resource than a guidebook. Purchase the guidebook for the current year. For unofficial, frank opinions about the quality of various services and the rip-offs to avoid, get a student guide. Because student guides are geared to the types of activities and the budgets that students want, they are also useful in alerting you to risks to avoid, tips for safeguarding your money, places to get reliable housing, and meals at a reasonable price. Unlike the guidebooks that address a general reading audience, they might suggest how you can save money when you are traveling on your own. They might tell how you can get a room in a university residence hall or in a monastery or other safe yet reasonably priced location while traveling. You need a guide with up-to-the-minute prices, addresses, schedules, and Web sites. Here is some of the information you can get quickly and easily with a guidebook:

- Various ways of getting to and from your destination country (airlines and major international airports serving the country, international train connections, and ships and buses for travel between neighboring countries).

- In-country travel options with schedule and cost comparisons, as well as main office addresses and contact numbers.

- Restaurant guides with different price categories, popular cuisine or diet preferences, and candid ratings. (Some cities also offer official lists on the Web.)

- Housing options, comparing various levels of comfort and price, with addresses, phone numbers, fax numbers, and even e-mail and Web sites.

- Admission cost of museums and exhibits.

- Estimated exchange rates, taxes, service fees, and incidental costs for each city.

- Emergency services—locations of hospitals, clinics, and other help.

- Heads-up about local safety issues and other things you need to know to have a safe, enjoyable visit.

- Rip-offs to avoid.

- Site-specific tips for handling your money: ATM locations, American Express Offices, banks that handle cash advances, and where to get the best exchange rates.

Some of the most popular student guide series are

- The Berkeley Guides
- Let's Go Guides—comprehensive guides to Europe, Eastern Europe, Southeast Asia, Central America, 23 countries, and five cities
- Lonely Planet guides—Geared to the student crowd and young travelers who like adventure and don't mind "roughing it," these guidebook series offer sound tips for saving money but also precautions to take and some risks to avoid for travelers with a student budget and lifestyle.

Many excellent guidebooks are published in each country for individual cities, historic monuments, or regions that you will visit. It is usually easy to find guidebooks when you arrive at the site. Most people want to read up on their destination in order to get the most out of their visit, but it is not always easy to get the information ahead of time. Most people borrow a guidebook that someone else has brought back from the site. Today, however, you can go to many publishers online and order guides to read in advance or contact distributors of travel guides via the Internet to purchase materials in advance. The only difficulty is that you must know the names of the publishers in order to find the sites easily. Most travel guides on the Net focus on providing links rather than access to published guides. In the following paragraphs, we give some good examples of regional guides.

Pitkin Guides are the most widely distributed source of information to help you get the most out of visits to English cities, monuments, and historic sites such as Wells Cathedral and Stonehenge.

Order directly from the publisher through the Pitkin Guides home page (www.britguides.com/).

You can order Pitkin Guides through a distributor in the United States, Bridgham & Cook, Ltd. It also sells a variety of other U.K.-related products:

Phone: 800-UK-BUYER

www.britishgoods.com/Pitkin_Books.htm

Several excellent guidebook series are available for France. For those seeking materials in French:

Editions Ouest-France
Edilarge S.A.
13, rue du Breil
B.P. 6339
35063 Rennes Cedex
France
Phone: 02 99 32 58 27
Fax: 02 99 32 58 30
www.editions-ouest-france.com/

Guide du Routard is the most popular series of guidebooks in French for the budget traveler. Published only in French, this guidebook is available in bookstores all over France. In the United States, try bookstores specializing in foreign language selections.

Michelin Green Guides are available for many parts of the world as well as for the individual regions of France. For the traveler who wants informative details about architectural history, archaeology, geology, and natural features, the Michelin guides are indispensable, compact, and lightweight enough to carry with you. They have only two drawbacks: The information is organized alphabetically by town. The result is that you might miss the flow of information as you travel between cities. Second, these are gold mines of information for the serious student of cultural history; if you are not in that group, they might be less helpful. To order Michelin guides for a variety of countries:

Rex Travel
100 N. LaSalle, Suite 2010
Chicago, IL 60602
Phone: 800-777-7739 or 312-641-6633
Fax: 312-641-6641
E-mail: vacation@rextravel.com

Michelin North America
P.O. Box 19008
Greenville, SC 29602
Phone: 800-223-0987
Fax: 864/378-7471
www.michelin-travel.com

China Guides series offers guidebooks with historical, natural, and architectural features of various regions of China. They are beautifully illustrated and feature photographs. They are printed on glossy paper and are heavy to carry, but nice to keep as souvenirs or to use in preparation for your travels. You can find them in the travel section of many bookstores or order them from Web bookstores.

Through the Moon Gate is a useful guide to the major artistic sites of China. Almost any study tour will visit at least three or four of the locations described in this publication. Look for comparable guides for other countries. This excellent guidebook is now out of print, but you can buy it from bookstores that stock used titles. You can find it on the Web at bookstores such as Powell's that carry used books (www.powells.com).

The Irish Tourist Bureau (Failte Bord) publishes guidebooks for all the counties of Ireland, but you cannot order them via the Web site (www.ireland.travel.ie/home/index.asp). You can buy them readily all over Ireland.

You can find the U.S. addresses of each country's cultural office and tourist board, if they have one in the United States, by starting at www.embassy.org and selecting the country. You can also find the addresses and phone numbers in the introductory section of many student guidebooks. Ask for lists of detailed guidebooks that you can order to prepare your travels.

Two useful guidebooks for all of Europe are:

- *Europe Through the Back Door*, a personal viewpoint on the Europe that experienced travelers and residents know best.

- *Mona Winks: Self-Guided Tours of Europe's Great Museums* (John Muir Publications), an enjoyable read and a comprehensive guide of all the major museums. This book helps travelers interested in art history plan their travels around Europe so that they can see museums of greatest interest to them.

You can order both of these titles from the book providers on the Web.

For detailed guides to sites in Asia, Southeast Asia, Central and South America, and Africa, see helpful suggestions for further reading in guidebook series mentioned here.

The Best Way to Use the Internet

As in so many other fields, the Internet has added a whole new dimension to study abroad because of the timeliness of the information available and the ease and low cost with which material can be transmitted across great distances. For certain purposes, the Internet helps greatly with advance planning for study abroad. For students, parents, and advisors, the Internet can save time and steps. It helps to avoid confusion, bringing the other side of the world into instant focus.

The hypertext format of the Internet, with one page leading to another, related page, is slow when it comes to comparing profiles of information from different sources. The only way you can nail down the same facts about each program is to print everything and start making lists. When it comes to comparing complex sets of discrete information, the Internet cannot help and might be even more time-consuming than traditional resources. The catalogs can do all of that work for you much faster! After you've made your overall comparisons, however, the Internet is great for quick access to details.

The Internet is slow and unhelpful if you are trying to make comparisons between destinations, programs, and countries. Descriptions usually don't contain much historical detail and extensive reading matter.

The Internet is a great source for some valuable information such as:

- Updates of time-sensitive information such as visa requirements
- Introductions to museums and historic sites, brief descriptions of the collections, and information about admission fees and hours
- Forms you can print
- Quick connections to supplementary resources
- Scholarship information
- Internship information
- Organizations providing services to students abroad

- Cultural organizations
- Host institutions overseas
- Travel information
- Train and flight schedules
- Airport maps
- City maps
- Bus schedules
- University services (opening hours and so on)
- Practical information about getting to the program site
- Passport and visa information
- Newly released materials
- Bookstores and other suppliers from which you can quickly order books and materials
- E-mail connections you can use to send requests for information and receive speedy replies

Many Web sites have handbooks of information for special groups. They provide the same material that used to be printed in flyers. Getting this material from the Internet saves time, money, and paper because you can read the material without having to send for it and you print only what you need.

Basic facts on study abroad is a free handbook from the Institute for International Education (IIE) that you can download (www.iie.org/svcs/bfacts/).

Information for women, a second handbook at the IIE Web site, offers practical tips for women going abroad as students, parents, or employees.

Transitions Abroad offers a free handbook written by William Hoffa on its Web site, www.transabroad.com.

Both *Transitions Abroad* and IIE have Web sites with program information; however, the detailed IIE listings are available only to authorized users such as study abroad advisors. You can go to the sponsoring colleges and universities from its main Web site.

The key to success in using all these information resources is combining them effectively. Start with careful consultation of experts at your institution, use the catalogs as you start your search, and make strategic use of the Internet and other media as you refine your plans, start gathering details, and begin making final arrangements for your trip.

Just the Facts

- Use catalogs to make fast objective comparisons of program features.

- Consult brochures for details but look for content, not slick presentations.

- Use the Internet for timely information, details, schedules, and a variety of support services.

- Get first-hand advice from study abroad advisors and faculty.

- Talk to returning students before you decide which program is for you.

Unofficially...
Don't neglect other media when looking for information to prepare you for the history and culture of the countries where you are thinking of studying. Audio-Forum (www. audioforum.com) offers a complete series of more than 80 travel videos, plus CDs, audio cassettes, and more than 100 films to prepare you for knowledgeable travel and study almost anywhere in the world.

Before You Apply

GET THE SCOOP ON...
Deciding what courses to complete before you
go ▪ Choosing the right time to study abroad
▪ Doing your cultural homework ▪ Honing your
language skills ▪ Getting the scoop on health
and safety

PART II

Doing Your Homework

Chapter 6

Before you finalize your choice of program, there are some important things to think about. What are all the things you need to take care of before you study abroad in order to get the most out of the experience and make a smooth transition when you return to the United States? Have you considered all the options and programs that are available to you? What courses are best to take before you go? Should you complete major requirements at your home institution or overseas? What prerequisites should you take to get ready for your program? How much language preparation will you need before going abroad?

Getting Degree Requirements Out of the Way

Depending on your field of study, you might find it pays to take as many of your degree requirements as possible at your home institution. Many schools set minimum requirements for the number of credits in your major field of study that you must take on campus. Check to be sure that you will be able to meet

A Student Speaks Up
The best advice I can give other students is to read up on the country you are going to and plan to get out and see as much as you can. It is exciting to be surrounded by so much history and tradition, and you should know what you are seeing.

that minimum without the courses you plan to take abroad. The courses from your overseas program might still count toward degree requirements over and above the minimum number that you have to take on campus.

In addition, some departments at some institutions take the position that no other academic program can duplicate their unique facilities or the concepts and skills they want students to acquire in introductory courses for their specific degree program. They feel that the training students receive on the home campus provides the only satisfactory avenue toward completion of the basic elements of the degree program. Therefore, they might not allow transfer credit to meet any of those foundation requirements.

Finally, most institutions set a cap on the total number of hours of transfer credit that can apply to your degree. All the rest of your credit must be earned on campus. Have you already received transfer credit for some advanced standing courses you took in high school or for credit transferred from another U.S. college or university? Find out how much additional transfer credit you can apply to your degree.

If your institution or degree program requires you to complete all or most of your concentration requirements on your home campus, you should plan ahead to make sure that you can fulfill this portion of your degree requirement. Save electives and (if possible) general education requirements for your study abroad experience. In reality, you gain the most from study abroad when you allow the maximum flexibility in the program of study you take abroad. This allows you to take full advantage of what is offered through the program that you could not get at home.

Choosing the Right Time to Go Abroad

Choosing the right time to go abroad depends on your major field of study. In some fields, particularly in psychology, American training programs set requirements that differ considerably from those in other countries. The European approach to psychology, for example, is reputed to center around statistics. If you are a psychologist in training, you should consult with your study abroad advisor to find the right time to go abroad. You might need to complete all your basic coursework in psychology in the United States and choose elective courses, refining your second language skills, taking courses that count toward general education requirements, or simply broadening your background, in Europe. On the other hand, psychology courses in the U.K. and Australia transfer quite well to the American student's degree program.

Students preparing for medical school often hear that they cannot study abroad because they need to take science courses in a certain sequence and because they must cover certain basic material in preparation for their qualifying examinations (MCATs). You might hear that these requirements interfere with studying abroad during your junior year. If that is the case, why not consider study abroad during an earlier semester? Many direct enrollment opportunities and sponsored programs have no inherent requirement that you must complete two years of university study in the United States before enrolling.

Another solution is to go abroad *after* you have applied for medical school and taken the MCAT

A Student Speaks Up
I want to study in Australia because I am an anthropology concentrator and I have an opportunity to take courses on Aboriginal religion, music, and art on this exchange program. These are courses I could never take anywhere else in the world. I will take the foundation courses at my home campus before I go.

Watch Out!
If you go abroad during your senior year, you might need special permission to be away. Be aware that transcripts are often slow to arrive from overseas. Many institutions do not send grades for spring semester or a full year of study until the end of July. You might participate in the graduation ceremony but get your actual diploma a few months later.

examinations, during your senior year or right after graduation. Some students defer the start of their graduate degrees and study abroad after earning their undergraduate degrees. Ask your study abroad advisor what arrangements your institution is willing to make in order for you to go abroad during one of your last semesters. A final option is to study abroad in the summer so that you do not interrupt your schedule for admission to medical school.

As you review the courses you hope to take abroad, be sure to discuss the curriculum carefully with a professor in your field of concentration. Universities in other countries might organize the curriculum differently. A professor in the field can assist you in determining where the course you plan to take fits in the American curriculum. For example, American language and literature programs usually organize literature courses by the century in which the works were written. A student going to Germany might find that the courses are organized by the names of specific writers. Sometimes, they are organized by literary genre (poetry, fiction, or theater). To help you decide which courses to take, your professor might need to provide you with a list of important writers from a certain century or from a certain genre.

A student going to study physics might need to take the course descriptions to a professor in the physics department to find out how the two programs interface. It might be necessary to send e-mail messages to the physics department at the host university to get more information about the sequence of courses.

Preparing for Life in Another Culture
Once you have chosen your destination, take courses and read up on the language, culture, and

history of the region. Living in another country, even if you speak the language, involves some profound changes and adjustments. Any preparation you can make in advance helps reduce the difficulty of this process.

Intercultural Press offers a series of books on intercultural communication for students, scholars, and business people. Each book compares U.S. culture to another country's way of handling interpersonal relationships. Works currently available include books comparing American culture with that of Arabs, Filipinos, Thais, Greeks, Germans, Japanese, Australians, French, Russians, Eastern Europeans, Chinese, Mexicans, Israelis, Spaniards, and the peoples of sub-Saharan Africa. Also available are books describing ways of doing business effectively, books for women in business around the world, and a range of other materials offering strategies for making the best out of the differences:

> Intercultural Press
> P.O. Box 700
> Yarmouth, ME 04096
> Phone: 800-370-2665 or 207-846-5168
> Fax: 207-846-5181
> E-mail: Books@interculturalpress.com
> www.interculturalpress.com

The *APA Insight* guides, available from Impact Publications, offer glances into the country, people, and culture of more than 100 countries, as well as cities and regions of the world. These are primarily guidebooks, although they are enriched by series of articles on the most significant aspects of the history, economy, culture, and natural setting of the country. Two other series more specifically address the task of learning how to live and work with people in other cultures. The *Culture Shock!* series offers

Unofficially...
Did you know
that many
Europeans, par-
ticularly the
French, learn as
children to dis-
trust strangers
who smile a lot
in public? Their
culture teaches
that people who
have legitimate
business adopt a
serious expres-
sion in public.
People who
approach
strangers with a
smile appear sus-
picious and
untrustworthy.

studies of the people and cultures of 47 different countries. *Culturegrams: The Nations Around Us* is a set of cultural studies to help prepare people for living in other countries and communicating with the people. Volume 1, *The Americas and Europe* and Volume 2, *Asia, Africa, and Oceania* are available individually or as a two-volume set for $80. Check whether your library carries reference materials of this type and encourage it to enlarge its collection of materials to prepare students for sojourns abroad. Ask your professors for suggestions of texts to check out of the library for pre-departure reading:

Impact Publications
9104-N Manassas Dr.
Manassas Park, VA 20111-5211
Questions and orders: 703-361-7300
Fax: 703-335-9486
E-mail: Careerinfo@impactpublications.com
www.impactpublications.com

Broaden Your Perspective by Crossing Disciplines

In addition to reading about the cultural differences that you will encounter, you should do some background reading on the history and economy of the country. Each of the books in the Intercultural Press series offers some suggestions for additional reading. Ask your language professors for additional materials to prepare you more thoroughly for living in another culture.

If you know that you will be taking courses in a specific discipline (such as philosophy, art history, or science), take the time to cross disciplines and read about the country you are going to visit from a completely different perspective. For example, if you know that you will be taking history courses, why not read something about the country's contributions to science? If your interest is business, spend a little bit of time finding out more about the country's art or music. If you intend to study literature, why not read up on the industrial revolution in the host country or its achievements in engineering or architecture? You will find that each area in which you read deepens your appreciation of the subjects you will study while you are there. Anything you can do to deepen your understanding of the culture will help you appreciate the way in which instructors in another country approach their material.

Get a map of the country as soon as you decide where you are going to study. As you read, use the map to orient yourself to the country's natural features and to the physical and historical relationship between the various cities and regions of the country. A map also helps you understand the country's relationship to other nations in the region you are studying.

Talking to Other Students

As soon as you begin to think seriously about participating in a particular program or going to a particular country, seek opportunities to meet students from the country who are studying at your university. Attend dinners and social events celebrating the culture that interests you. Ask them about family customs, universities in their home country, and some of the major differences they encountered when they first came to the United States. International students will appreciate your interest in their country and will offer interesting perspectives on American culture as well as insights into their own.

Above all, you should make an effort to discuss your study abroad plans with American students

A Student Speaks Up
Learn a little Italian and be familiar with the art. Read up about it. It is really thrilling to be surrounded with so much beauty. You will enjoy it much more if you know a little about it before you arrive. Knowing some Italian before you go will be very helpful during the first couple of days while you are getting started with classes.

who have just returned from study in that country. Of all your information sources, returning students can offer you the most immediate and practical advice as you make your preparations for study abroad. Ask the program administrators for the names of students who have recently participated, and contact them for advice.

Don't be surprised if the international students and returning students express strong opinions about American culture and policies. They might criticize or express appreciation for some aspects of American life that you have never thought much about. In these discussions, you will probably begin to realize that the United States is an object of intense interest to the other people of the world. However, you might be surprised at what you learn about the opinions other countries have of Americans and the United States government.

Spend a little time learning more about your own country's history, culture, and political climate. As you will learn from returning students, people in other countries regard American students abroad as representatives of their country and its culture. People will challenge you with questions about the United States. Sometimes, they will know more than you do about your country's history and its involvement in the affairs of other nations. At times, you might be called upon to explain American customs or to justify government policies about which you do not know very much. You will probably start reading the news with a new awareness. You will begin thinking about aspects of life in the United States in new ways and might want to read up on history and government of the United States. This exposure is another one of the benefits of study abroad. Even before you go, you start becoming more aware of the ways in which your culture has shaped your attitudes and the things you take for granted. You will probably become more interested in your responsibilities as a citizen. As you prepare to go abroad, you will begin to become more informed about U.S. policies that interest or concern the people you will meet in other countries.

Special Information for Women

The Institute for International Education prepared a special set of guidelines for women who plan to live or study abroad. See the IIE Web site at www.iie.org. The guidelines remind women of questions they should ask if they plan to take children with them or set up a household in another country. Women should make a particular effort to find out as much as possible about cultural attitudes in other countries. In some countries, women do not have as much independence as women do in America. Women students should be aware of any precautions to take when they go out alone in public, day or night. If you plan to enroll in a program sponsored by an American university, you should ask about safety precautions for women and ask for orientation materials on this subject. If you plan to enroll directly in a university in another country, it is essential to gather as much information as possible about precautions you should take for your safety and comfort in public.

For more detailed information, see Nancy J. Piet-Pelon and Barbara Hornsby, *Women's Guide to Living Overseas* (2nd ed.) Intercultural Press, 1992.

Honing Your Language Skills

Whatever language you are studying, study as much of it as you possibly can before you go abroad. Being able to speak a second or third language is a valuable

A Student Speaks Up
The grandmother in my Japanese host family yelled at me for not using the highest form of respect. I was just a beginner and didn't know the forms. The other host families explained to her that a beginner wouldn't know the proper expressions. Everyone learns about language in a host family situation!

skill. You can make constant improvement in your proficiency as long as you keep in constant practice. No amount of advance preparation is too much, and no amount of language study that you do overseas is too much. Don't confuse the number of hours of language you need to complete a major in a subject with the amount that you need for optimum proficiency. Even when you complete an undergraduate language major, you have only gone part of the way toward achieving advanced proficiency in a language. The more preparation you do before leaving the United States, the more confidence you will have in your skills, the more progress you will be able to make when you get to the country, the more people you will meet, and the more friends you will make. Once in country, you will be able to move from intermediate to advanced proficiency and take full advantage of the best courses available at the host university.

Language teachers recommend that you enroll in as many language courses as you can fit into your schedule before you go abroad. Even though you might be trying to complete foundation courses in other fields before you go abroad, include at least one language course in your program of study each semester. If a language course is difficult to work into your schedule during the academic year, consider an intensive summer program to help boost your skills. Take advantage of opportunities to practice the language whenever you can. Participate in a language club, a film study group, or the activities of a language house if there is one on your campus.

Talk to native speakers of the language as often as possible. Get to know some international students or newcomers to the community from the country you are going to. If your institution has a volunteer program for community service, ask whether you can tutor people who want to work on their English skills in return for helping you to practice their native language. Terry Marshall, author of *The Whole World Guide to Language Learning* (Intercultural Press), designed a set of practical guidelines for building your language skills through carefully planned conversations with a mentor. He originally developed the method to help anthropologists, Peace Corps workers, and other professionals learn languages for which there was no written grammar. Later, he refined the method to help people practice any language through carefully planned conversational practice. Using his method might help you develop a useful language partnership with a newcomer to your community. If there is no formal volunteer program, ask graduate students or university employees from the country that interests you whether they have a spouse or friend who needs help with English in return for helping you to practice your language skills.

If your university does not offer courses in the language of the country you are going to, or if you plan to take beginner-level courses in the language when you get to your destination, start working on it before you go! You can select from a wide range of learning aids, including books, videos, and audio cassettes, to help you start your language study before you arrive in the host country. Beginning to practice the new language before you go will help build your confidence during those first few weeks when you are covering the basics in class. Even a few phrases will help you feel more independent. You will be able to go out, use the bus, shop, and ask directions much sooner.

A Student Speaks Up
Come with a knowledge of basic phrases. The first week is difficult if [you do] not [know a little of the language]. Get some tapes or a video or a book to read up. Don't just depend on the students who know more Italian.

Beginning books and self-teaching materials are available for virtually all the modern languages. There are three basic types of teach-yourself materials: books and workbooks, cassette tapes, and videos. The last two usually come with written materials. These materials might take the form of a manual or a complete textbook.

Books range from small reference books of practical phrases to extensive grammar books with workbooks or sets of written exercises. If you plan to enroll in a grammar class when you arrive in the country, look for written materials that give you a lot of basic conversational phrases and practical vocabulary. The 10 Minutes a Day series (Bilingual Books) offers practical conversational materials in 10 modern languages. You can cut out stickers for commonly used items and paste them on everyday objects all over your room so that you can start learning useful expressions in the new language. The more necessary those items are in your daily life, the faster you'll learn the vocabulary in the new language. The more time you put in writing out the suggested exercises, the more comfortable you will become with the vocabulary and with the basic grammatical patterns of the new language. This practice will help you learn to speak the language more quickly. Unfortunately, working with a book does not teach you how to pronounce the words and phrases.

To get an accurate model for pronunciation so that you can understand native speakers and pronounce the phrases correctly, look for an audio cassette or video series. These materials come with manuals that are sometimes fairly detailed textbooks. The best is a video program. Watching the speaker's facial expression and the position of the

mouth is a great aid to comprehension and pronunciation. On the other hand, the cassettes are
convenient for your car tape deck or portable cassette player.

Audio Forum offers a comprehensive supply of
all types of language instructional materials and has
videos of many parts of the world, including cities
and regions within countries:

> Audio Forum
> Jeffrey Norton Publishers
> 96 Broad St.
> Guilford, CT 06437 USA
> Phone: 800-243-1234 or 203-453-9794
> Fax: 203-453-9774
> E-mail: info@audioforum.com
> www.audioforum.com/

Using a good search engine, you can obtain the
names and addresses of other language resource
centers from which you can order materials.

Although you should begin studying the basics
of the language with a skilled instructor as soon as
you arrive, it will take you some time to build up a
basic command of grammar and learn how to form
original sentences in the new language. This is why
you will benefit from learning as much as you can
before you go. If you take a short course or spend
some time each day learning basic phrases and
vocabulary before you travel, it will help you navi-
gate in the new country during the first few days.
You will not feel helpless if you know you can make
your way to your lodgings, speak to your hostess,
and go out on your own to make simple purchases.

If you are an absolute beginner, you can find
combination cassette and textbook programs that
offer you a helpful introduction to the language.

Listening to the cassettes will make you more comfortable understanding native speakers when you first arrive, and practicing phrases will give you the confidence to get around when you first arrive in the country. Your classes with native speakers will quickly develop your skills further. If you are at the intermediate level but feel that you have forgotten during the summer many things you learned in last year's language classes, you can buy "survival" guides that refresh your memory of basic grammar rules and get you into practice again with some helpful exercises and readings. Just getting back into the language is like a warm-up for an athlete or performer; it brings back your skills and gets you ready for the next stage in learning.

If you don't expect to study the language of a country you will be visiting, you can purchase phrase books and dictionaries to help you get around in basic communication. This approach might be more effective than trying to do everything in English. People always appreciate a visitor's efforts to use the language of the country. No matter what your skill level, you should have a good dictionary on hand. Ask your teachers for suggestions. You might choose to purchase one after arriving in the country, but make sure you have one on hand.

Instructional materials are available for virtually every known language on the planet. Investigate the materials available and enjoy the process of picking up a new tongue or refining your skills in one you haven't used in a while.

Videotapes are increasingly popular. Examine a selection at any large bookstore and choose the one that is right for your level and time frame. The more opportunities for practice you give yourself, the

Watch Out!
You should have a dictionary, but be careful how you use it, especially if you get one with definitions in English. Remember that English words can have many different meanings, and you might pick a word in your second language that corresponds to the wrong one!

better. Computer language series and Web-based programs are newer methods.

More advanced speakers who want to brush up their skills can use conversational guides and guides to colloquial language. Whatever method you choose and whatever level you select, you must practice to benefit from the materials. Writing out exercises is an excellent way to practice. The more you write, the more familiar you will be with the patterns of the new language and the more readily you will learn to speak it.

No matter how much language study you have had, you will run into new words and phrases as soon as you arrive in the country where the language is spoken. Get a good pocket dictionary to help you decipher menus and messages while you build your language skills. Consider brushing up your language skills even if you plan to take many or all of your courses in English. The amount of language skill you have will greatly enhance your ability to make contacts and cope with difficulties. You will be joining a vast network of internationally aware people from other countries. Even if you do not speak the official language of the country you are visiting, your ability to use more than one of the world's languages will be useful to you, and you can make valuable connections by helping other travelers.

Gathering Health and Safety Information

While you are still in the preliminary process of gathering information about your destination and program of study, you should get as much information as possible about health and safety issues in the country or region or for the type of program in which you will be participating. For information

Timesaver
To gain time and take more classes in the host university, do as much work in the language as you can before you go. A summer school class or a lot of work with textbooks, cassettes, and videos can help you maximize your classroom time in the country.

about health risks and recommended precautions to take before travel to various countries, see the Center for Disease Control Web site at www.cdc.gov/travel/index.htm.

If possible, arrange to obtain any recommended immunizations from your host university or a local travel immunization center, or take the information to your own physician. Find out whether a physician in your area has some expertise concerning immunizations for international travel. Often, you can find known specialists for each region of the world. Ask about an expert on the region where you plan to travel.

It is essential to have a medical and dental examination before you go to any country in the developing world and to ensure that you have the immunizations recommended by the Center for Disease Control. Gamma Globulin is a protection against hepatitis, which is widespread in China. Proof of yellow fever immunizations is required with the application for a visa in Ghana. Anti-malaria medication is also a necessity in Ghana and in many other tropical countries. Be sure to review the necessary immunizations early in your planning. You might have to allow plenty of time to begin your shots and other medications prior to departure.

The World Health Organization is increasingly concerned about the spread of highly resistant strains of tuberculosis. In some poorer countries where the disease is on the increase, the available vaccines are too expensive to distribute to the population. Take note of any recommended precautions if TB is on the increase in any area you plan to visit. You will note that some countries require chest x-rays for students planning to remain for a semester

Unofficially...
While traveling in Shanghai, a colleague got appendicitis and had an immediate operation. I speak several European languages. If the hospital staff member did not speak much English, I tried another language. While in China, we made good friends among teachers or travelers who spoke no English.

or year. These x-ray screenings are intended to prevent further spread of drug-resistant strains of the disease. For information about measures to prevent the spread of disease, see Chapter 17, " First Things First: Getting Settled."

A special committee of NAFSA, The Association of International Educators, meets regularly to study health and safety issues. The committee arranges for workshops and informational sessions at national and regional conferences to assist program administrators in evaluating the safety of their programs. In 1998, NAFSA, in collaboration with a task force of other professional organizations, drew up a set of guidelines that program administrators and participants can refer to in evaluating program safety issues. The Health and Safety committee offers workshops and sets standards of best practice to heighten public awareness about safety issues in study abroad.

No program can guarantee 100 percent protection against all illnesses, natural events, and mishaps that could befall students studying abroad. You have to be responsible for remaining alert, following instructions, and exercising reasonable care. Whether or not you safeguard your own welfare and possessions might be a combination of circumstances, your judgment, and the best services and information the program can provide you.

To determine the general safety and the quality of public health in a country where you would like to study, the first place you should check is the Department of State Travel Information Web site: travel.state.gov/. To receive travel information by e-mail, click on the button provided on the Department of State travel warning page for further information. The Department of State offers a

Bright Idea
In countries where tap water is not safe to drink, you need to take extra precautions to keep skin abrasions and minor infections clean and disinfected. Take plenty of antiseptic cream with you, and be especially careful to keep cuts and scrapes clean and protected while they heal.

Watch Out!
While crossing a London street late at night after leaving a pub, several students were struck by a car. They forgot to watch for traffic approaching from the right. The doctors sent one student home to recuperate because a misstep during healing would aggravate the injuries to her knee. The student made a full recovery and completed the program.

publication that you can download, *A Safe Trip Abroad*, which offers advice about protecting yourself and your possessions.

You can order it from the Superintendent of Documents, U.S. Government Printing Office, Washington, D.C. 20402, or via the Internet at www.access.gpo.gov/su_docs, or read and download a variety of travel documents on the U.S. Department of State, Bureau of Consular Affairs Web site http://216.200.80.33/travel_pubs.html.

Additional information about travel to specific regions is available on the State Department Web site. Additional flyers that you can download include judicial information for some countries, information about transfer of money in emergencies, and medical information for U.S. citizens traveling abroad.

It is helpful to compare the information provided by the U.S. State Department with information you can get from other health and safety sources. The London Foreign and Commonwealth Office (which has the same role as the U.S. State Department) is at www.fco.gov.uk. Information from the Foreign Affairs office of the government of Australia is available at www.dfat.gov.au/consular/. The Canadian Foreign Affairs Office is at www.dfait-maeci.gc.ca/travelreport/menu_e.htm. It is useful to compare the viewpoints of several governments on safety risks. To put all the recommendations in context, compare the Department of State's travel warnings with information that other countries give their citizens about travel in the United States.

Next, review the health and safety guidelines developed by NAFSA (The Association of International Educators). You can access them from the organization's home page: nafsa.org. These are recommendations for the best practices to ensure health and safety in the administration of study abroad programs. If you are interested in a program by an American college or university, you should request further information directly from the program about health and safety precautions you should take, as well as measures the program has in place to protect the welfare of participants. Consult with your study abroad advisor as well.

Program administrators can subscribe to several private information services providing monthly newsletters. However, the information they publish is primarily for business travelers and tourists. For information about subscribing to these services, see these Web sites: Pinkerton Global Intelligence (www.pinkertons.com/pgis) or Kroll & Associates (www.krollassociates.com).

In general, American program administrators rely on the government information sources listed earlier and on their private networks of information sources within the host country. These include university administrators and faculty, travel agencies that provide services to study abroad programs, and diplomats and professionals living in the countries. Other sources include Fulbright Centers in many parts of the world and university alumni working in various countries.

If you plan to enroll directly at a program in another country, the responsibility rests with you to review and assess the safety of the program. You need to determine whether you are comfortable with the level of the host institution's commitment to hosting international students. If you are unsure whether the institution will provide you with safe, reliable housing and instructional facilities, you should contact your study abroad advisor for advice.

Just the Facts

- Choose the best time to go abroad.
- Save as many electives as possible for study abroad.
- Learn as much as possible about the culture you are going to visit.
- Study languages as much as you can.
- Know where to get health and safety information before you go abroad.

GET THE SCOOP ON...
How to figure out the real cost of your program
▪ Factoring in other charges ▪ Financing your
program with financial aid ▪ Finding other funding sources ▪ Creative approaches to financing
international study

Figuring Out the Cost of Programs and How to Finance Them

Chapter 7

Afterfter choosing a program that fits your
needs and study plans, you need to make
sure that it can fit your budget as well. In
addition to the program fee you find in the
brochures and catalogs, there are other expenses to
consider. Before you figure out the amount of financial aid you need and how to finance the program,
you need to be sure you understand what all the
expenses will be.

Interpreting Cost Information

The following sections discuss the basic elements of
a study program. When you compare the cost of various programs, be sure that you know which costs
and services are included in the program fee and
which are additional expenses that you have to pay.
Some programs include almost all of these elements
in the program fee. Fees for other programs cover

only a few of these items, which makes their fees appear lower, at least initially. When you begin calculating how much you will pay to make your own arrangements for the items that are not included in the program fees, the costs of different programs begin to look more similar. A program that appeared to be a bargain at first could end up costing more money than a program that charges a higher, but comprehensive, program fee.

Instruction

The instruction cost, sometimes listed separately as tuition, is frequently a part of the program fee. The cost of instruction for a prestigious private university program might be a substantially larger part of the program fee than for an equally prestigious state university program. A program offering instruction by U.S. university professors might cost more than a program that hires instructors locally. A program with a large staff to attend to your needs might cost more than other programs but might also provide more individualized service. In some cases, you might decide that the extra cost is worthwhile.

International Airfare

If airfare is not included in the program fee, you need to estimate what it will cost you to make your own travel arrangements. You can begin by checking the prices quoted by consolidators in their ads in the travel sections of big city Sunday newspapers. Chapter 14, "Travel Options," tells you more about cost-cutting strategies for arranging your international travel.

On the other hand, experts caution you to be aware that international travel is only a small part of your total program cost. Do not feel that you have to pay thousands of dollars more for a program just because airfare is included.

Domestic Travel

Domestic travel includes the cost of getting from your home to the point of departure and from the point of arrival to the actual program site. Even if the program fee includes international airfare, you probably need to pay your own way from your home to the international departure point. Don't underestimate this expense. The price of a domestic plane ticket to get you from your home town to the departure point could increase the cost of participating in a program. If you are going to be away for a whole year, you might have to purchase a separate one-way ticket each way for your U.S. travel.

After your flight arrives at the international airport nearest your destination, you might have to travel some distance from the airport to your program site. There are a number of advantages to choosing a program that includes in its fee all arrangements for travel from the arrival city to your final destination. First of all, if this is your first international flight, it is quite reassuring to have someone from the program meet you and make all the arrangements to get you to the program site. You will not have the anxiety of finding your way through a large international city to a hotel and then making the connections to your program site. Moreover, the program can handle baggage for the entire group, which is a convenience when you are tired from your overseas flight. You have a chance to get to know participants from other schools on the way to the site, and you can relax and enjoy the trip.

If you choose a program that requires you to stay overnight in a major city before checking in for your international flight, the cost of your meals and overnight lodging also adds to your expenses. Then, you need to calculate the cost of the trip to the final destination. Each time you make a transfer with luggage, be sure to add in the cost of taxis and luggage carts. Getting from one place to another with luggage in tow is always going to involve expense unless you plan to travel light. Add about $1.50 for each luggage cart and anywhere from $5 to $20 for a cab, depending on the cost of services in the city where you are staying.

Lodging

If housing is included in the program fee, it is much easier to calculate your total cost for the study abroad program. On the other hand, this may give you fewer options to choose from. More information about housing choices is included in Chapter 10, "Registering for the Program."

Students going to Europe or Japan should expect to pay at least as much for meals as they do for a full meal plan at their home institution. If the program offers you housing in a residence hall with meals provided, compare that cost with the cost of a residence hall plus a full meal plan at your home institution. You will not find as much variety in institutional meals as you do at an American university. They do not represent the country's best cuisine. However, the combination package may be a reasonably priced option, and there are advantages to living in a residence hall with local students (see Chapter 10).

Utilities

If the program offers the option to rent an apartment, be sure to inquire about the monthly cost of utilities. Bear in mind that it costs much more in other countries to provide the amount of hot water, electricity, and heat Americans are used to. In Europe, a student should estimate at least $40 to $60 each month above the basic rent to cover the cost of utilities if they are additional.

Additional Meals

Be sure to calculate the additional cost of meals that are not part of the basic package. These might include meals on excursions, meals during a big city stay (allow at least $30 a day for meals in big cities), lunch, or perhaps breakfast. If you will live in a residence hall or apartment with cooking facilities, you can probably stretch your budget by shopping and preparing your own meals. Much depends on your versatility and ingenuity as a cook and your ability to use foods that are locally plentiful and therefore inexpensive.

Security Deposits

Find out whether you will be expected to pay a security deposit when you move in to your lodgings. This deposit could be as much as one month's rent, payable in cash when you move in. Be sure to budget for this if it is not included in the program fee. This charge might be assessed as a non-refundable cleaning fee or room damage deposit fee.

In Japan, new tenants are expected to pay "key money" to the landlord to ensure a good relationship. Owners of any decent apartment expect to receive this from a new tenant. "Key money" is a gift to the landlord. For a family expecting to live in the same location for many years, the amount could be as much as $10,000. For a student renting a modest apartment, it might be $1,000 to $2,000. Be sure to inquire whether your apartment arrangements include the expectation that you will pay key money.

Watch Out!
If you plan to stay over an extended vacation, find out whether housing will be available, whether meals will be served, and whether there will be an additional charge. You might need to budget for alternative housing and meals during that period.

Local Transportation (Getting from Your Residence to Classes)

Daily transportation is another cost the program should indicate, although it probably will not include the cost in the program fee. If you are studying in a big city, the cost of the bus or subway and the time involved in getting to and from classes are major factors. In most cities, subway travel costs at least $2 a trip, and costs increase depending on the length of the commute. Student passes help to reduce the cost, but they could be a $25-to-$30 item in your monthly budget. Students older than 21 years of age might not qualify for student discounts on public transportation in some countries.

In many localities, a bicycle is very useful for getting around quickly. It saves on bus fare, provides some exercise, and gets you to places the bus lines do not go. If you plan to purchase one, investigate the cost of used bicycles. Unless you have cross-country touring in mind, you don't need to purchase an expensive bicycle. Sturdy models for commuting are usually available. You might be able to line up a used bicycle left behind by a student who followed the program the previous year. Whatever your choice, be sure to register the bicycle with the local police or university security office. Lock it to bicycle racks provided for the purpose, and don't leave it overnight on the street, even if you lock it. This is a good opportunity to emphasize safety: Observe local traffic patterns and be cautious until you become familiar with local hazards.

A Student Speaks Up
We wondered how so many thousands of bicycles could flow in all directions in Beijing, sometimes straight at one another, with so few collisions. When two cyclists approached one another, one would jerk the front wheel to show the side on which he wanted to pass, and the other would give way.

Excursions

Your program will undoubtedly include some planned excursions. (Check whether meals are included.) Always budget a little bit extra for meals in unfamiliar locations because you might not have time to shop around for the best meal deal. Are some excursions an optional extra? If so, you probably want to take advantage of them and factor these costs into the total cost of the program.

Personal Travel

If your program does not include many excursions, you will want to travel independently to see the country. On longer breaks, you might even visit other countries in the region. Train travel can be very expensive. If you purchase a rail package before leaving the United States, such as a BritRail pass or a Eurail pass, you select the number of days of travel you want and the length of time during which the pass will be valid. You get the most value out of your pass if you plan to travel long distances on certain days and then spend time visiting a city or region by using local transportation. Nonetheless, a basic rail pass costs several hundred dollars. The price increases the more travel days you include and the longer it is valid.

In addition, you need to calculate the cost of hotels and meals. (Remember, meals cost more when you don't know the area and you don't have time to shop for the best price.) If you plan to do some travel on your own, this is the time to start doing some research and considering your itinerary. The first thing to do is shop for a guidebook. Be sure that the guide you select reflects your interests and lifestyle. A guide designed for vacationing professionals, business people, or families might not reflect the things you want to do. Many of the recommendations for hotels, restaurants, and recreation might be beyond your budget. Purchase the current year's edition of a good student guide for the country that interests you.

Using the guide, start to put together a day-to-day itinerary that includes the cost of train fare between locations that interest you (with or without a student pass), budget hotel rates, and meals in the cities you would like to visit. Begin putting together a daily budget. You should plan on a bare minimum of $60 a day, allow no less than $100 per day for any time spent in major cities, and think of $125 as the most you'll spend for any day you will be traveling and arriving in unfamiliar places.

After a week of business travel in Japan as a member of a delegation from my university, I felt brave enough to try a Saturday afternoon excursion on my own. Using my limited recognition of characters and the instructions a friend had written for me, I took the subway to the train station ($3) and boarded the train for Kamakura ($7). A monsoon was coming in, but I was leaving Japan in several days and was determined to see the Great Buddha. Arriving at Kamakura, I found the little trolley that goes to the village of Hase ($2). I hadn't had lunch, but I bought some ice cream and tea from the station platform vending machines ($3). At Hase, the monsoon was bearing down, and my shoes took that moment to spring a leak. Still, I followed signs with rough drawings of a seated Buddha, fell in with a small procession of raincoats and umbrellas, and sloshed determinedly toward the Kotokuin Temple. At the temple, I paid my admission ($5) and bought a little English guidebook ($3). The Great Buddha was extraordinarily beautiful, even wearing a mantle of rain. I spent an hour or two admiring the graceful figure from every angle, walking around the sheltered walkways and the little temple garden. The peaceful look of compassion and dignity on his face was far more moving than any photograph had ever led me to expect, and the guidebook contributed a great deal to my appreciation of the artistry and symbolism. The weather did not permit a view of the sea and did not encourage visiting the other temples of the area. Instead, I chose the craft shops and took the opportunity to do my gift shopping ($100). At about 4:00, I splashed back to the trolley ($2), returned to Tokyo by train ($7), and (because it was dark by the time I got back) took a cab 1 mile to my hotel ($20). Triumphantly, I joined my friends for dinner ($15) to tell them about my excellent adventure. My total expenditure for this afternoon excursion was $167 ($67 without the gift shopping). My hotel bill was reasonable for Tokyo ($80). I'd heard that Tokyo is expensive, but the individual items on this outing were quite reasonable (except for the cab fare). The point is that when you set out to visit the historic monuments you've traveled so far to see, in any city in the world, even small charges begin to mount up.

Unofficially...
The faculty say to bring twice as much money and half as many clothes as you think you'll need. This is good advice.

Books, School Supplies, Computers, and Telephones

Books in other countries can be just as expensive as in the United States, but you might end up spending less on textbooks. It is possible to do a lot of the reading in the library. In fact, many of the assigned readings might come from books you can only find in the university library. You might end up purchasing only the books you want to keep as reference materials. Many language programs include the texts in the tuition. However, don't forget to budget at least $75 for a good language dictionary if you are concentrating in the language. For a short-term program, a lightweight pocket dictionary may do. Most programs provide you with an estimate of the cost of other books and school supplies. Paper products can be more expensive in lands where trees are relatively scarce, but it is still better to buy your supplies on site in order to have the proper format for your class assignments.

Many students ask about taking computers or purchasing them in the country. Before you decide about this expense, find out whether your professors are likely to expect printed assignments. In many countries, carefully hand-written papers are customary for most assignments. Purchasing a computer to take with you or acquiring one in the country will add quite a bit to your program expense, and it might not be entirely necessary. In addition, you will require a converter for any computer built for American current. A printer with its own adapter and converter is necessary if your goal is to print assignments. The biggest expense associated with a computer might be a telephone line so that you can use your modem to access the Internet. Installation of a telephone line is expensive. In most other countries, you have to pay a hefty security deposit as well as a month's payment in advance. You are charged for every call to connect with the Internet, including local ones. If your server is in another city, which is more often the case in other countries, you have to add long-distance charges to the cost of your computer. Again, in most cases, this expense is not a necessary part of your program, but an expensive extra.

If you telephone friends and family frequently, your phone charges can add up. Installing your own phone in your residence and paying for individual calls is very expensive outside the United States. On the other hand, you can go to a phone booth or to the post office and use a phone card or credit card to call home.

Moneysaver
In many cities, you can purchase a local phone card for use in public pay phones. These are much more readily available in other countries than in the United States. You can purchase the cards in different denominations. You avoid the inconvenience of getting change when you need to use the phone.

You can also use a credit card or telephone company calling card in many telephones. If the phone has a place to swipe a credit or debit card, you can simply swipe the card in the sensing device and charge your call. If you plan to use a telephone company credit card, you need to make sure that you have the access number for placing credit card calls outside the United States. Most long-distance services are only too happy to provide potential customers with information about how to use their product overseas.

Laundry and Incidental Expenses

Laundromats are expensive. You can easily spend $3 or more to wash and dry a load. It makes sense to plan on doing a lot of hand washing and to make sturdy clothing such as jeans that last several wearings. Consider toilet articles and other small expenses. Use of an Internet access service, photocopying, purchasing film, and developing photos are other potential costs.

Passport and Visa Fees

Depending on your age, a new passport costs $45 to $65. Visa fees and associated costs vary from country to country. They range from $30 or $40 to as much as $300 for countries that require medical examinations and immunizations.

Insurance

Even if you plan to continue using the insurance coverage you now have, you should consider the cost of medical insurance as one of your necessary expenses for study abroad because most programs, and many countries, require you to have it. In some cases, the program requires you to enroll in a mandatory insurance plan (usually around $150 per semester).

A Student Speaks Up
An apartment downtown is expensive. Bills are expensive. The cost of maintaining an American standard of living is expensive.

Be sure that your estimate of program costs includes all of these elements. Look for as much of this information as possible in the material the program provides.

Watching Out for Hidden Costs

Many students fail to anticipate the number of unforeseen service charges, taxes, fees, and penalties that officials can charge people when they move from place to place and from country to country. If your parents have moved from one state to another recently, they can tell you that the process of moving from one jurisdiction to another, even within the United States, is full of hidden costs. Study abroad students are not alone in running into these expenses. The important thing is to plan ahead and allow for some cushion in your budget for the unexpected. You should allow a minimum of $200 per semester to cover the unforeseen costs of transferring your money, your possessions, and yourself from one country to another.

When you exchange money, change traveler's checks, send payments, and pay security deposits, you should expect the process to cost money. You have to pay banks to prepare cashier's checks, change money, and send wire transfers. At the end of the year, if you get a small security deposit back in the form of a check in foreign currency, you might not be able to convert it to dollars without paying service charges that consume the entire amount. With careful planning and good advice from program administrators, you can anticipate or minimize some of these charges, but you cannot expect to eliminate them all. They are one of the costs of doing international business. You should not expect your program to anticipate them all or to help you pay one they did not tell you about.

In addition to the costs of transferring money, you should expect to pay some fees for issuance of a residency card and other necessary items such as fees for a bus pass, various taxes and surcharges, and an extra transcript or copy of your birth certificate that some official might require. Because local administrations and even national governments can start imposing such fees or requirements without notice, neither you nor your program can possibly know about all of them in advance. The wisest thing to do is budget for miscellaneous incidental expenses as one of the costs of study abroad.

Service Fees Your Home University May Charge

When you study abroad, your college or university study abroad office provides some services to help you remain connected to the institution. You will probably register for study abroad so that you can transfer credit or simply make a smooth transition when you return to campus. Many colleges and universities impose a service charge for helping you with these arrangements. Over the years, various study abroad professionals have tried to keep data on the fees charged by different universities. Some institutions ask students to pay a small amount ($50 to $100) to register for study abroad. This is the only money the student owes to the home institution for the summer, semester, or year abroad. The charge helps to cover international and long-distance phone calls, mailings, and other expenses associated with keeping the student connected to the institution. Some institutions charge higher study abroad registration fees. Another group of institutions charges full tuition to every student who goes abroad or to every student who goes on one of the institution's programs. Still others charge full tuition plus a study abroad service charge, which

A Student Speaks Up
It cost $20 for our first telephone subscription of two months. The second month again cost $20 for two months plus 18.6 percent tax on the itemized bill. The installation tax was $21, and the "regularisation" of the subscription was $9, a total of $70! When you add on all your calls and the VAT (tax) of 20.6 percent on those calls, it can be expensive.

A Student Speaks Up
My college allows a certain number of students to study abroad every year. The student pays the usual amount of tuition and the college pays all the financial aid the student would normally receive. However, they only do this for a certain group of students. Anyone else who wants to go abroad just withdraws from school.

can be as much as $2,000 above regular tuition. They might provide an extensive range of services for this fee, to help students prepare for study abroad.

With this much variation in the fees institutions find it necessary to charge, it is important for you and your family to inquire about this well in advance. You are entitled to find out what services or educational programs are provided. You might even decide to attend one university or another on the basis of what you learn about registration for study abroad.

Financing Study Abroad
Applying for Financial Aid
The first office to contact concerning funding for study abroad is your financial aid office. Even if you do not normally qualify for assistance in the form of scholarships or loans from the institution, you might be eligible for loans to help offset the cost of study abroad on one of your home institution's programs. Make an appointment to discuss the types of assistance that are available and the application procedures.

Federal Aid
It is possible to apply federal financial aid in the form of loans to study abroad. Colleges and universities ordinarily establish policies about allowing students to take this aid with them. If you are going on one of your institution's own programs, you should not have any difficulty finding out about the procedures for applying for federal aid. You and your parents need to fill out the Free Application For Student Aid (FAFSA) and submit the supporting paperwork. Even if you do not normally qualify for assistance under the federal loan programs, your

institution might require you to complete these procedures. This process might be necessary in order to consider you for other loan options that are available, especially if you are planning to participate in one of your college's approved study abroad programs. Do not be discouraged by the paperwork. If you need financial assistance to study abroad, persevere and complete the papers.

If your institution does not assist you in applying for federal aid for participation in certain programs, you might be able to apply independently or through the sponsoring institution. Be sure to ask your study abroad advisor and the program sponsors for advice about this if you run into any difficulties with your home institution's policies. For more information on federal financial aid and study abroad, consult the federal financial aid Web site: www.ed.gov/offices/OPE/Students.

For a U.S. Department of Education guidebook to help you understand financial aid, go to www.ed. gov/prog_info/SFA/StudentGuide.

The Department of Education guidebook does not provide specific assistance with applying for financial aid to study abroad. Therefore, the materials are most helpful to you if you work through them with the assistance of your study abroad advisor and financial aid advisor.

If you decide to apply for financial aid to study on a program that is not sponsored by your own university, but offered by another American university, you will probably be instructed to complete a form called a *consortial agreement*.

This form is an agreement signed by you, by your home institution, and by the host institution or sponsor. The form confirms the cost of the program and certifies that you are applying for federal financial

Watch Out!
It is relatively unusual for students to apply for financial aid through the sponsoring institution rather than through their home institution. Most program sponsors do not have enough financial aid staff to help anyone but students registered at their own institution.

aid through only *one* of the two institutions. This is fair because it ensures that students do not get aid twice for the same educational experience. The program sponsor provides an estimate of the total cost of participation in the program. Your study abroad advisor reviews the budget, adds any additional costs that need to be part of the budget, and confirms that you will be able to transfer credit for the program back to your home institution. Then, the financial aid office completes the process of packaging the aid for you.

If you decide to apply through the other institution (the sponsor) for financial aid instead of through your home institution, the consortial agreement is similar. However, at the end of the process, the sponsor completes the process of packaging the aid.

Other Types of Loans

If you are not able to apply for federal financial aid through your home institution, your next step should probably be investigating other types of loans through private lending institutions. Your home university might be able to provide you with the information to get started with this process. You can apply to a number of private lending organizations. The main difference in applying for assistance through these sources is that the interest rates might be higher, there are no outright grants available, and you might need to start repaying the loan earlier.

Ordinarily, you and your family must complete the FAFSA in the same way as if you were applying for a federal loan.

Scholarships

You should inquire about a number of scholarship sources.

First, ask whether your university offers any special scholarships for students participating in the approved programs of the university.

Secondly, review scholarship options available through sponsors of programs that interest you. AIFS and IES both offer merit scholarships and other scholarship assistance. The National Council on U.S.-Arab relations provides substantial funding to support its summer program in Damascus.

Finally, consider the many prestigious scholarship competitions offered by national organizations. Use the Web sites and addresses in this chapter to request information. In most cases, you need to apply through your institution if you are enrolled at a college or university. Find out who the program advisor is for each of the scholarships. Arrange to meet with the advisor well in advance of the time when you hope to study abroad. Gather all pertinent information about application deadlines, qualifications, and admission requirements. Remember that the application deadline for many of these awards is a full 12 months before your program of study would begin. Find out what sort of prior experiences enhance an applicant's chances of qualifying for some of the most competitive awards. Be sure that you make arrangements for strong letters of support from faculty who know a lot about you and the academic project that you intend to carry out if you receive the scholarship.

The University of Michigan Web site for study abroad offers links to other information about scholarships and funding for study abroad as well as opportunities for work and internships and fellowships for study abroad. Scholarships from various national and international organizations are described in the following sections.

A Student Speaks Up

I dreamed of going to Africa. I applied for admission to a program in Ghana and drew up a proposal to film the program and use it to publicize the college, the academic division offering the program, and international studies. I received over $3,000 to carry out the project.

National Security Education Program

The National Security Education program offers scholarships to U.S. citizens enrolled at two- and four-year colleges or universities for summer, fall, or spring undergraduate or graduate language study in critical areas of the world (Africa, Asia, Eastern and Central Europe, Latin and South America, and the Middle East). Certain service requirements apply. You should review the requirements carefully to see whether you would agree to these requirements if offered a scholarship. Students in the following fields are especially encouraged: agriculture and food science, business, computer science, economics, engineering, health and biomedical science, history, international relations, political science, and applied science. For more information, contact:

> National Security Education Program
> Institute of International Education
> 6th Floor
> 1400 K St., NW
> Washington, DC 20005-2403
> Phone: 800-618-NSEP or 202-326-7697
> Fax: 202-326-7698
> E-mail: nsep@iie.org
> www.iie.org/nsep/

Reference Service Press is a company which disseminates information about all types of financial aid. Their publications include: Financial Aid for Study and Training Abroad, 1999-2001 ($39.50), and Financial Aid for Research and Creative Activities Abroad, 1999–2001 ($45).

> Reference Service Press
> 5000 Windplay Dr., Suite 4
> El Dorado Hills, CA 95762
> Phone: 916-939-9620

Fax: 916-939-9626

http://www.rspfunding.com/

Many other Web sites, including several developed by other universities, take you through so much material you will never cease to find new opportunities for work, internships, and fellowships for study abroad.

CIEE

CIEE offers partial scholarships to cover international travel expenses for students planning language study in a country outside of Western Europe and North America. One goal of the scholarships is to encourage minority students to study abroad. If your institution is a member of CIEE, it can nominate a student each term. Contact your scholarship advisor for further information about the recruitment process.

Rhodes scholarships for a year of study at Oxford University are available for U.S. citizens, ages 18 to 24, who will complete a B.A. degree before going into residence in Oxford. Citizens of 16 other countries can also apply within the jurisdiction of their own countries. If you are not a U.S. citizen, check whether your country is also eligible to send students to Oxford. Universities and colleges usually nominate the candidates. Interested students should make inquiries many months in advance of the deadline, which is October 1 in the fall of their senior year in college. You need time to prepare your application and to complete selection procedures at your home university:

Office of the American Secretary
The Rhodes Scholarship Trust
P.O. Box 7490
McLean, VA 22106-7490

The Marshall scholarships were developed by the British government to thank the United States for assistance provided during World War II. More than 40 students receive the awards each year. Marshall Scholars must study for at least two years and ideally earn a degree at any one of more than a hundred universities and university-type institutions in Britain. In a limited number of cases, a scholar can receive an extension for a third year. Former recipients include Bruce Babbitt, Secretary of the Interior, and U.S. Supreme Court Justice Stephen Breyer, presidents of several colleges and universities, writers, and scientists.

The British Council coordinates the administration of the program in the USA on behalf of the British Embassy. Regional British consulates also have information about the program. Consult the British Council home page for information about the scholarship and the address of the regional office of the British Council for your area:

> The British Council
> British Consulate General
> 3100 Massachusetts Ave. NW
> Washington, DC 20008-3600 USA
> Fax: 202-588-7918
> E-mail: study.uk@bc-washingtondc.
> bcouncil.org
> www.britishcouncil-usa.org/usabms1.htm

The Rotary Foundation provides funding for a range of international service projects, including funding for about 1,200 students to study abroad each year. Scholarships of as much as $24,000 per year enable students to study for a year in a country they have not recently visited. Applicants must have completed two years of college and be citizens of countries with Rotary clubs. Applicants apply through their local Rotary club, provided the club participates in the scholarship program. They cannot be related to current Rotary club members. Students with disabilities are encouraged to apply. For further information, contact your local Rotary club or the campus Rotary scholarship advisor or consult the Rotary Foundation national headquarters:

> One Rotary Center
> 1560 Sherman Ave.
> Evanston, IL 60201
> Phone: 847-866-3000
> Fax: 847-328-8554
> www.rotary.org/foundation/index.htm

Fulbright and related fellowships are offered to graduating seniors, young professionals, artists, and graduate students to more than 100 countries. Although you can apply independently, colleges and universities usually nominate the applicants. Those interested in applying should check months in advance of the October deadline in order to comply with institutional procedures for nominees for the award. For additional information, contact:

> Institute of International Education
> 809 United Nations Plaza
> New York, NY 10017-3580
> www.iie.org/fulbright

Other Ways of Financing Study Abroad

Cindy Chalou has created a Web site at Michigan State, "Study Abroad, You Can't Afford *Not* To Go," a compilation of ingenious suggestions by students for financing study abroad (studyabroad.msu.edu/finance.html).

A Student Speaks Up
In 1997, I proposed that Rotary International help re-establish some Rotary clubs in Palestine. Rotary and a scholarship from my home institution helped me put the process in motion. Out of this project grew an English as a Second Language teaching project.

World Teach, an organization that trains and places beginning teachers around the world, has a "Fundraising Ideas" Web site as well (www.worldteach.org/funds.html).

Here are some other suggestions: First of all, write a statement of purpose, explaining why you want to study abroad and how it will help you meet your goals. Using this statement of purpose, develop a series of proposals that you might use to solicit funding from various sources. If you come from a small town where you and your family are well known to the community, see whether you can apply for a loan from a local bank. Incorporate something of benefit to the community into your experience. Submit a proposal to your church, temple, or synagogue explaining how study abroad will help you meet your goals, how it might benefit the church in some way, and how you need scholarship support. Similarly, develop a proposal to submit to a non-profit or charitable organization in your community whose goals might be compatible with some of your objectives for going abroad.

Take an extra job or organize a fund-raiser for your project, making the event of mutual benefit to you and to a sponsoring organization. World Teach suggests that you make this event an awareness night for the part of the world where you want to go. This is an excellent opportunity to create global awareness in your community. Develop a civic project related to your study abroad destination: What about establishing a sister city program for your community, beginning with the town where you plan to study abroad? Offer to carry advertising for local community enterprises with you and design a cooperative project between your community and enterprises or institutions in the host country.

If you are participating in a program sponsored by your host college or university, offer to do some videotaping or filming for the institution; design it to be a component of the orientation for the program. Contact the admissions office and offer to film some study abroad program activities as a recruitment tool for the institution. Write a proposal to the alumni society and to the admissions office, offering to serve as liaison to your institution's alumni in the host community. Offer to set up a chapter of the alumni society and to serve as a recruiter of international students in the host city. You might offer to coordinate some informational sessions to tell about your university and show videos of the college to interested secondary students in the city where you are going.

Contact a regional or state chamber of commerce or small business association to see whether you can get some funding for an initiative they want to start at your destination. Offer to contact some businesses in the host city to establish cooperative linkages.

Upon your return, give informational presentations about the region you have visited. Keep the connections strong and build upon them. If you did not get funding for the first trip, begin working toward your next one.

Just the Facts

- Get complete information about study abroad costs before seeking funding.

- Find out about special costs related to the country where you are going.

- Contact your financial aid office early to make sure you qualify for aid while studying abroad.

- Plan early to apply for prestigious national award programs.
- Use ingenuity in developing proposals for funding from civic and other groups.

GET THE SCOOP ON...
What your college can provide ▪ How the study
abroad office can help you ▪ Special study
abroad experiences ▪ Policies that strongly affect
your choices and costs ▪ Avoiding problems if
you don't enroll in your college's program

Making Your Home University Your Study Abroad Ally

Of all the factors in making your study abroad experience a success, the services provided by your home institution's study abroad office are the most important. Your study abroad advisor has access to sources of information about health and safety factors in various parts of the world and can help you to find a program that is both reliable and educational, as well as one that will fit with your program of study at your home institution. It is important to recognize that your home institution's policies will influence where you can go and how your credit will transfer. If you are thinking about study abroad, you should investigate study abroad opportunities and policies before you select a college or university. Make sure that your goals are compatible with those of the institution you select so that you and your college or university can work closely together to plan a rewarding experience.

As a reader of this guide, you probably consider study abroad to be an important part of your plans for college. Therefore, you should consider your choice of a college or university very carefully. If you have set your sights on a particular destination or program, you might find your plans incompatible with the policies of a college or university that you were seriously considering. Ask each college as much as you can about international education and study abroad policies. Otherwise, you might be disappointed when you encounter limitations to your choice of programs or to the amount of financial aid available for the program you choose. It's best to find these things out before you enroll!

Information Available Through the College Study Abroad Office

The study abroad office on your campus is your greatest ally in helping you to find a good program, to prepare for study abroad, to arrange for financial aid, and to bring credit back. Be sure you meet the study abroad advisor when you visit any college campus. These are some of the things to ask to make sure the institution's study abroad policies fit with your goals:

- Ask how many official or approved programs are available and where they are.

- Find out whether the programs are island or direct enrollment programs (see Chapter 2, "A Quick Guide to Types of Study Abroad Programs").

- Find out how many courses are available and how credit transfers.

- Ask whether students can select programs other than the college's official programs.

Watch Out!
I was really disappointed to find out that my college had no program at Oxford except for one with American instructors. I was interested in philosophy and economics. I thought the philosophy selections were really "Mickey Mouse," and there were no economics programs. I enrolled directly at one of the colleges of Oxford, but I couldn't get financial aid for the program.

- Find out whether any financial aid or other financial resources are available.

- Ask whether scholarships are available and how difficult it is to get one.

- Ask about admission requirements for the college's official programs. Is there a minimum grade point average or another admission requirement?

- Ask whether the study abroad office assists with travel arrangements or information for students going abroad on other programs.

- Ask whether information is available about non-credit programs, work, and teaching opportunities abroad.

- Find out whether the office provides returning students with assistance in planning for a career with an international focus.

Bright Idea
If you're interested in teaching, investigate opportunities to teach abroad through programs that train you to teach English as a second language. I taught English in China for a year and this opened the door to some opportunities to do interpreting and translating for several international conferences and to assist some scholars doing research on the ancient remains found in the Western deserts of China.

Find out whether the college offers a health insurance plan that will cover your medical expenses while you are abroad on an official college program. Before selecting the college you will attend, find out whether the study abroad office can advise you if you want to go to a different program (one that is not an official college program). Find out whether the study abroad office can help you assess programs that are not on the official list. Some students are interested in going abroad to study a language that is not offered at many colleges and universities in the United States. Examples might include Thai, Danish, Czech, Amharic, Korean, or Welsh. Find out whether the college will allow you to earn credit for studying a language that it does not offer. Find out whether there is a way for you to meet the college's language requirement through study abroad.

Bright Idea
Why not contact BUNAC or CIEE and make arrangements to work for a summer or a semester after completing your study abroad program? Earn some money to cover travel in your leisure time, and get to know the people of the country from a whole new perspective.

How the Study Abroad Office Can Help You

The study abroad office can provide you with a great deal of assistance in finding the right program. The office can provide a lot of background information about programs and international activity in general. These are some of the services your study abroad office might provide. It probably maintains a library where you can browse material and catalogs from institutions all over the world. Some study abroad offices also contain videotapes, CDs, and computer terminals from which students can search a database of programs. They might organize information sessions where you can meet program representatives, meet returning students, and get first-hand information about programs. The information sessions might discuss the culture and provide background about the history and special features of the location.

Many institutions organize study abroad fairs where you can meet returning students or program representatives and learn about programs to which you might want to apply. The study abroad office might also arrange for visiting program representatives to set up information tables on campus where students can drop by to ask questions.

One of the most important roles of the study abroad office is to help you make arrangements for the approval and transfer of the academic credit you hope to earn from your study abroad experience. The office provides information about what you need to do to get approval from the academic departments and to make sure that the credit earned helps you to meet requirements for your major, minor, or general degree program.

The study abroad office or another office on campus keeps you informed about study abroad scholarship competitions announced by other organizations and foundations or refers you to the proper office on campus for this information.

The study abroad office might manage several study abroad programs operated by your home institution. Many colleges and universities offer their own group programs. They design the programs, develop the budgets, hire program staff, recruit students to participate, and organize pre-departure information sessions. Sometimes, they open the programs to students from other colleges and universities. Applying to a program offered by your own institution has many advantages. Program officials know you and the professors who recommend you. The courses usually fit your institution's degree requirements. Application and registration might be simpler. The orientation will probably take place on your home campus, and you may know other program participants.

Your advisor can help you meet the language proficiency requirement at your institution through selection of an appropriate study abroad program. If your institution offers a language, you usually have two ways in which to meet the language proficiency requirement. First, you take the required number of language courses on your home campus. Second, you arrange to transfer credit for courses you took somewhere else, which have been approved as equivalent to your home institution's courses.

Your home institution faculty and study abroad advisor can help you find a language program that the department recommends. This is an important choice and one that you need to make in close consultation with instructors and advisors at your home institution. The faculty know the reputations of

Watch Out!
Scholarship competitions often have early application deadlines. I wanted to attend a program in Egypt during my junior year. I began applying for an NSEP scholarship a year in advance! The application required a complete program budget, letters of reference, and transcripts. I was interviewed by a committee at my college. It was worth it when I got the scholarship!

many programs. They will encourage you to enroll in a program that will help you make enough progress to enroll in the next course level when you return. Get as much information as possible about the grammar and vocabulary that are covered in any language courses you take. Some programs cover a great deal of colloquial language material but do not provide a full academic term of instruction in grammar.

Your study abroad office might be able to help you if you would like to meet the language requirement through study of a language that your institution does not offer. Some institutions have a system whereby students can meet the language proficiency requirement in a language not offered by the school. The chair can approve transfer credit for academically rigorous courses in the language offered at an accredited institution in another country. Some schools might also be willing to arrange for a native speaker to evaluate your proficiency in the language after you return from study abroad. The language department can select a qualified native speaker to evaluate your ability to converse in the language, your mastery of certain grammar patterns, and your vocabulary.

An important responsibility of the study abroad office is to organize orientation sessions to help you get ready for life in another culture. The sessions might last a few hours, an entire day, or more. Some institutions require you to enroll in a complete course to provide you with a better understanding of the process of crossing cultures. Others offer a course on the culture of the country where you are going. Pre-departure orientation sessions offer tips about health and safety, travel planning, and other

A Student Speaks Up
Even though there was no scholarship money available, my advisor encouraged me to apply anyway. Later, the Office of Student Services got more scholarship funds for study abroad, and I received a partial scholarship to cover the costs of my study abroad program. It pays to let people know what you need so that they can look for ways to help you.

useful advice to help you get the most out of your study abroad experience. There may be a session on etiquette in the country you are going to.

Another task of the study abroad office is to coordinate exchange programs allowing you to pay tuition to your home institution and switch places with a student from an institution in another country. It also wants to help you find out about financial assistance such as institutional scholarships, grants, and federal financial aid to help defray the costs of your study abroad experience.

Some institutions are able to provide college health insurance to students going on the institution's study abroad programs. This can be a real advantage to a student who cannot use family health insurance overseas. Be sure to ask your family health insurance company about its policies for covering you if you study abroad.

When you choose a college or university, find out whether it offers a student health insurance plan that remains valid while you are abroad. Some school insurance plans cover participants in the college's study abroad programs. This offers some real advantages. Each time you change insurance plans, the new plan might refuse to cover a medical condition that existed before you enrolled. If you choose a plan that remains valid while you are abroad, your medical care is covered before you go abroad, while you are away, and after you return. This is a plus if you develop a continuing medical condition. The insurance will cover treatment of any condition you had before you went away. If you develop a new medical condition overseas, the insurance will continue to cover treatment after you return.

Unofficially...
I received a call from a parent whose insurance company has informed her that if her daughter is out of the country for more than 90 days, her insurance will be terminated. The student was just about to leave for her junior year abroad. The student will be covered overseas by an international health/medical insurance policy. That one terminates when the student returns to the U.S.

Limits to Study Abroad Enrollment

Institutions vary in the policies they set about giving permission to students to study abroad. At some institutions, it is possible for everyone to study abroad who wants to go, whereas other institutions might set limits on the number of students approved for study abroad.

Some institutions, particularly small, private ones, set numerical limits to the number of students approved for study abroad. They do this so that all needy students in the approved group can receive financial aid according to their level of need. The institutions advise the chosen students carefully as they select a program and might provide a series of planning and orientation sessions to get them ready to go. Students might need to apply to the study abroad office early in the fall semester of their second year in college in order to receive approval and sponsorship.

Other institutions set a grade point average limit and allow students to go abroad only if their academic records reach a certain level. If your grades do not reach the appropriate level, you have two choices: You can study hard, wait for a year, and apply again, or you can withdraw from the school and enroll in a program that accepts you. At the end of the study abroad experience, you can reapply to enter the college or university, but you might not be able to transfer the credit.

Some institutions focus on managing a select series of programs that they consider to be very high quality. They carefully choose students to participate in them and limit the number who can enroll. To get into the program, you might have to reach a certain level of language proficiency. You might also

> ❝
> Our university approves a dozen students each year for study abroad. We help with program selection and financial aid. Unfortunately, others going abroad get no aid. They withdraw from school in order to go on other programs. Often, they do not return but transfer to another institution after study abroad.
> ❞

have to convince the selection committee that you are ready for the challenge of living in another culture. If you do not get into the institution's approved programs, you might have to withdraw from school and make other arrangements on your own.

Many institutions have a strong commitment to preparing students for life in another culture. Some colleges carefully define the types of study abroad experiences that they approve for students. They might establish a minimum period of time (one month, one academic term, or one semester) that students must live in another country in order to earn credit for the experience. They might require that students study a language. Some colleges require all students to enroll in a preparatory course prior to study abroad. Depending on the college's mission, the course could be an introduction to the study of non-Western cultures or some other course that helps students understand and appreciate cultural differences.

Many colleges screen students to make sure that everyone who goes abroad is ready for the challenges of crossing cultures. They might create an application that carefully screens students. You answer searching questions about how ready you are to live in a non-Western culture. The selection process might include interviews with the selection committee. If you are not ready for the experience, you might not get to participate the first time you apply.

Institutional policies about transfer credit have improved greatly over the years. For many decades, students have been able to go abroad to study a language, especially if they were majoring in the language. In the past, however, some institutions refused to transfer credit for any other subjects.

A Student Speaks Up

My undergraduate college did not accept transfer credit for study at any other institution, in the U.S. or abroad. The only students who could transfer study abroad credit were language majors taking courses abroad in the language they were studying. A classmate of mine who went to Oxford was not able to transfer any of the English literature courses she took.

If you are interested in study abroad, you should check the transfer credit policies of colleges and universities before enrolling. Make sure that you can transfer credit for the type of study abroad experience you have in mind. Ask whether you can transfer credit if you select a program that is not on the college's list of official or approved programs.

Institutions that select and prepare only a small number of participants for study abroad have good reasons for choosing to handle study abroad in this way. Small institutions have to budget carefully. They might have only a small staff available to help students. To ensure the best possible service and preparation to students who go abroad, they decide to limit the number who can benefit from the opportunity.

A high grade point average is not the only indication that you are qualified to participate in a program. Be sure to find out what other qualifications are important to the institution. Ask what the criteria are for admission to its study abroad programs. Consider whether you are ready for the differences you will encounter in another culture. What experiences have you had that might show whether you are able to adjust to new foods, new living conditions, and unfamiliar climates, customs, and activities? How big an adjustment will the institution require you to make? Do you welcome the challenges of a life that is really different from your usual routine? What aspects of your life are the hardest for you to change? Do you get satisfaction from being able to adjust to difficult living conditions? These questions might be important to consider before you enroll in a college that offers a small, select range of study abroad options.

Financial Aid and Credit Policies

If you need financial aid in order to study abroad, an institution's financial aid policies can have an important effect on your choice of programs. Here are some of the policies that various institutions follow.

Some institutions offer a limited choice of programs but encourage all students to go abroad, and they provide financial aid: Some institutions try to arrange for *all* interested students to go abroad or off campus. They charge full tuition to all students and cover the full cost of study abroad through tuition. This allows everyone to participate in study abroad or off-campus programs if they want to do so. Those requiring financial aid receive the same level of assistance that they receive on campus. However, students must participate in the institution's own programs in order to receive these benefits. This policy helps make study abroad affordable if you require financial aid to participate and if you are interested in the programs the institution offers. You will not be able to obtain financial aid to study abroad unless you choose one of the institution's programs. You might experience some difficulties transferring credit if you choose a program that is not on the college's approved list.

All students can go abroad, and the institution offers a variety of programs, but aid only applies to an approved list of programs: Some institutions allow all students to go abroad who want to do so. They do not charge full tuition to students who go abroad.

Unofficially... Our application for study abroad asks, "What do you think will be your biggest problem in adjusting to life in Japan?" One student wrote that he loved American foods and would have a hard time with a new diet, living with a Japanese family. The admissions committee made the student wait for a year. He still had trouble getting used to different food but liked the country in other ways.

They help you choose programs that are compatible with your interests, academic goals, and finances. They usually have a procedure for you to follow to arrange for the credit to transfer back to the institution. However, they only allow financial aid to apply to a specific list of approved programs. Depending on the size of the institution, this list might be fairly large. If you do not need financial aid, you will find this policy convenient. You will have a wide choice of study abroad options. However, if you need financial aid, you can find your choices more limited.

Out-of-state students and in-state students may encounter differences in program affordability: If you are considering enrollment at a large state university, you might find that the institution offers a wide range of programs and has a liberal policy allowing you to go on any program you choose. However, you might still find that there are some obstacles to study abroad. Out-of-state students might receive certain advantages. It is often cheaper for them to go abroad than to pay the cost of study on campus for a semester or year. They might already receive financial aid from the institution that they can apply to participation in one of the institution's approved programs. On the other hand, if you regularly pay low in-state tuition, you might find that study abroad costs more than you pay to attend the institution. You might not receive enough financial aid to offset the cost of the study abroad program in which you want to enroll. Often, the university's own programs

are affordable (at least with the help of financial aid). However, your choice of program is
once again limited to the institution's
approved program list.

The object here is not to paint a gloomy picture.
It is simply to point out that you need to ask a lot of
questions before you choose a university or college.

Pitfalls to Avoid

If you review all the options available through your
college and still want to study abroad on another
program, you can do several things to make sure it
works out. If you don't take care of each of these
aspects, you could have difficulties when you return.
Your study abroad advisor is the person who can
best advise you about the reliability of the program,
even if it is not one the institution approves. Find
out how you will make sure the program is reliable
and whether it can handle any health and safety
issues that arise. These are some of the criteria the
office might use to determine whether the program
management is likely to be responsible and reliable.
Following are some of the questions you might ask
about the program.

Is it a reputable program? Is it listed in the
Peterson's or IIE catalog on any of the study
abroad Web sites offering programs to American
students? Is it listed on any of the large university
Web sites such as those of the University of
Michigan, the University of Minnesota, or the
University of California?

Does an accredited, degree-granting university
award credit for the program? Regardless of the
quality of the program, many colleges do not recognize credit unless it comes from an accredited,
degree-granting institution in the host country or

Moneysaver
I pay out-of-
state tuition.
There is a pro-
gram in Australia
that is a tuition
exchange. I
really wanted
to enroll but
couldn't pay out-
of-state tuition,
airfare, housing,
and expenses. My
study abroad
advisor found
another arrange-
ment for going
to the same uni-
versity. Every-
thing was
included, and it
still didn't cost
as much as going
to my home uni-
versity for a
semester!

A Student Speaks Up

My family wanted me to participate in a great French language program, but I couldn't get any credit for the program because it wasn't offered by a degree-granting institution. After a lot of research, I found an American university that sponsors the program. The study abroad advisor approved the program. I had a great semester and got to travel before the program began. All my credit transferred.

an accredited American university that serves as the institution of record for the program. Most colleges and universities require that credit come through an accredited U.S. college or university. Many also accept credit through a recognized degree-granting university in the host country. Most institutions cannot offer credit for study abroad taken through a junior college or community college, unless the credit was earned prior to your admission to your present four-year college or university. Check with your study abroad office before you go abroad to make sure that the credit has the potential to be approved by your home institution.

Does the credit-granting institution have a strong academic reputation? Is the sponsor an American college or university with a solid reputation and a list of other study abroad programs? Does the sponsor list this program on its Web site of approved programs for its own students?

Will your home institution approve the credit? Will it allow you to apply the credit to your concentration requirements, or will it just be elective credit?

Does the institution subscribe to the NAFSA health and safety guidelines? (You can view the guidelines on the Web at www.nafsa.org.)

Does the institution grant credit to a large number of programs managed by other organizations and institutions? Look favorably on programs sponsored by American institutions that are closely involved in the program. Give them bonus points if they send their own faculty to serve as program directors and work closely with staff and faculty in the host country to ensure the quality of the program.

Find out who will be accountable if things do not go well. If there is a problem with housing, for example, or travel arrangements, is there someone in this country to whom your family can turn to address the matter?

Do program administrators participate actively in organizations that support and strive to maintain high quality in international education, such as CIEE or NAFSA?

Will the academic standards and interests of the students, faculty, and home stays be compatible with yours? Are you used to fast-paced language courses with highly motivated students who participate actively and want to be challenged? Do large numbers of students from your institution enroll directly in universities in host countries? Be careful not to choose a slow-paced program in which the students do not work as hard.

Make sure the language proficiency you gain will enable you to enter the next language level when you get back. Discuss this thoroughly with your study abroad advisor and with faculty from your language department. Some programs cover a great deal of colloquial language material but do not provide a full academic term of instruction in grammar. You probably want to complete a full semester or year of language study and enroll in the next higher level upon your return. Or is there a way to meet your institution's language requirement with a language not offered at the university?

On the other hand, you might prefer a program that puts less emphasis on the language and offers a more relaxed pace, allowing plenty of time for social and cultural interactions with your host families and with each other. You might want to find a program from an institution that promises a sociable, close-knit group. You might look for program materials that promise sufficient free time for leisure activities and travel.

Review the program materials carefully to be sure that the educational goals are compatible with your interests. Some programs place a strong emphasis on courses and activities that help you develop intercultural understanding. There might be opportunities to meet community groups, interview civic leaders, or participate in volunteer activities after class. Others address development issues and take students to inspect farms, factories, and commercial enterprises. If you have always dreamed of exploring museums and visiting the great architectural monuments of a country, a program that emphasizes commercial or social development might not stimulate you. If you like outdoor activities and spend your vacations hiking and camping, a program that considers the natural and geological features of the country might suit you well.

How will you stay in touch with the home university? Will you be able to register for study abroad and get all the services the students get when they go on the university's own programs?

What will happen to your student loans? Make sure that you will not lose your status as a full-time student while studying abroad on another program. If this happens, you could be required to start repaying student loans. To maintain your student status for loan purposes, your home institution needs a system that reports you as earning credit toward your college degree while studying abroad, regardless of whether you are enrolled in the college's own program or another study abroad program.

Students sometimes ask about going abroad immediately after they graduate from high school, *before* they enroll at the college of their choice. If you are considering this option, make sure that you and your parents can finance the program without receiving financial aid through a college or university in the United States. Find out what the procedures for transferring credit will be and whether the credit can be approved. Ask for recommendations. The process might differ from the way the institution handles other types of transfer credit.

Some students are interested in programs involving extensive travel, but no extended stays in any country. If you are considering such a program, find out whether your college will approve the credit you earn.

Applying Credit from Abroad to Your U.S. College Degree

There are various ways to handle transfer credit on programs that your institution sponsors or approves. Ideally, the credit should be handled according to a system that makes it convenient for you to see how it fits into your degree program. Some college programs are pre-approved so that every student knows exactly how the credit from each course transfers to the degree program.

Some colleges assign regular course numbers from the college catalog to all the courses students can take on official college programs. The students receive full credit and earn letter grades that appear on their transcript, just as if they had taken the course on the college campus.

The grades students earn while on study abroad programs do not always figure in their grade point

A Student Speaks Up
I chose this college because I liked their program in China. I got a list of courses and knew exactly how the credit would transfer. If the college runs the program, credit arrangements go much more smoothly. They held the orientation right here on campus so you can meet the other students. Orientations for other programs were too far away for me to attend.

Unofficially...
The older genera-
tion of my family
speaks Italian,
but none of us
kids learned it. I
would like to
know more about
my heritage and
use Italian to
meet the lan-
guage proficiency
requirement at
my college. I
asked the study
abroad advisor
and learned that
I can take begin-
ning Italian in
Italy. The chair
of the modern
languages
department says
she can approve
the credit.

averages. This depends on the policies of the individual school. Many institutions process credit for
courses taken at other institutions as transfer credit.
This means that the credit hours appear on the student's record, but the grades do not appear. Only
courses taught by the school's own professors can
figure into the grade point average. Find out what
your home institution's policies are.

Some courses might count toward concentration
requirements; because of the importance of study
abroad to learning a second language, language
majors usually can count the credit toward their
majors. Check with your concentration advisor to
see whether the department recommends particular
programs.

Just the Facts

- When deciding where to go to college, find out
  about study abroad opportunities.

- Your study abroad office provides numerous
  services to help you plan.

- Find out whether financial aid help is available.

- Make sure you qualify for programs your college offers.

- Look out for policies limiting your program
  choices.

- Get help evaluating programs your college
  does not sponsor.

Making It Happen: Applying and Preparing for Study Abroad

PART III

GET THE SCOOP ON...
Assembling the documents you need ▪ Selling
yourself to the programs ▪ Making your choice
▪ Making alternate plans

Applying for Study Abroad Programs

Chapter 9

Before You Start

As you gather the applications you want to submit, you'll find that most programs want you to submit a set of materials by the application deadline. Therefore, it makes sense to start the process early and to plan ahead to have on hand the items most programs want.

The first thing you need is a large supply of identity photos. Well before you begin your application process, find the least expensive way to get a supply. How many will you need? It depends on the number of applications you submit. For the program you finally select, you need at least eight. If they don't request them before you leave, take them with you to the country because you'll use them once you're there.

Arrange to get passport-size or small ID photos, the kind they also call wallet size. They should all

179

Watch Out!
If you forget to sign your passport before you submit your visa application, the consulate mails the documents back to you for your signature and you have to send everything again by registered mail. This could cause you to miss important application deadlines.

present the same view of you, much like the photo on your driver's license, your campus ID, or the smallest size of those grade school photos your Mom used to send to the relatives every year. They should show your face in a space about $1 \times 1^1/_2$ inches. If you wait until the last minute, you could spend from $7.50 to $10 for each pair of passport-size photos you purchase at a photo shop. The shop takes them with a quick-developing camera and can only prepare two at a time.

If you choose to use a snapshot, come up with a good one, order a lot of duplicates inexpensively, and be ready to cut them to the dimensions the program requests. The visa office might insist that they all be duplicates of exactly the same shot, so whatever option you choose, plan to start with at least a dozen—more if you want to apply to several programs.

What are all those photos for? Program resident directors like to compile a photo chart of the arriving students to help the staff and the students get to know one another. If there is a host family coordinator, she will want one. Your host university overseas will require a photo for the card that admits you to the dining hall and another for your registration card. If you get a student bus pass, you need at least one photo, maybe two. A residency card will require one to two photos. Your bank might want one copy to place on your check-cashing card and one for the application it keeps on file. If you have any photos left over, they make nice remembrances to give your host family or friends.

Getting Your Passport

Another item you should have on hand well in advance is your passport. Depending on the complexities of the visa application process for the country where you intend to go, the program might want your passport number on the application itself. If you are planning to go abroad for the summer, you might need to supply your passport, or the number, very soon after applying for the program. If the program application materials do not tell you how soon you need your passport, contact them for information or ask your study abroad advisor.

The State Department Web page provides detailed information concerning all aspects of passports, including instructions for applying for one and the application forms to use (www.state.gov/www/services.html).

You may have appeared on your parents' passport if your family traveled abroad when you were a child. However, if you have never had a passport of your own, you should begin the process early. You need the following documents before you begin the application process. Please make sure that you allow enough time to assemble them.

Proof of U.S. Citizenship (One of These)

Previous U.S. passport.

Certified birth certificate issued by the city, county, or state.

(If you were born in the United States but do not have a birth certificate available, you can order a certified copy from the clerk of the county in which you were born. Many county offices now have Web sites. Go to the county clerk's page. In some cases, an application to order a birth certificate is available on the Web.)

Consular report of birth abroad.

(If you were born overseas, you should check with your parents and make sure that you

A Student Speaks Up
I couldn't believe how many photos I was going to need," one student writes. You need several for the application, two especially prepared ones for your passport application, and one for your international student identity card. Others are for the application to the host university, and from two to eight will go on copies of the visa application.

Moneysaver
If you call photo shops in department stores or malls ahead of time, you might get a good deal on a large quantity. If you are lucky, you can find a photo-mat machine and get inexpensive black-and-white wallet-size photos. Or get a friend to take some photos of you and select one that includes a good one-inch square view of your face.

allow enough time to order a birth certificate in order to get your passport.)

Naturalization certificate.

Certificate of citizenship.

If you do not have any of these, the State Department Web site lists some other documents that you can provide and detailed instructions about how to get them:

Letter of No Record issued by the state stating the name, date of birth, years searched for a record, and that there is no birth certificate on file for the person.

AND

Other documentation of birth in the U.S. such as a:

Baptismal certificate

Hospital birth certificate

Census record

Certificate of circumcision

Early school record

Family Bible record

Doctor's record of post-natal care

You Will Also Need

Two passport photos, 2 × 2 inches in dimension.

(The application forms and the State Department Web site tell exactly the dimensions and pose required.)

Two copies of the application form. There are several easy ways to get the form. The State Department Web site indicates which of the following is nearest to your city or town:

Your county courthouse or circuit court-house.

Certain (Class II) post offices. (You can check the web to see if your post office qualifies.)

Or you can download the application directly from the Web site: (travel.state.gov/passport_services.html).

If you have never had a passport before, you need form DSP-11.

If you are renewing a passport and meet certain requirements, you need form DSP-82.

Proof of Identity

Previous U.S. passport

Naturalization certificate

Certificate of citizenship

Current, valid driver's license

Government ID: City, state, or federal

Military ID: Military and dependents

Work ID: Must be currently employed by the company

Student ID: Must be currently enrolled

Merchant Marines card: Also known as a "Seamen's" or "Z" card

Pilot or flight attendant ID

The Application Fee

For those age 16 and over, the fee is $60.

For those under the age of 16, the fee is $40.

Renewals are $40.

If you are applying for the first time, you must submit the application in person at the county

Watch Out!
Remember to sign your new passport as soon as you receive it. This is an important element in proving your identity. The signature on your passport is used to confirm the authenticity of your signature while you are abroad, each time you sign travelers' checks or a credit card bill, register at a hotel, or fill out any official document.

courthouse, district circuit courthouse, or a qualifying post office. For further information, see the Web page or the application form or contact your county courthouse.

Ordering Transcripts

Timesaver
Allow at least 10 days for ordering your transcripts. Order them well in advance of the program deadline. At certain times of the year, the registrar's office might receive many requests for transcripts for graduate school and job applications, and it might take some time to get an official transcript.

Another item you need quite soon is an official transcript for each program. You probably need an official transcript from each college or university attended. If you have not yet enrolled in college, a high school transcript is required. You can order an official transcript from your registrar's office. Indicate whether it should be issued to you to send with the application or mailed directly to the program admission office.

If you need a transcript from a high school or an institution that you are no longer attending, do not worry. Your records are available, and you can order the transcript. Just allow enough time to request the document and arrange for sending it before the deadline. To request a transcript to go directly to the program, be sure that you provide a complete mailing address.

Lining Up Letters of Recommendation

The letters of recommendation are one of the most important parts of your application. The program will be looking for evidence of your ability to work well with groups, your adaptability and flexibility in new situations, and your interest in the subject matter the courses will offer.

Who should write your letters of recommendation? Students often worry about whether their professors know them well enough and would be willing to write letters on their behalf. Sometimes, they turn to work supervisors or even friends instead of faculty to obtain letters they think will be favorable. This can be one of your most serious application mistakes! Consider carefully what the program writes about itself. Will you be in a traditional classroom situation? A field study? Will there be volunteer activities? Will you be living and spending time with a small group of fellow participants over an extended period of time? Request a letter from someone who can describe your level of maturity, intellectual aptitude, and readiness for the type of program for which you are applying. A professor will be able to say the most about your academic strengths.

First, professors probably remember you better than you think and keep records of your work to help them remember you. Secondly, the program is interested in receiving at least one letter from someone who can comment on your academic work. Ideal instructors to write letters of recommendation are:

- The instructor of a seminar who got to know you well through class discussion and also saw your work on papers.

- The instructor of a lab who worked with you and observed your ability to solve problems and work with others.

- Your advisor, who should have a good sense of your academic goals and the way they fit into your plans for life after college.

If the program expresses interest in letters from other persons who know you well, then you might want to solicit a letter from a resident assistant, a work supervisor, or your supervisor when you worked as a camp counselor. Think about people who can write about:

Bright Idea
If you do well in a course with a professor you really like, ask for a letter of recommendation. Ask the professor to write a letter and send it to your career placement file or keep it in a computer file. When you decide what type of program you will apply for, the professor can review the letter on file, revise it to suit, and meet the deadline.

- Your ability to work with others

- Your flexibility in new and unexpected situations

- Your maturity

- Your willingness to work with people from diverse backgrounds

- Your willingness to participate in group activities and to contribute to them

Make sure that your references know exactly what is expected of them and make it easy for them to write a letter for you. Allow them plenty of time to prepare a letter for you. Be aware that they are busy and might need plenty of advance notice to prepare a good letter for you.

If you think your professors do not remember you well enough, arrange an appointment with them. Be prepared to tell them in five minutes or so why you are interested in the program, what you hope to accomplish, and how the program fits with your academic goals. Talk a little bit about why you want to go to the country you have chosen and your interest in the culture. Consider this meeting as a mini-interview that the professor will use to round out the impression of you that she acquired while you were enrolled in her class. She might ask you some questions about your interest in the program to gain a better understanding of your preparedness for the program. The professor might ask some questions to get an idea of your maturity, adaptability, and ability to handle new and unexpected situations.

Provide your references with an addressed envelope. If you are expected to collect and return sealed letters of recommendation, let them know that you will pick up the letters from them. Make sure that your references know the deadline for submitting letters. Call or write to send them a polite, grateful reminder before the deadline. Be sure that you thank your references, whether or not your application is successful. Let them know the outcome of your application. After the program, tell them about the experience and let them know how much you appreciate their helping you to prepare a successful application. These steps ensure that the same people will submit letters on time and will be willing to recommend you again in the future.

Other Items—Signatures

Check well in advance of the deadline to see if your parents' signatures must appear on the application form. Allow plenty of time to discuss the program with your parents. Allow them the opportunity to read the program materials, agree to any financial commitments and payment schedules that are outlined in the application, and sign the application where necessary.

Similarly, if a signature is required from your study abroad advisor or academic advisor, be sure that you plan ahead to obtain it. The advisor might require you to complete some steps before she can approve your application. Don't expect busy faculty and administrators to sign forms upon demand. Most teachers and administrators take their responsibility for approving your application very seriously. They have a right to keep your file for a day or two so that they can find an appropriate time to review it carefully before approving it. If you wait until the last minute to submit your application and insist that the advisor sign your forms immediately, the study abroad advisor might not regard this procrastination favorably. Waiting until the last minute to

A Student Speaks Up
I felt nervous when I went to ask my professor for a recommendation, but she encouraged me strongly. She even called the study abroad advisor and recommended me for the program. She also got some suggestions from the advisor for places where I could do my research. She was so helpful that I was really glad I had asked her.

complete these steps is not a good sign that you are serious about your application. Remember that the advisors and other faculty are looking for indications that you are well prepared for the program and mature enough to comply with any requirements the program might impose for your well-being, safety, and academic benefit. Waiting until the last minute to request approval does not make a good impression.

How Many Applications Should You Submit?

The good news is that applying for study abroad programs is not as competitive as applying for admission to a college or university. You do not need to apply to a large number of programs, provided you make sure of the following:

- You will be able to submit all the necessary materials by the program deadline.

- You meet the admission qualifications for the program. (Discuss your qualifications with an advisor or instructor if you are unsure about this.) Qualifications might include the following:

  - You meet the minimum grade point average and minimum number of semesters of language study.

  - You have taken all of the specific prerequisites for the courses offered on the program.

You should also consider admissions policies. Is there a limited enrollment? In conjunction with the previous question, is there a rolling admission policy? (That is, does the program accept qualified students only until the program is full?) Is priority given to students at the sponsoring university, to residents of the state in which the sponsor is located, or to some other select group?

If any of these factors suggest that you might not be accepted to the program that is your first choice, then be sure you apply to one or more back-up programs.

Writing Your Personal Statement

Tell the program about yourself. One of the most important parts of the application is the personal statement. (Some programs call it a statement of purpose.) Programs want to know whether their goals are a good fit with yours. On a study abroad program where there may be a small group of people and a limited program of study, it is essential to determine that the group will function well together and that students will have a serious interest in the courses. It's also important to have a group that will cope well with unexpected situations and enjoy learning from a new culture. Depending on the focus of the program, your personal statement might be more important in getting you into the program than your grade average.

State clearly how the program will help you meet your personal goals. Answer some of the following questions:

How will it help you meet degree requirements?

What personal interests do you have that fit with the program destination?

How will it help you achieve your career goals?

Does the program offer you an opportunity to develop another facet of your interests and talents— perhaps allow you to explore a subject not in your degree program? This might be a good point to mention. Help the program to see you as a person

Moneysaver
In general, you can expect a favorable response if you meet all the admission requirements, submit your complete application by the deadline, and fall within any category of students to be given special consideration. You can save money and avoid losing deposits by applying early to your first choice. Apply to others only if you do not get into your first choice.

of many talents and interests who intends to combine all of them in a creative and satisfying adult life.

If your grade average is a bit short of the minimum, you might refer briefly to any special factors that you want the program to consider. Do not dwell on the negative aspects of your academic record, but be sure to make a brief reference to any special factors to explain a grade average that does not reflect your real abilities:

- Did an illness force you to drop a course?

- Did you choose some inappropriate courses during your first year in college, perhaps in subjects that did not utilize your real abilities to the fullest?

- Do your recent grades show steady improvement now that you have found where your talents and interests lie?

Point out steady improvement, special achievements, and good grades in courses that directly qualify you for the program. Keep in mind that a willingness to take risks and to perform less well in a new subject, one that you want to learn more about, is actually a strength. It is a good indicator of your willingness to explore new cultures and to learn from new and different experiences. Being willing to make mistakes is a sign of courage and adaptability.

Discuss some of the things you want to learn. Mention aspects of the host culture or the courses that stimulate your curiosity and suit your special talents. Provide examples of previous situations in which you showed adaptive flexibility in adjusting to new surroundings and circumstances. Call attention to some special achievements that gave you satisfaction and that show how much you will benefit from the program.

Above all, look at the process of applying to the program as an opportunity to review your talents and interests and describe the things about yourself that make you a unique individual. Applying for this program is good practice for other situations, such as job applications, in which you need to see yourself in the best light in order to convince others of your abilities and qualifications.

Sending Your Application

Once your application is ready, re-read all the instructions carefully and double-check the completeness of your forms. Did you sign every place that requires a signature? There may be several different places where you need to sign the forms. You must sign your passport, any visa application forms included in the application materials, and any other separate documents included in the packet.

The application will probably ask where the transcript should be sent at the end of the program. Do not assume that it should go to the registrar. It should probably be sent to the study abroad office at your institution. Allow time to check with the study abroad office so that you fill out that part of the form correctly, but above all, make sure that you do provide the information to ensure quick processing of your credit at the conclusion of your program.

Next, make complete copies of everything you are sending to the program. Give a copy to your parents or to the study abroad office. This step is a safeguard in case the application gets lost in the mail. It is a good idea to mail the application yourself. Campus postal services might delay your application for many days or even lose it.

Consider sending the application by overnight delivery or by registered mail so that you have a way of tracking the package and confirming delivery. Be sure that you follow up in approximately 10 days to be sure the application arrived and is being reviewed. If you do not hear from the program within three weeks of the time your application arrives at its destination, check again on its status.

When the Study Abroad Program Responds
Choosing the Best of Those Who Chose You

When the program notifies you of acceptance, you should have all the information you need to decide whether you intend to accept a place on the program. If not, be sure that you get the materials or information you need to make your final decision. Prompt receipt of registration materials and other program information is a good indicator of whether the sponsor runs the program efficiently and responds promptly to the needs of the participants.

Discuss the decision with your parents and advisor. If the program is your first choice, be sure that you respond and submit all deposits by the program deadline. Many students relax after learning of their acceptance and fail to take note of important registration deadlines. Be sure that you read all program materials with great care and follow the written instructions for course registration, housing selection, visa application, insurance information, and all other necessary registration materials (more about this in a later chapter).

Read your program checklist, make a copy for your parents, and post it in a prominent place so that you can meet all the deadlines. If you receive financial aid, find out what you have to do to apply your aid to the program you prefer. Discuss your program options with a faculty advisor and with your

Watch Out!
Submit all registration materials on time. Failure to do so might mean that you miss out on critical travel arrangements, room reservations, and other arrangements for the participants. If the program is your first choice, don't lose your chance to participate.

study abroad advisor to help select the program that accords best with your needs. If you feel you need further advice, consult with the career planning and placement center on your campus.

Let's assume that you have read the other chapters in this book and have applied to programs that are well run, that you have already gathered information about health and safety issues, and that you have reviewed information about the courses you will take on the program. The best way to choose from a number of good options is to consider what you want most to do and think you will enjoy the most.

Select a program that will help you complete your graduation requirements on time, but don't force yourself to choose a program that is not your first choice because you think it will guarantee you a job after college. Many successful and well-paid careers have grown out of interests that did not seem "practical" at first glance. Don't select a program because it is the first choice of your friends. Remember that you will make new friends on your program, from among people whose interests coincide with yours. Your best long-term program choice is the one that fits best with your real interests and aptitudes.

Watch Out!
Some programs close after receiving a certain number of deposits or after the deposit deadline. Read the admission material carefully and review it with your parents. Be sure to send in your deposit by the deadline.

What to Do If You Are Not Accepted

If you do not get accepted to the program you really want, you should find out whether the decision is negotiable. One of the most frequent common reasons for rejection of applications is that they are incomplete. Find out first of all whether all the essential elements of your application arrived and whether it is too late to supply the missing materials. Ask a faculty member or advisor to call and make sure that there were no misunderstandings concerning your qualifications for the program.

If you learn that you did not meet the program admission requirements, you should meet with your study abroad advisor and find out why. Discuss other program choices and spend enough time to find another program that is a better fit. Call or fax your follow-up program at once to see whether there are still spaces available. Many programs do not fill all their openings and might be able to accommodate a few late applicants.

If your application was unsuccessful because the program is full, find out when final deposits are due and whether you can remain on a waiting list. Make sure the program administrators know how interested you are in participating. This interest might be influential in creating a space for you.

Some students whose parents know influential people might get a family friend to put pressure on the program administrators to accept you. Be very careful about this strategy; it could backfire on you. A better idea is to ask your family friend to call to ask the program director for advice or guidance. Get the program directors on your side in helping to find you another suitable program. This is a more tactful approach. and it might encourage the admissions committee to take another look at your application. If they realize how much you want to participate in the program, you might even move up from the waiting list.

One summer, the administrator of a prestigious junior year abroad program in London persuaded the host university faculty to create some additional spaces for qualified students who were extremely eager to participate. He then called all over the world to locate students at the top of the waiting list and inform them that they had been accepted for the academic year about to begin.

Just the Facts

- Plan ahead to gather all application materials before you have to apply.

- Apply early for your passport.

- Allow plenty of time to get the signatures you need.

- Choose a program that you will enjoy.

- Submit your deposit and registration on time.

- Don't give up if your first choice does not accept you.

GET THE SCOOP ON...
Completing program registration procedures ▪
Choosing the housing that's right for you ▪
Nailing down your course selections ▪ Figuring
out how your credit will transfer

Registering for the Program

Chapter 10

You've been selected for the program you want and now you have to make some choices and register for the program. Signing up for the best program involves a careful review of all the papers and materials you receive. Be sure that you review the deadlines carefully and submit all the requested material by the due date. Students sometimes challenge programs concerning the necessity for photos and other documents. Cooperate with your program administrator by submitting all the requested material by the deadline. The photographs might be required for your visa application or for other documents that the sponsor needs to prepare for the entire group. Failing to meet the deadline could delay arrangements for the whole program.

Choosing Housing Options

Choosing your housing options and your courses involves some important considerations. Understanding cultural differences plays a large role in

Watch Out!
I was accepted to a study abroad program in Florence but was really distressed to discover that they enrolled students as soon as they sent in their deposits and closed the program when they reached their limit. Read the materials very carefully, and be sure you know when and how to reserve your place.

selecting your options. Before selecting housing, you need some background about housing arrangements in other countries. It will help you make sure that you get what you were hoping for.

Home Stays

If you are interested in choosing a home stay, it is very important to know what to expect. In many parts of the world, people live in a city-like atmosphere even when the town is fairly small by today's standards. The centuries-old cities that used to be surrounded by walls retain their narrow streets and crowded city centers. Many people still live in apartments located close to the historic city centers rather than in shady outlying suburbs filled with separate houses. Therefore, whether you are going to Japan, Spain, Germany, or Argentina, if you choose a home stay, it is as likely to be in a large apartment as in a house. Be aware that apartments are sometimes called flats in other parts of the world.

One of the reasons for the predominance of apartment living in many of the world's cities is that cars have only recently become practical in many countries. Until fairly recently, people were obliged to walk or use public transportation, and many still prefer to live close to the city center or close to public transportation lines. Even rapidly expanding modern cities have retained an urban appearance with many apartment buildings. Doors opening directly on the street are typical. In some locations, houses open directly onto the street but are built around an open courtyard or a walled garden. From the street, nothing is visible but walls. This arrangement ensures the residents' privacy, something that city dwellers value.

Visitors from other countries are sometimes surprised to visit American cities where they drive through mile after mile of tree-shaded houses surrounded by lawns and gardens. "There isn't any city!" they might exclaim. If you have a strong preference for an American-style home rather than an apartment, you should discuss your expectations with the program administrator.

Another factor to consider is the possibility that your home stay will be shared with one or more other international students. Some people simply have rooms available and like the company of international students. The hostess might have various reasons for renting rooms to students. Many couples whose children have grown and left home have extra rooms to rent. Others might see the arrangement more as a source of income than as a cultural experience for the student. Sometimes, a single parent needs the income to help maintain a large apartment.

In Latin America, living with a host family is an important way of establishing a secure place in the community. Your host family makes sure that you get safely to and from classes and afterschool events and watches out for your welfare in other ways.

Ask the program administrators about the educational purpose for the home stays they arrange for program participants. Indicate your preferences. If you are looking for a true family atmosphere in which you can spend a lot of time learning about the culture, talking to your hostess, and improving your language skills, you can find a program that selects host families with this objective in mind. However, you need to ask or you might be disappointed.

A Student Speaks Up
I will never have another host family. The mother borrowed at least $200 from each of us, took in extra people in violation of her contract, and took advantage of our inexperience in other ways. It took a while before we realized it and complained.

**A Student
Speaks Up**
Check out the
history of the
apartment build-
ing. Older, down-
town ones
probably have
six-legged ten-
ants! My apart-
ment was over a
former restaurant
in an old build-
ing. The roaches
were so bad that
I finally got the
program to
relocate me.

Do not expect to have a room of your own in which to study in the evening. In many parts of the world, dinner is served late. After the meal, the family watches television together or talks until bedtime. After dinner, students might go out with friends or visit with their families, if they live at home. Unlike Americans, families in other parts of the world might not expect students to require a private place for after-dinner studying.

Bedrooms might be small, shared with another person, and not designed to afford privacy. In Japan, for example, housing is extremely expensive and families adjust to the small quarters by using their space for many different purposes. Beds might be mats that are spread out at night and taken up during the daytime. Because of the high cost of electricity, bedrooms in many parts of the world might not be well lighted for reading late at night. Students often study during the day, in the university library or in a café. To get the most out of a home stay arrangement, you might need to organize time differently from the way you plan your days in the United States.

You should not expect to use the host family's phone frequently. In many parts of the world, not every family has a working phone. In most countries, users are charged for each phone call, even for local ones. If you have a laptop with a modem, you should not expect to monopolize the family's telephone line to use e-mail or the Internet. Check with your program about arrangements students usually make for going online. Many sign up to use Internet access service at a cyber-cafe or arrange to use facilities at the university library.

Following are some of the questions typically found on a housing preference questionnaire:

Housing Plan

Would you prefer a house (the number of home stays in suburban-style houses can be very limited in some cities)?

Can you go up and down stairs?

If you lived in an apartment, would you require access by elevator?

Smoking

Indicate whether you prefer:

a smoking household

a non-smoking household

doesn't matter

Pets

Would you prefer a home with no pets?

With cats only?

With dogs only?

With small dogs only?

Allergies

Do you have any serious allergies?

If yes, please describe.

Meals

Are there any foods you cannot eat?

Are you a vegetarian?

If yes, do you eat eggs and milk products?

Special Needs

Do you have any medical conditions or physical limitations of which the host family should be aware?

A Student Speaks Up
Get a program with a home stay. Our house mother was fantastic, and she cooked us the most delicious meals. Every night, we would sit at the table and try to talk Italian with her. It was the best part of my stay.

Location

Would you prefer to be close to the city center?

Close to the university?

Commuting

What is the farthest distance you would be willing to travel by bus:

Five minutes?

Thirty minutes?

One hour?

(In some large cities, such as Tokyo, it could easily take one or two hours to commute from some locations.)

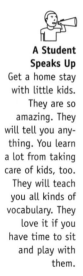

A Student Speaks Up

Get a home stay with little kids. They are so amazing. They will tell you anything. You learn a lot from taking care of kids, too. They will teach you all kinds of vocabulary. They love it if you have time to sit and play with them.

Children

Would you prefer a family without children?

With small children?

With teenagers?

Religion

Would you prefer a family that practices the same religion that you do?

If so, please indicate what religion:

(It might not be possible to accommodate all religious preferences.)

Interests

Please describe your interests and hobbies. Indicate which of these you would most like to share with your host family.

Free Time

How would you prefer to spend your time after dinner?

Studying alone in your room?

Visiting and watching television with the family?

Going out with friends?

If you decide to live with a host family, consider some of the basic rules of etiquette to observe and make sure that you are comfortable with them before you sign up for this arrangement.

Be sure that you are prepared to accommodate yourself to the family's rules. Let them know about your comings and goings and when you will have friends visiting. If you have meals with the family, be punctual (or a little early) and willing to help with the dinner preparations if it is expected. Let the family know in advance if you do not plan to be home at a regularly scheduled meal time. Keep your host family informed if you plan to be out late at night or if you intend to be away. Your family might want to lock up the house and turn out the lights by a certain time of night.

Most visiting students share a bathroom with family members. Don't monopolize the bathroom, and be sure that you work out an appropriate schedule with the family. Check to be sure that you aren't using too much hot water. Even though you are treated as a member of the family, be courteous and do not use other family members' toilet articles unless specifically encouraged to do so.

Because of the cost of food and electricity, you should not raid the fridge unless specifically invited to use certain snack foods. Be careful not to open and close the refrigerator door or use the electric stove too often. In some countries, people are extremely conscious of the effect on their electric bill.

Bright Idea
Some programs offer students housing arrangements in residence halls and apartments but establish contact with families in the community purely for social interactions. You might gain just as much culturally from contact with a family that invites you regularly for dinner or family excursions.

66

My wife and I had guests and stocked our Heidelberg apartment fridge with beer and soft drinks. The next morning, the landlady confronted us with a precise count of the times we had opened our refrigerator door!

99

If you think you will not feel comfortable accommodating yourself to these basic rules of courtesy for living with a host family, you might want to consider another housing option.

In some countries, it is difficult to find a family that does not smoke or own a cat or a dog. Some dogs that people keep to help guard the house are quite hefty, considering the small size of the quarters in which their owners live. If you are sensitive to animal hair or to cigarette smoke, be sure to check with the program administrators about the advisability of signing up for a host family.

Residence Hall

Choosing a residence hall instead of a home stay has some advantages, but again, you need to be aware of some differences between American college residences and those in other countries. One advantage of the dorm is that you will live with other students and will have the opportunity to meet people your own age, with similar interests. Many students hope for a roommate who is a native speaker of the language and citizen of the country they are going to. In many countries, rooms in student residences are singles.

There are some exceptions to this. Chinese university dormitories house as many as eight Chinese students to a room, but the foreign student dormitories where American students live usually have doubles and triples. In many residence halls, each student has a sink in the room, which is a convenience. Toilets and showers are shared, with one or two per floor. Usually, men and women live on separate floors or in separate wings of the building.

American students are often disappointed with dorm rooms in other countries because they are used to spending a great deal of time studying in their rooms and they expect a lot of space and light. Even if your room is a single, you should not expect it to be a spacious one in which you can comfortably spend most of your time. Student rooms are often small and not well lighted. However, as mentioned earlier, students in other countries can plan to study during the daylight hours and in a location other than their rooms. When the weather is mild, they might study outdoors in a park or on the university grounds. They can also study in school libraries or in cafes. After dinner, in many cultures, is the time to get together with friends or family members.

Telephone access in older residence halls is usually extremely limited. Most have a single phone for each floor or one per building. However, the popularity of computers has increased the demand for telephone lines in individual rooms. Modern dorms might be fully equipped with multimedia facilities, including phone jacks for the use of modems. Ask about the type of residence hall you will find at your host university or program.

In the British Isles, you often have a choice of accommodation. You can choose to live in a residence hall with meals included. All the residents eat together in a dining hall (also called a commons), which is a good way to get to know the other students. If you prefer, you can choose a room in a self-catering (which means you fix your own meals) residence hall. In these halls, the rooms are arranged around central kitchens where the students can prepare their own meals. One advantage of the self-catering rooms is that they are open during vacation periods, whereas the halls with meal service might close. Another advantage is that you

Bright Idea
Arranging to room with a student who does not speak English, or making friends with one after you arrive, will do a lot for your language skills. To get the most out of your friendship, the two of you need to speak in the language you are there to study.

Watch Out!
We had meal ser-
vice during the
regular terms,
but the entire
residence hall
closed during
vacations.
Students in self-
catering halls
were able to stay
and cook meals
during the
breaks.

can probably make some good friends among the students who share your kitchen.

There are cultural differences in the amount of social activity organized by the residence halls. In British culture, the residence hall might be a center of social activity, somewhat like the American dormitory. In Australia, campus life might center around residential colleges, with sports and other activities organized by the colleges. In France, the residence halls might not have as many organized activities. You might have to make more of an effort to get to know people and find activities to share. However, if you make the effort, you will make friends and you might actually get to know more French students than you would in a home stay. Students report that German and Danish residence halls are friendly places where they make many friends.

European universities usually offer meals in large student restaurants. They are called the Mensa in Germany and *restaurants universitaires* (nick-named *resto-u*) in France. Any student, whether living in a residence hall or not, can get an ID card for the student restaurant and purchase meals there. The restaurants are located in various places throughout the city. Meals in student restaurants, whether in the dorm or located throughout the city, are notoriously basic and repetitive. However, they are reasonably priced and help you stick to a budget.

It is a good idea to budget some money for eating out from time to time. You should take advantage of the country's specialties and vary your diet. Most student residence halls around the world have hot plates on each floor, and some might even have a tiny refrigerator. Like most of the other students, you can vary or supplement your diet by shopping in the market for food to keep in your room for lunches and snacks. An insulated bag is a good idea for keeping cheese or yogurt cool. Refrigerated foods should not be left at room temperature for more than one to two hours.

In many residence halls, students get together and cook meals, with each person contributing something. This is a great way to meet other people and an especially good way to meet other international students. They might introduce you to some delicious dishes from their homeland. Don't be shy about striking up conversations with other students in the halls. Gradually, you will get to know people just from asking them for information and saying hello on a daily basis, and some interesting friendships will develop.

Renting an Apartment

Some students have the option of finding an apartment to share with another student. In the United States, an apartment offers many advantages. You can keep your own hours, entertain or study as much as you like, play your own music, prepare meals in keeping with your tastes and schedule, stock your own refrigerator, and even keep pets such as fish. You might be able to zip to campus in a few minutes by bike or by car. Once again, it is important to consider what this living arrangement means to students in other countries. Although privacy and flexibility are certainly advantageous, you might not have some of the other benefits of a student apartment in the United States.

Although people fall in love with animals in other countries and sometimes want to bring their new pets back to the U.S., you must go through considerable red tape to do so. You must provide proof

Watch Out!
Be sure to check security carefully in residence halls and make sure your windows and doors have solid locks. Avoid first-floor rooms. Even residence halls that appear to be safe frequently experience petty thefts. There have been reports of assaults.

❝

When the cook got a little dog, we became fond of him and complained when the health department sent the dog away. We later realized he was being fattened up for cooking. Finally, we got permission to take the dog home to the U.S. with us, and he is now a San Francisco resident.

❞

of immunizations for rabies and other diseases and put the animal through a lengthy quarantine. Investigate U.S. and local regulations thoroughly, as well as checking with the owner of your residence, before acquiring a pet.

Property is much more expensive in other parts of the world than in most parts of the United States. For instance, if you live in the Southeastern United States, your idea of a good price for a clean, well-maintained apartment in a safe area is far less than what you have to pay in London, Paris, or Tokyo. In any country, the prices are much higher in the center of town or near the university than in the outskirts. Moreover, student apartments have the same limitations that home stays and dormitory rooms do, in that the rooms are apt to be small and more useful as a place to sleep than as a place to spend many hours studying.

If you choose an apartment far from the university in order to save money, it could mean a commute of one to two hours in some cities. A city bus has to get through city traffic. In places such as Beijing, Tokyo, London, and many other parts of the world, traffic congestion is increasingly problematic. Therefore, a smaller place and a more expensive location close to the university might be worthwhile.

Some programs require students to find their own apartments, but others offer a choice of recommended housing. This generally causes students a great deal of anxiety and stress. You can contact an apartment locating service to arrange for your own housing. In fact, even when the program offers you a choice of apartments, you are not obligated to select the housing chosen by the program. In some

cities, finding your own apartment might be sufficient and cost about the same price as the options
the program arranges for you. In others, you might
find that the program arrangements are the most
convenient.

Selecting Courses

The courses you select should be as close as possible
to the ones that were approved for you. Notify the
program of your course selection as soon as you register. This will ensure the best chance of getting the
courses you require.

Curriculum—Some Differences to Consider

The term *course* applies to an entire program of
study. When the program materials ask you what
course you want to study, you should answer "art history" or "anthropology." When the materials ask you
to list the individual classes you want to take, then
you list what we consider courses—such as "19th
century French painting" or "The novels of Thomas
Hardy."

In most countries, students are accepted into a
specific department or field of study. Their degree
program is already set. This means that each academic department can decide what first-year students
must study, as well as each step along the path
toward their degree. It is not as necessary for them
to advertise the course content in a catalog in
advance (although some universities are starting to
provide more information as a result of the increase
in exchanges). This means that it might be somewhat difficult to get course descriptions, unless you
plan to take courses offered year after year with little change. Most program sponsors try to identify
courses that are offered consistently each year and

Watch Out!
Be cautious
about living in
unsafe areas.
Although you
want a central
location, follow
the recommenda-
tion of your
housing coordi-
nator and select
housing that
ensures security.
Avoid ground
floor lodgings
and areas that
are unsafe after
dark. Check door
and window
bolts before
agreeing to rent.
If necessary, buy
your own locks
to reinforce any
that do not seem
secure.

are certain to have spaces available for international students. Ask the program to provide you with a description or reading list for each of the courses that are sure to be offered.

Confirming Your Course Selection

To select your courses, confer with a professor or advisor in your field of study. Because the courses might be organized differently, you might need assistance identifying the topics listed in the host university catalog that match with requirements you have to meet at your home institution. For instance, your university catalog might list a three-credit course in 19th century French literature. The host university might list instead a group of one- or two-hour seminars on individual authors or on various themes or topics. An advisor can help you choose suitable classes to meet your requirements. Be as flexible as possible, choosing alternates whenever necessary. You might find that one class is full or not available for the term you will be there. Having a second and third choice already selected is helpful.

Send your selection of classes to the program as soon as you can. You might not be able to make your final selection until after you arrive. On the best programs, an academic advisor is assigned to help you select your classes and find the best topics to fit your home university requirements. In some situations, classes might be full. You might be encouraged to take courses that have been popular with international students in the past. If the program is in English, you should not necessarily be encouraged to take classes that work better for non-native speakers, those whose native language is not English.

A Student Speaks Up
The more advance information you get about your courses and the more planning you do, the better. At the same time, you need to be flexible and ready to shift your plans if necessary. Get some extra courses approved as a back-up.

Comparing Credit Systems

The university you are going to attend might convert all course credit to the American system. If the program is operated by an American university or if an American university sponsors the program, you can expect clear information about the amount of course credit you will receive. However, if you are enrolling directly in a university that uses another system, the credit system might require some interpretation or explanation. Consult your study abroad advisor about the way your home university will convert the credit you earn to the American system. Read your college catalog to be sure that you understand your institution's transfer credit policy. The following system might be the one your institution uses.

A full-time course load at the host institution is compared to a full-time load at your home university. Let us say, for example, that the host university awards approximately 120 units of credit for a full year of study, and your home university awards approximately 30 semester hours of credit for a full year of study. This means that four units taken at the host university are equal to one hour of semester credit at your home university. On this basis, if you successfully complete a 20-credit course at the host university, your home university will convert that credit to five semester hours of credit.

If, on the other hand, the host university awards 24 credits for a full year's work, and your home institution awards 30, one course that is equal to four credits at the host university will transfer as five semester credits at your home institution. Again, this is assuming that your home university uses this

Bright Idea
Take along a course catalog from your home university and a copy of your transcript so that you can show your academic background. This might be helpful in showing that you have the prerequisites to enroll in a class that interests you.

**A Student
Speaks Up**
I was worried
because a full-
time load in
Australia is only
12 credits for a
semester,
whereas I needed
15 semester
hours to gradu-
ate on time.
Fortunately,
when the credit
was converted to
the American
system, it came
out to 15.

basis for determining transfer credit. Other systems may apply. Check with your study abroad advisor before leaving the campus to find out how the credit will work in your case.

Choosing Payment Options

Some colleges and universities handle all program payment arrangements for students. All that you need to do is arrange to pay your tuition at the regular time. At other institutions, you are responsible for paying the program fees directly to the program and arranging to meet all your other expenses yourself. If you are expecting financial aid to help cover the payment of some of your expenses, it is very important for you to stay in close contact with your study abroad office, the office of financial aid, and the program sponsor. Work closely with all three offices on the timing for distribution of any financial aid you are to receive. It is your responsibility to make sure that all payments are made by the payment deadline. If the funds cannot be released at the proper time, you might have to make other payment arrangements to meet the program's registration and payment deadlines.

Delayed Payment

Many colleges allow students and their families to pay tuition on an installment plan. Your parents make regular payments to their account, and the tuition management company pays your tuition on the date when it comes due. If your college is paying the program fees on your behalf, and you pay full tuition to the college, you should have no difficulty continuing with your tuition payment plan in the usual way. If you are responsible for paying the program fees directly to the program, you need to contact the tuition management company and the program sponsor to see whether a payment plan can be arranged.

Normally, you and your parents are responsible for contacting the tuition management service that pays your college expenses. You must ask whether it will agree to adjust the usual arrangements for paying tuition to your home university to help you pay for your study abroad program. These are some of the details you must work out:

- Tuition management plans pay only for the regular academic year. If your program includes all or part of a summer term, your family might need to make other arrangements to pay that portion of the program fees.

- The company must agree to make the payment to the program sponsor instead of to your home university.

- The company must agree to make the payment by the payment deadline.

- If your program fees are a different amount from the tuition you regularly pay, the company must agree to restructure your family's payments to accommodate the difference.

- If the company cannot make payment by the program's deadline, the program sponsor must agree to wait for the payment.

- If the company cannot change the payment amounts, you need to make other arrangements to pay any balance due.

- The company needs to send written confirmation of the agreed-upon terms to the program sponsor.

Normally, tuition payment companies make a single payment each semester to your university.

Watch Out!
I had been in China for six months when the program called my mom to say that the tuition payment program had not paid anything on my program fees. They pay only in the fall. Because my grades for summer had come in, they thought I was back on campus and paid my school instead of the program.

These payments come at the beginning of the regular fall semester and the beginning of the regular spring semester at your home institution. Be sure to document the payment schedule clearly. Make sure that your program has complete information about the payment dates and that these dates are acceptable.

Loans

Your program might start earlier or later than the school year at your home institution. This could have an important effect on the timing of financial aid payments you are scheduled to receive.

For some types of aid, the financial aid office might be able to make the funds available at the time your program begins. The earlier you check with the office of financial aid, the greater your chances of working out the timing for the release of funds so that you can pay your program fees when they are due.

Some federal financial aid disbursements are not made until the end of the add/drop period for the regular academic term at your home university. This is the point at which your student account office normally confirms that you are enrolled as a full-time student. For the semester or year that you are studying abroad, the student account office will confirm that you are registered for study abroad on an approved program. Some student account offices send a form to the program administration to confirm that you have actually enrolled in the program. When the program sponsor returns the form, your student account office can confirm your status and the money can be released. Naturally, this process takes some time.

If this is the case, you should check with your program to see whether it will accept certification that your financial aid is on its way and wait for your payment. If this is not acceptable to the program, you might need to make special arrangements to pay the deposit or the program fees before the program begins. A short-term loan might be necessary to ensure that your program enrollment is complete. When your financial aid payment arrives, your family can repay the loan. Ask your financial aid office for suggestions about how this has been arranged for other students. Be sure to check with the study abroad office as well.

You might be able to apply directly to the program sponsor for financial aid. If you do this, the program asks you and your home institution to complete a consortial agreement to confirm that you are receiving financial aid from only one source. (See Chapter 7, "Figuring Out the Cost of Programs and How to Finance Them," for more information.)

Your financial aid office might be able to refer you to private lenders to obtain supplementary funds so that you can meet the full cost of your study abroad program. You might also need to apply to your family's bank or to a lending institution in your community to arrange for a short-term loan to meet program deadlines.

While you are abroad, your family needs to remain in close contact with the program sponsors and all the offices responsible for disbursement of funds to meet your program costs. Never assume that everything is going as smoothly as it usually does when you are on your home campus, even if you are receiving all the financial aid that you normally receive. The fact that you are studying abroad

A Student Speaks Up
My school will not release financial aid to pay the program until we actually enroll. Therefore, programs always have to wait for their money until they return the form that says we are in the country and enrolled in classes.

makes all the financial aid arrangements non-routine. It is easy for clerical oversights or computer errors to occur. Each time your parents receive a payment from your home college or a loan company, they should double-check with the program sponsor to make sure all program payments have been made.

Just the Facts

- Follow program registration instructions and meet all payment and registration deadlines to secure your place on the program.

- Review housing and meal choices carefully and be sure you know what to expect before you decide.

- Select your courses early, and be sure you understand the course selection procedures.

- Nail down the process for converting credit to your home university's credit system.

- Work closely with your financial aid office to ensure timely payment of your fees.

GET THE SCOOP ON...
Nailing down credit for your courses ▪ Planning
ahead to meet degree deadlines ▪ Reserving a
place on campus for your return ▪ Making sure
of financial details

Making Final Arrangements with Your Home Institution

A fter you choose your program and register for it, your next step is to make sure that your home university has all the necessary information about your plans to study abroad. This is the time to take care of all the details to ensure that you stay in touch with your home college or university while you are away and that you make a smooth return at the conclusion of your study abroad. Some students advise themselves by reading through their college catalog before they go abroad. They might simply assume that they can make all the arrangements for transfer credit and degree requirements after they return. This could be a serious mistake! Be sure you check carefully with all the important offices on your campus. Know the requirements to earn credit for everything you plan to accomplish on your study abroad program.

Getting Course Approval

Arranging for transfer credit involves several important steps. Your first stop is the study abroad office. You need to make sure that you get approval for the courses you plan to take overseas. Some schools take care of this after the student returns, but many require you to get approval before you go. Ask the study abroad advisor on your campus about the procedure. Find out who will evaluate and approve your credit. At some institutions, approval comes from the chair of the department that would offer the course if you took it on your home campus. At others, a dean or study abroad advisor might be designated to evaluate the credit. Some students first ask the dean of students or the academic advising office for advice about this. They might be sent to several different offices before they find the correct one. The *best* place to start is the study abroad office. If that office does not evaluate the credit, it is sure to know who does and what you must do to transfer the credit back to your records.

Your next step is to compile all the information that is available about the courses you intend to take. Some colleges and universities determine all the course numbers in advance for the programs they administer. This makes it easy for you to complete the credit approval process. If you plan to enroll in an island program, with courses designed especially for American students, it might be relatively easy to contact the program sponsor and obtain course descriptions and information about any prerequisites. They might even be printed in the program catalog. Many students prefer the convenience of this type of program because it speeds up the approval process.

On the other hand, direct enrollment at a host university in another country has many cultural and educational benefits. Don't let the additional time and care involved in getting your courses approved deter you from choosing a direct enrollment program. Many universities in other countries do not publish detailed descriptions of their course offerings prior to the start of classes. Nonetheless, even if the course descriptions are not published in advance, you can still arrange for approval of your transfer credit. By assembling a file for each course as described here, you have a good chance of arranging approval for your courses prior to enrollment or after your return. Some students can arrange to fax or e-mail information about their courses as soon as they obtain it. If you cannot obtain this information before participating in the program, prepare a file for each course you take. Place a cover sheet on each course, including the following information:

- The number of hours per week the course meets.

- The number of weeks the academic term or semester lasts.

- The reading list.

- A syllabus, if available, showing the topics covered.

- The course level. (Introductory, intermediate, advanced? Are there prerequisites?)

- The basis for grade.

- The grading system at the host university. (Your study abroad office will probably supply this for you.)

- The primary approach used in the course. (Is it history? engineering ? economics? public health? sociology? philosophy?) The answer determines which department at your institution would probably give you credit for it.

Include as much information as you can provide about the number of courses in a full-time load at the host university. You can often find this information in a university catalog or even on the university Web site. If your study abroad office does not have the information, ask the program sponsor or international student advisor at the host university to write a note confirming the number of courses in a full-time load.

Others ask students to confer with each department chair to decide individually what the course numbers should be. Expect this to take some time. Plan ahead to allow plenty of time to complete this step before you leave campus at the end of your last term before you study abroad. This is a very important step in your credit approval. Therefore, you should call ahead to make appointments with each of the faculty members you need to see. Remember that a large number of students might be requesting this service and the professor might not be in the office all the time. During exam periods, most professors have different schedules, just as students do. They might also have to be away at out-of-town meetings. This is why it is better to allow plenty of time for this process and to make an appointment instead of just dropping by.

After you get all your courses pre-approved, you will turn the information over to the office that records the credit on your transcript. On your campus, it might be the study abroad office or the registrar. Make sure the information is on file before you leave for study abroad.

Before you meet with your advisor or chair, put together a little file, including an unofficial transcript showing the courses you have already taken and descriptions of the courses you plan to take. Include a copy of the statement of purpose or personal statement that you submitted to the program. The transcript will help the chair make sure you do not get the same course number on your record twice, creating a problem that could take some time to correct. This file of information about you will assist the chair or other college official to approve the credit in the way that is most appropriate for you and your program of study.

Credit

Take copies of all the material you have assembled to your meeting with the person who will determine the number of credit hours you will receive for your courses. If the host university does not convert credit to semester hours for you, your study abroad advisor should be able to explain how your university will calculate the weight of the courses you take.

Some universities that work closely with American universities are aware that this information is important. If the university publishes a catalog, it might provide information about how to convert its credit system to semester hours. Somewhere in the catalog, you should be able to find information about how many courses a degree candidate must take each year and the other steps to completing a degree. Look for the requirements for individual programs of study, such as religion, engineering, accounting, public policy, biology or economics. If you have any difficulty with this, request

Unofficially...
If a student takes the equivalent of a full-time load for a full year at the host university, our college regards this as equivalent to 30 semester hours in the American system. If a student takes less or more than a full-time load, we calculate the increase or reduction in credit in proportion to this basic formula.

assistance from the person or office to which you submitted your program application.

After you determine the way in which the credit hours will be calculated, you need to arrange for review of the individual courses to determine the equivalency. The equivalency is the course number from your home institution catalog that is placed on your transcript to confirm that you have transferred the credit earned abroad.

Independent Study

Every so often, a student abroad discovers a gold mine of information for an exciting research project or an opportunity for an internship with some research possibilities. If there is no credit associated with the activities, students can request the chance to carry out an independent study project working with a professor on their home campus. Generally speaking, it is difficult to get approval for an independent study project after you arrive overseas. It is much better to develop a project with a professor prior to your departure and to obtain clear guidelines for an independent study project in advance. If your instructor knows your background and capabilities and has already given you some readings and some guidelines to follow, you might find it easier to communicate while you are overseas. Occasional contact for advice and guidance goes more smoothly. You can tell your instructor what sort of material you are finding and get some specific suggestions for giving form to your project.

Many experts feel that it is best to carry out your independent study project without being too dependent upon telephone, fax, and e-mail while your work is in progress. They prefer to arrange for the host institution to evaluate all your work and award credit that can be transferred to your home institution.

If you come across a valuable research opportunity after you arrive in the country, the best approach is to see how it might be incorporated into the courses you are taking at the university. The guidance of experts who are close to the material will be more informative for you, and the arrangements for credit will go more smoothly.

Journal Writing

Some study abroad programs require students to maintain journals as one basis for their grades in one of the program courses. Often, the journal is evaluated on a daily or weekly basis. This is a really valuable opportunity. First, it is an excellent way to record the people you meet and the contacts you want to follow up on later in your stay or upon your return. Secondly, you will be surprised at how many details are forgotten even a few weeks after the events when you are in such a new experience. A journal helps you review the various stages of your experience and refreshes your memory. Third, journals help you develop your powers of observation and your analytical skills. They help you to prepare any reports you are required to submit and provide information about courses you take that need to be evaluated for credit upon your return. A journal can be the nucleus of an ongoing research project or a creative writing project. After your return from study abroad, your notes serve as an invaluable record of your experience.

If you have the opportunity to compare your journal with others from your class, you discover the power of your own observations and gain confidence in your ability to express your views. The

**A Student
Speaks Up**
Some of the
entries in my
journal were
unique observa-
tions that I trea-
sured after I got
back. They
brought back the
smells and
sounds so
vividly. I remem-
bered watching
the family across
the street pre-
pare breakfast,
filling their
beautiful little
coffee pot, stop-
ping frequently
to pet the head
of some little
animal I couldn't
see. Everything
came back to life
when I reread my
journal.

variety and originality of the comments will impress you. Journals can serve as the basis for valuable class discussions during the program.

As you complete your final preparations, you might want to collect a small bibliography in prepa-ration for a journal. These readings will provide some filters through which you can review your daily experiences and react to them. Here are some types of readings you might consider:

- The autobiography of a noted citizen of the country, ideally one in which the writer is addressing an audience of non-compatriots and trying to help readers understand the country better

- Travel writing of a well-known person who visited the country a long time ago so that you can contrast your own reactions to that person's

- A book about the technique of crossing cul-tures, such as a brief history of the country

- A history of philosophy seen through that country's history

Internships

Some academic programs have very clear guidelines for internships that are a necessary part of the degree program. If you have enrolled in an intern-ship program, check with your concentration advi-sor before your departure to make sure you know what requirements you must meet to receive credit for the practical training you will receive.

Some institutions or departments award credit only for an academic course associated with the internship. Other departments have special internship courses. They might set specific requirements for awarding credit for an internship completed overseas or through any other institution. Check with both your study abroad office and your department to make sure you meet the requirements for receiving credit. In some cases, a student is required to complete a learning agreement document to receive credit for an internship. Investigate all these requirements with care.

Consulting with Your Department or Concentration Advisor

Your next step is to contact the department in which you intend to major to make sure that the credit earned abroad will apply to your required program of study. Be sure to allow plenty of time for taking care of this before you leave campus. Your concentration (or major) advisor will tell you what courses you have to take after you get back. If you don't meet to discuss this with him or her before you leave, you might end up having to take an additional course after you get back, perhaps delaying your graduation!

You also need to ask what steps the other students in your class will take in their degree program during the semester or year you are away. Many institutions have students officially declare their concentration at the end of their second year or at the beginning of their third year at the university. If you will be overseas at that time, you need to find out what steps are required and complete them before you go. If you need to send anything from overseas, be sure you know the deadlines and obtain copies of all the required papers and descriptions of any files you need to compile in order to declare your major (concentration).

A Student Speaks Up
As a teaching intern in a British school, I was required to enroll for independent study credit at my home university. At the conclusion of my teaching duties, I prepared a complete report to submit to my home university. This enabled me to earn the credit and helped the next intern prepare for the project.

Graduating When You Return

Some students go abroad at the very end of their
college or university years and expect to graduate as
soon as the credit transfers from their study abroad
experience. Find out what you need to do to graduate when you expect to do so. Most students are
expected to file an application to graduate, an intention to graduate, or some other formal paperwork
so that the registrar's office can check the records,
make sure everything is in order, and prepare the
diploma. Find out those deadlines so that everything goes smoothly for you.

Honors

Unofficially...
Internet video
conferencing
makes it possible
for students at
our institution to
collaborate on
research projects
with students at
a partner univer-
sity in Japan.
Scholars can
complete pro-
jects begun
abroad or confer
with professors
at home.

Most professors want to discuss honors projects in
person with students who want to work with them on
a senior research paper. If you want to do honors
and have not yet developed a project, you might
want to meet with the professor you want to work
with prior to your departure. Find out what sort of
materials to gather and how you can take advantage
of the courses available at your host institution to
put together the nucleus of a research paper. The
professor might have valuable suggestions about
libraries or other sources of information to consult
while you are in the country. He or she might be
able to arrange for you to meet and interview people significant to your project. You can discuss data
that you could start collecting while in the country,
such as newspaper articles or statistics.

If a very good idea occurs to you while you are
abroad, you might have to wait until you get back to
start working with a professor on a research project.
By then, the material you want to work with will be a
long way away. You can take better advantage of your
time abroad if you meet with a professor before you

go to find out what type of material you should think about collecting.

Thanks to increased improvements in e-mail connections, you might be able to work on your project with supervision from your home campus while you are abroad.

Important Offices to Check with Before Leaving Campus

Registrar's Office

Find out who enters the credit on your transcript upon your return and who should receive the official transcript showing the credit you earned while abroad. Be sure that your program knows which office should receive the transcript and sends an official copy directly to that campus official. Records that you receive and carry back might not be accepted.

Students often ask whether they should register for courses for the coming semester even though they know they are going to be abroad. The best advice is "Play safe." Register for those courses. When you finalize your plans and officially withdraw from school or register for study abroad, your name will be removed from those registration lists. If your plans change at the last minute because of a family emergency, or if some other unexpected event causes you to cancel or postpone your plans, it could be difficult to register late in the classes you need to take on your home campus. Until your plans are final, therefore, many registrars advise you to hold your place in your classes.

Be sure that the registrar will list you as studying abroad during your absence. The study abroad office might take care of notifying other offices

A Student Speaks Up

As a student in China, I met a colony of artists who live and work together near Beijing. I interviewed them and used the material for my senior thesis. This led me directly into a graduate research project. I got a fellowship to go back to China and continue my research on the artist's colony's dealings with Chinese officialdom.

Unofficially...
We keep students in their classes until three weeks before classes begin, just in case they have to change their plans.
—A registrar's office official

about your status. Be sure you know who will keep records of your mailing address while you are abroad and notify that office as soon as you have an address.

Dean of Students Office

On some campuses, a single office coordinates all of the steps to register you for study abroad. On others, you might need to check with individual offices and notify them of your plans. If your campus is in the second group, you probably need to visit the dean of students office to withdraw formally from the college and indicate your intent to return after study abroad. Some other offices you should check include the university post office, telephone or e-mail service, and other student accounts.

Do not be surprised if some university offices send mail to your campus address or to your home address, even after you register for study abroad and provide an overseas address. Not all university offices use the same database for addressing mail to students. Be sure to notify the campus post office of your forwarding address and your intent to return to campus after you study abroad. If necessary, you should also provide a forwarding address to the U.S. post office where you usually receive mail. Most U.S. mail is not forwarded overseas. Your parent or guardian might need to open your mail and send you the most important items.

Before you leave campus, be sure that you notify your telephone service that you are leaving. (Tell the campus phone system you will be returning.) Make sure your account is paid in full and that your telephone service knows the date when you will no longer be responsible for calls made from your current number.

Be sure your accounts are all paid in full. Unpaid phone, library, or other bills can have a bad effect on credit in more ways than one. Unpaid bills on your university account might hold up disbursement of financial aid, release of transcripts, and processing of your credit. Be sure to take your checkbook with you so that you can clear up any unfinished business, but try to clear up everything before you leave campus.

Forward your e-mail. Increasingly, American students use e-mail to receive communications from friends, family, academic departments, and study abroad programs. If you can keep your present e-mail address and forward your e-mail to another address, it is a convenient system for staying in touch while you are away—as long as you don't let it interfere with getting the most out of your study abroad experience! You can get a universal e-mail address at yahoo.com, netscape.com, hotmail.com, or any one of a number of other Internet e-mail providers. This allows you to check e-mail anywhere that you can access the Internet. Internet access services are available all over the world in public libraries, universities, hotel business centers, and private Internet service centers. Students can drop into services in Ghana, Nepal, Iceland, or Mexico City to send and receive messages. But don't rely on it too much. You didn't go overseas to look at computers!

Confirming Registration and Housing for Your Return

Check with the housing office about reserving a place for the semester of your return. Is there a deadline for payment of the housing deposit? Write it down or provide it to your parents. Does someone

Watch Out!
While abroad, I needed to order a transcript to apply for a scholarship, but I had an outstanding phone bill and there was a hold on my account. It took several weeks to get the bill paid and the transcript released.

on campus need to select your room for next year?
Take care of arrangements with that person. Do you
want to sign up for any special interest housing or
serve as a residence hall supervisor? Pick up the
applications and take them with you, noting deadlines and deposit requirements. The American college calendar will not be on your mind when you
reach your destination, so be sure you and your parents note these deadlines so that they don't get overlooked.

At some institutions, you might need to complete your course selection for the semester of your
return before you depart. Other institutions will
mail you packets of registration materials. Still others will allow you to register online if you can access
the Web. Find out what to do if you need to change
your schedule after you enroll for classes abroad,
what to do if the mail does not arrive, or what to do
if you cannot access the Web. International communication today is speedy and convenient when
the systems are working well, but it is easy for something to go wrong. Be sure you know what back-up
arrangements are in place so that you won't have to
worry about missing a registration deadline.

Nailing Down Financial Aid Arrangements

Be sure you clarify the final details about your financial aid for the term. Even though you regularly
receive financial aid from your institution, you
might need to make special arrangements for your
study abroad time.

The Office of Financial Aid

Be sure the office of financial aid has an official
budget from the program showing what it will cost.
The study abroad office often prepares or approves

this on your behalf. The study abroad office will try to make sure that all the costs of study abroad are included in the budget so that your financial aid package is adequate.

You might be asked to sign a consortial agreement. This is an agreement signed by your institution, by you, and by the program sponsor, stating that you will not receive financial aid from both institutions. Ask your study abroad advisor for assistance with this procedure if you have any questions.

After you find out how much financial aid you are eligible to receive, you must decide how much you want to borrow. There might be some additional papers to sign. Most financial aid offices disburse the aid after the term starts at your home institution, sometimes after the add/drop period for classes. Your study abroad program might begin before that date. Find out whether you can make arrangements for the aid to be released earlier. If this is not possible, you might need to make temporary arrangements to pay the program fees and repay yourself when your student loan or grant money comes.

After the financial aid office has confirmed the loans, grants, and other assistance you will receive, it is important to leave clear instructions about where the money is to be sent. Be sure to find out which office will take care of releasing the funds when they become available. Usually, it is the student accounts or bursar's office that arranges to disburse, or pay out, the funds.

If you expect to be abroad when the money comes through, provide the address where the money should go. Most students indicate their permanent address. Some can make arrangements for deposit of funds directly to their bank account.

Timesaver
Get information from the program about all costs. These include program fees, international travel, meals, lodging, books, deposits, local transportation, incidentals, visa, and immunization charges.

Sometimes, the money can go straight to the program.

Before you leave campus, be sure you know exactly how financial aid payments will be provided and the approximate time they will be issued. Will the money automatically be applied to program fees? Will a payment be sent to your home for you or your parents to pay the program? If the check is made payable to you, you need to leave instructions for your parents about how the funds are to be handled.

Most students going abroad leave a power of attorney with their parents. This paper authorizes your parents to sign important papers for you while you are away. In case your financial aid check arrives at your home after you go abroad, a power of attorney gives your parents the authority to endorse the check for you and deposit the funds to your account. They can then arrange to send payment to the program. With a power of attorney, your parents can also clear up any small business matters requiring attention after you leave your college campus. For example, they can pay your phone bill or a library fine if you had a small balance at the end of the year.

Forms for signing a power of attorney are available at business supply stores. In some cases, the form can be filled out, signed, and notarized at the same location. Notaries work in banks, real estate offices, law offices, loan companies, and several locations on your university campus. Check with the president's office, the business office, or the financial aid office. Your parent's business might have its own notary.

Finally, just to compare notes, you might want to look at these Web sites prepared by four different universities to get their students ready for study abroad:

University of Wisconsin Steven's Point
www.uwsp.edu/acad/internat/boards/announce.htm

Cornell University
www.einaudi.cornell.edu/cuabroad/handbook/index.html

University of Wisconsin Milwaukee
www.uwm.edu/Dept/International/StudyAbroad/forms.html

Queen's University, Kingston, Ontario
quic.queensu.ca/outgoing/index.html

Special thanks to Angela DeGruccio for compiling this information. For further information, contact:

Angela DeGruccio
Program Associate
Global Campus Study Abroad
University of Minnesota
Phone: 612-626-7134
Fax: 612-626-8009
E-mail: degru002@umn.edu
www.UMabroad.umn.edu

Watch Out!
The accounting office sent my father a check with a note that this was an overpayment. He used it to pay bills. Unfortunately, the money was supposed pay my program fees. It took us two years to pay back the program fees. I almost didn't graduate on time.

Just the Facts

- Make sure your credit arrangements are complete before you go abroad.
- Check with all the key offices on the campus before you leave.

- Nail down all your home institution's requirements for independent study, internships,
  honors papers, and other special projects
  before you go.

- Make sure financial aid arrangements are
  clear.

GET THE SCOOP ON...
Why you need a visa ▪ What you need to apply
for a visa ▪ How to apply ▪ Saving time and
eliminating uncertainty

Chapter 12

Applying for Your Visa

What Is a Visa?

A visa is a permit issued by the foreign affairs or state department of a country. It allows you to *enter* the country. Visas are usually stickers placed inside your passport. In most cases, you must apply for it in your own country *before* you travel. Because of an agreement between many developed countries, some citizens do not require visas when they go to each other's countries for short stays of less than three months, for business purposes, or as tourists. However, the purpose for which you enter a country must agree with the visa you receive. You cannot apply for most types of visas, or change visa types, once you are in the country. To enter as a student for a stay of longer than 90 days, you must apply for a visa before you travel. In other words, you cannot enter the country as a tourist and then register as a student. Similarly, you cannot get a short-term work visa and then enroll as a student.

In some countries, student visas might be valid only for a short period of time, perhaps for a period

**A Student
Speaks Up**

Getting a visa for study in Australia was a long process. After I was admitted to the university, I sent a check in Australian dollars for insurance. They sent me an admission certificate to send to the embassy with my passport and application. Then, I needed a health examination. At last, I got my visa!

of three months. This gives you enough time to enter the country during the period before the academic year usually begins. Upon arriving, you are expected to register at a university and obtain a residency card confirming where you will live while you are a student there. After you obtain the card, it becomes the proof of your right to remain in the country. If you go to a country as an intern for the summer and then begin a study program in the fall, you will probably require another visa and might have to return home between the two experiences.

When to Apply

It might take as long as four months to obtain a visa for certain countries. Therefore, you should apply for the visa as soon as you receive the necessary documents confirming admission to the host university overseas.

If your program is under the sponsorship of an American university or organization, it should provide you with instructions about this procedure, help you get the admission document, and arrange for your visa. Some programs can arrange for your visa through a company that specializes in offering this service. If your program does not provide this assistance, the information in this guide will help you make arrangements. Be sure that you will be in the United States and have your passport available to apply for the visa. You might not be able to apply from abroad.

Where to Apply

Each country that has diplomatic relations with the U.S. has an embassy in Washington with a consular section, plus one or more consulates in different regions of the country. A consul is a person with the authority to represent his or her country's government in another country. The consulates are the offices of the consuls. They are authorized to issue visas to people who want to enter their country. The safest way to apply is to go to the consulate in person, but this might be difficult for you if you live a long way from the nearest consulate. If you go in person, be sure to call ahead and check the office hours of the visa section. In some cities, the office might be open only a few mornings or afternoons each week. You can also submit your application by mail; however, it takes much longer to apply by mail and certain restrictions might apply.

Getting Instructions from the Web

For detailed instructions about most visa application procedures, visit the Web site www.embassy.org. Click on the letter for the country where you will be studying. Instructions for a student visa application appear on the country's Web site. If you do not find a button for visa applications on the country's home page, choose the button for the cultural section. The U.S. Department of State has a 35-page overview of visa requirements for short-term visas and business travelers, providing information and embassy addresses for all the countries that have diplomatic relations with the United States. You can review the Web page at travel.state.gov/foreignentryreqs.html.

On the Web, you can get information about express passport application services and companies that process visa applications. These services might be of benefit to you if you live a long way from the nearest consulate for the country where you are going. However, by consulting the information about student visas that is available from the various embassies and from your program sponsor, following

Unofficially... American students entering Great Britain to study don't need to apply for a visa in advance. However, you get a stamp in your passport when you arrive in Great Britain, which is technically a visa. You just need your letter of admission, passport, and plane ticket in hand. Student visas are valid for six months or more and allow you to work in Britain.

Timesaver
Contact the country's consulate for your region before making a trip there and make sure when the visa section is open. Except for the consulate general at the country's embassy in Washington, the visa offices might be open only certain days or parts of days.

the instructions carefully, and sending your documents by registered mail, you might be able to handle your application yourself just as easily. This could save you some money.

Be aware that fees and procedures are subject to change. Sometimes, these changes are reciprocal. If the United States changes its policies for international students coming to study in this country, other countries might change the requirements they set for U.S. citizens applying for visas to study in their country. Checking the Web will give you the most current information.

The following visa companies provide assistance to applicants for student visas:

> Visa Advisors has an online book to help
> applicants apply for visas.
> 1801 Connecticut Ave., NW
> Washington, DC 20009
> Phone: 202-797-7976
> Fax: 202-667-6708
> www.visaadvisors.com/

> All Points Visa
> P.O. Box 30874
> Bethesda, MD 20824
> Phone: 301-652-9055
> Fax: 301-652-4161
> www.allpointsvisa.com/

> Travisa has a directory on the Web with
> offices in many locations.
> Phone: 800-222-2589 or 800-421-5468
> E-mail: questions@travisa.com
> www.travisa.com/

Travel Document Systems
734 Fifteenth St., NW, Suite 400
Washington, DC 20005
Phone: 800-874-5100 or 202-638-3800
Fax: 202-638-4674
E-mail: info@traveldocs.com
www.traveldocs.com/

Documents You Usually Need

The most important document you must submit when you apply for a visa is your passport. This is your proof of citizenship. Your visa is placed inside it. Instructions for obtaining a passport appear in Chapter 9, "Applying for Study Abroad Programs." Remember to sign your passport before you apply for a visa. Be sure you have a passport in hand at least six months before you intend to study abroad. For some countries, you might need all of the time prior to the start of the program of study to complete the visa application process. Make sure that your passport is also valid for at least six months after you are scheduled to leave the country. Some countries do not issue a visa to persons whose passports expire less than six months after they plan to leave the country.

You need two to six identification photos, usually 2" × 2" passport-size photos. This includes one photo for each copy of the application form that is required and additional photos as required for other forms.

You have to provide any payment required by cashier's check or money order. Consulates usually accept cash payment when you apply in person. If you apply by mail, they prefer a cashier's check or postal money order. Check the Web site for the

Watch Out!
Be sure to keep an eye on the country's Web site and note any changes in the application procedures for student visas. Countries change their visa application procedures and fees periodically, without notice. Changes might extend to documents required, the amount of time required to process the visa, or whether you can submit your application by mail.

Bright Idea
Sign your passport right away! Before mailing documents to the consulate, check and recheck every item carefully to make sure you signed every place where a signature is required. One program had 10 percent of the students' passports returned because students forgot to sign them.

current fee, which might vary as the exchange rate fluctuates. Consulates do not accept personal checks.

Make sure to include all the copies of the application form, completed and signed. You'll be asked for a document confirming your eligibility for a student visa. This usually comes from the host university and confirms that the university has admitted you for a period of study as a visiting student.

In addition, you often need a financial guarantee. This is a statement from your bank or a notarized statement from your family or from the program sponsor confirming their intention of providing you with funds sufficient to cover all your expenses in the country.

The following is a summary of student visa requirements for frequently visited countries. Visa information for other countries is available at the consular section of the embassy Web page for the country of interest.

Australia

Australia requires a certificate of eligibility from the host university and a health report prepared by a physician on the official Australian government form. Procedures are being simplified for American students. Watch the Australian Web site for further information (www.embassy.org).

Austria

The first application for a residence permit must be submitted from abroad (as a rule from your home country) before coming to Austria. The application form is sent to you by the respective Austrian university or college as soon as you contact that university or college for admission. Forms are also available at the Austrian embassy or consulate. Complete the form and submit it either to the university that will admit you, to an Austrian consulate abroad, or to an office granting residency permits. See the Web site for details (www.austria.org/visa.htm).

Canada

Students going to Quebec *must* obtain a visa from the provincial government in addition to documents from the Canadian embassy and present them with their passport at the border, together with financial certification and a letter of admission from the host university. It might take one to two months to obtain the documents from Quebec. These are required to enter Canada if you plan to study in Quebec. For other provinces, apply for the visa to enter Canada at the border. For further information, contact the Canadian embassy or your host university:

> Embassy of Canada/Ambassade du Canada
> 501 Pennsylvania Ave., NW
> Washington, DC 20001
> Phone: 202-682-1740
> www.embassy.org/embassies/ca.html
> www.cdnemb-washdc.org/
> (Canadian Embassy)

China

No mail-in applications are accepted less than one month before departure. Requirements for a six-month student visa include two admission documents provided by the host university (a certificate of admission and a certificate of eligibility) plus an application completed and signed by the student. The time required to obtain documents from the host university is at least one month (www.embassy. org, choose China, the cultural section).

Costa Rica

Apply to enter Costa Rica as a tourist. After enrolling at a university, apply to the immigration department, or apply through the university, to change your status to student. You receive a temporary permit to remain while studying (www.costarica.com/embassy/).

Ecuador

U.S. citizens staying for more than 90 days must apply for a visa. Documents required include passport, medical examination, police record, return plane ticket, certificate of course registration in a university in Ecuador, and proof of ability to meet all costs of stay. For details, visit the Web site (www.ecuador.org/visa.html#Visit and Non Resident Visas).

France

Students must obtain a long-stay visa (valid for three months) and apply for a residency card after they arrive in France, within a three-month period. For further information, contact your program or the French consulate Web site (www.france-consulat.org).

Germany

Students obtain a residence permit upon arrival. A medical examination might be required. Clearance from the police station in the city where you have your permanent address or your college police station, proof of sufficient funds, and health insurance are all required (www.germany-info.org/newcontent/index_students_scholars.html).

Ireland

For a stay of longer than 90 days, apply for alien registration within the first 90 days to the department of justice. Present passport, application form, photos, and evidence of financial support. See Web site for details (www.irelandemb.org/living.html#stu2).

Israel

U.S. citizens do not require a tourist visa. Students should complete an application on the Web, with a letter of admission from an Israeli university, a round-trip ticket, photos, and mailing charges. See the Web site for details (www.israelemb.org/visa.htm#student).

Italy

A visa is required for students. Consulates general are not located in Washington, but in other U.S. cities. Click on the consulate for your region. Go to the section on visits and visa (visti). The application is available on the Web, and there are instructions in English, although some of the pages leading to the visa page are not in English. For application instructions, go to www.italyemb.org/italcons.htm.

Japan

Some types of student visas might take several months. Submit a passport, photos, visa application forms, available at the embassy, or consulate documents certifying the purpose of the visit, or a certificate of eligibility issued by the host university. For further details, inquire at the ministry of foreign affairs or at the embassy or consult the program where the application will be made (www.embjapan.org).

Mexico

For U.S. students planning to enroll in Mexican universities and colleges for more than six months, apply in person and submit the acceptance letter from the school or university that you want to attend together with required photos, evidence of financial support, and certificate of good health. Within 30 days of arrival in Mexico, you must notify the proper authorities of the enrollment date and register at the National Registry of Foreign Citizens (www.embassyofmexico.org/english/main2.htm).

Norway

Students do not obtain a visa, but they are assigned an immigration number from the Norwegian consulate, which confirms that they have permission to enter the country and remain more than 90 days for study purposes. After entry into Norway, you need to apply for a residence permit. To be granted one, your study program must fulfil certain requirements. Furthermore, you must submit written proof that you are able to support yourself financially and that you have somewhere to live (www.norway.org/).

Russia

A passport, visa, and sometimes an original birth certificate are required. Consult your program sponsor for detailed instructions. Read the information at the Russian embassy Web page for further information about how to obtain a letter of invitation and arrange a visa. Students must get the business visa. You must go through a program sponsor and follow instructions meticulously (www.russianembassy.org/).

Spain

You might need to apply in person, but many sponsors arrange for visas for program participants through a visa agency. A medical certificate, a passport valid for six months after the conclusion of your period of study, confirmation of enrollment, and a financial guarantee are necessary. Contact your sponsor for more information. All student visas are valid for a period of 90 days from your entry day into Spain, during which time the student must contact the local authorities to acquire a student residency card. This "Spanish Student Residency Card" is then valid for as long as the student is enrolled in the program in Spain. See the New York Consulate Web page for information (www.spainconsul-ny. org/!consula.doi/!visastu.htm).

U.K.

No advance visa application is required for U.S. students studying in the U.K. Show your letter of admission from the British university to immigration officials when you arrive.

Financial Certification

Most countries require students and their parents to provide some certification that they have the financial resources to take care of all the student's needs while in their country. This helps to ensure that a student will not require financial assistance from the host country, either for medical treatment or living expenses. Sometimes, a sponsoring university provides a document showing that all of the program fees have been paid and the sponsor is providing everything the student needs. Sometimes, a statement or document needs to be notarized.

A notary public is an official licensed by the state to verify a person's identity when she signs legal documents. This helps to certify the truth of the information on the form. Notaries work in the offices of insurance companies, real estate brokers, banks, and law firms. You can also find them at your college or university; check the university directory or contact the president's office for assistance. You will probably find at least one notary at one of the following offices at your university or college: the

Watch Out!
For re-entry into the United States, you have to prove your citizenship or permanent residency in the U.S. A passport is the best proof of citizenship. For other acceptable documents, see the State Department Web site (www.travel. state.gov/ foreignentryreqs. html).

president's or dean's office, the dean of student's office, the school of business, the law school, the registrar's office, or the office of the comptroller (chief business officer). If you have a document to be notarized, do not sign it until you are in the notary's office. The official will ask to see identification, ask you to swear to the truth of the statement you are signing, and affix a seal confirming that the signature is notarized.

Health Insurance Documents

Unofficially...
Because many insurance companies use automated systems to process routine correspondence, and because employees who answer the phones might not have the authority to write special letters such as those the French consulate requires, I called the president's office of the insurance company to get personal attention to my request for a letter.

Some embassies require proof from your insurance company that your health insurance is valid in their country. The French, for example, require a letter from your insurance company on official letterhead confirming that your health insurance is valid in France. This statement needs to be in very clear English, understandable to persons who do not speak English well. Some insurance companies write letters in legal terms that are difficult for a non-native speaker of English to read and understand. The visa section might reject these letters and ask for clearer ones.

Other countries might require you to sign up for health insurance that meets their specification to give you a visa or residency permit. In Australia, the host university signs you up for the necessary insurance for international students before issuing you admission documents. In Germany, you must enroll in the insurance plan when you arrive and register for classes.

All students participating in study abroad programs should be sure that they have health insurance to cover their medical expenses while living in another country. In fact, most programs require you to enroll in some type of approved coverage, even if the host country does not require it as a condition of issuing you a visa.

All students participating in study abroad programs must be sure that they have health insurance to cover their medical expenses while living in another country. Ideally, you should continue your current coverage to ensure continuous coverage of any long-term treatment while you are abroad and after your return.

Check carefully with your regular insurance carrier concerning coverage in the country to which you are going. Find out whether your college or university student health insurance plan covers you while studying overseas during the summer as well as the academic year. If you are covered through your family's medical coverage plan, find out whether it will cover you overseas.

Check your policy carefully for special instructions concerning reimbursement of claims when you are away from the area where you usually receive medical treatment. In most cases, medical costs must be paid at the time of service and receipts submitted to the company for reimbursement.

Review the policy carefully for exclusions that apply to certain countries, situations, or activities. For example, if you plan to do any skiing, mountain climbing, scuba diving, or boating, you should make sure that your insurance covers injuries you might incur in these activities. Consider obtaining supplemental travel insurance if your regular policy does not cover such activities.

The following carriers offer insurance coverage that is valid for students abroad or for overseas travelers. Again, be sure to check the policy carefully for exclusions. Certain countries might not be covered

Unofficially...
When I broke my foot in a Paris youth hostel, my insurance paid my hospital charges and the hostel's liability insurance reimbursed the insurance company.

unless you request a special rider. You might not be covered for injuries incurred in water sports, other sports activities, riding on a motor scooter, acts of civil unrest, or war:

Associated Insurance Plans International, Inc. (AIP)
1301 S. Wolf Rd.
Suite 203
Prospect Heights, IL 60070
P.O. Box T
Wheeling, IL 60090-9021
E-mail: office@a-I-p.com

CIEE (medical and emergency evacuation insurance coverage provided by purchase of the International Student Identity Card)
205 E. 42nd St.
New York, NY 10017-5706
Phone: 212-822-2734
www.ciee.org

CISI (Cultural Insurance Services International)
102 Greenwich Ave.
Greenwich, CT 06830
Phone: 800-303-8120
www.aifs.org/java/US/aifscisi/index.htm

Hinchcliff International
11 Ascot Place
Ithaca, NY 14850
Phone: 607-257-0100
Fax: 607-257-3051

International SOS Assistance
Eight Nishominy Interplex
P.O. Box 11568
Philadelphia, PA 19116

Phone: 215-244-1500 or 800-767-1403 in U.S.
Fax: 215-244-2227
E-mail: scholastic@intsos.com

MEDEX Assistance Corporation
P.O. Box 5375
Timonium, MD 21094-5375
Phone: 800-537-2029 or 410-453-6300
Fax: 410-453-6301
E-mail: info@medexassist.com
www.medexassist.com

OMA Limited
Student Health Insurance
26 Quincy Ave.
Braintree, MA 02184
Phone: 800-767-0169
E-mail: omalimited@aol.com

PENTECO
1320 19th St., NW, Suite 420
Washington, DC 20036
Phone: 202-347-5575 (D.C. office) or
800-247-5575
Fax: 202-296-0007
E-mail: pentecorp@aol.com

T.W. Lord & Associates
International Benefits Division
25 Dodd St.
P.O. Box 1185
Marietta, GA 30061
Phone: 800-633-2360
Fax: 770-429-0638
E-mail: theplan@twlord.com
www.twlord.com

Timesaver
Send your visa
application and
supporting docu-
ments by Federal
Express. This
helps to protect
them by provid-
ing a routing
number to trace
the package. For
speedier return
service, include
an express enve-
lope and a
pre-addressed,
prepaid return
slip.

Required Immunizations or Medical Examinations

Other countries (including Australia) might require you to submit the results of a medical examination administered in accordance with their instructions (examples follow). This examination certifies that you are in good health, that you won't require any special treatment while in their country, and that you do not carry certain infectious diseases.

An increasing number of countries require visitors to take an HIV or AIDS test upon arrival or prior to issuance of the visa. Any person who is found positive might be required to leave the country. Some countries require proof of yellow fever immunization. Check the Web information to verify the latest requirements for the country you are going to. If a test is required, it is a good idea to get one privately, in advance, for your own peace of mind. You should also obtain any necessary immunizations prior to leaving the United States.

The following are just a few examples:

- Egypt requires all students to take an AIDS test upon arrival and proof of yellow fever immunization if the student is arriving from an infected area.

- China requires an AIDS test for stays longer than six months.

- France requires students to have a health examination from an authorized physician at the consulate or in France to obtain a residency card.

- Russia requires an HIV test no more than 90 days before departure for a stay of more than 3 months.

The document Health Information for International Travel is available for $20 from the U.S. Government Printing Office, from local physicians and health centers, or from the Centers for Disease Control. For further information, contact the Centers for Disease Control and Prevention:

> 1600 Clifton Rd.
> Atlanta, GA 30333
> USA
> Phone: 404-39-3311 or 877-FYI-TRIP
> Fax: 888-CDC-FAXX
> www.cdc.gov

Preparing and Submitting Your Visa Application

Read and follow the instructions very carefully. Assemble all the parts of your application exactly as instructed to do. Ask your study abroad office for assistance if you have any questions. Your address in the country, unless you have the exact address of the place you will be staying, will be the host university. Your contact person in the country will be the resident director of your program, if you have one. If you are not going with a group from a U.S. university and you do not have a resident director of your program, you should put the host university's international affairs office with which you have been dealing while making your arrangements. Your occupation is "student." Submit all the documents, with your passport, by registered mail.

A Student Speaks Up

Pay close attention to deadlines for providing passports and other visa documents. Get your passport well ahead of time if you are even considering study abroad. I waited too long and almost didn't get a visa because they needed my passport number to send the documents from Japan.

Watch Out!
The number of
your passport is
printed on the
Russian visa. If
you renew your
passport or
replace a lost
passport, the
passport number
will be different,
invalidating the
visa, and you
need to get a
new visa to enter
Russia.

Just the Facts

- Review visa application requirements for your country well in advance.

- Plan ahead to have the necessary documents, including a passport valid for at least six months after your stay.

- Send all your documents by registered mail or apply in person.

- Health and financial certification must meet the consulate's specifications.

GET THE SCOOP ON...
How to pay for your program ▪ How to get
money overseas for your own use ▪ The most
economical ways of handling your personal
funds ▪ Protecting your funds

Chapter 13

Sending Money and Making Payments

As you plan ways of handling your money for the year, you need to consider several different aspects of the task. First, you need to know how to send payments overseas without incurring unexpected charges for changing the money. Secondly, you need to consider the best ways of handling your funds when you arrive in the country. There are some tricks to getting the best exchange rates and avoiding hidden costs. Finally, you need to know about factors that can drive up the cost of living overseas and some strategies for keeping your expenses under control.

A word about calculating exchange rates: All big city newspapers publish the value of the dollar on the previous business day in the world's major foreign currencies. This information appears Tuesday through Saturday in the paper's financial section. You can also get this information on the Web at www.oanda.com/. The Web site gives the average value of the dollar in all the foreign currencies that can be exchanged for dollars. You can compare rates for any dates you choose and even obtain forecasts for the dollar's future value in some currencies. The rate provided by OANDA and by big city newspapers is based on the averages of the rates used by the biggest international banks for their best customers. Individuals who exchange money at a bank or currency exchange office might not get the same rate.

Keep in mind that there is both a "buy" rate and a "sell" rate, and they might not be exactly the same. In other words, if you have a traveler's check in dollars and you want to convert it to another currency (let's use Swiss francs as an example), the bank will be "buying" dollars from you. Therefore, if you look at the currency exchange chart posted at that bank, you look at the U.S. dollars "buy" column to see how many Swiss francs you can expect to receive for your dollars. Or you can look at the Swiss francs line and see how many the bank will "sell" you for your dollars. From that, you should then subtract any commission or service charge that the bank collects for its services. If you have Swiss francs in hand and want to change them back into dollars, you look at the U.S. dollars "sell" rate to see how many dollars you will get for your francs. Or you look at the Swiss francs line to see how many the bank will "buy" for $1. Again, you have to subtract any service charge or commission.

When you look in the newspaper or on the Web for the rates, remember that banks do not give individual customers the "best" rates. Your chances of getting the best published rate are greatest when you withdraw the local currency from an ATM using your U.S. bank card or debit card. The next best rate

Watch Out!
Look closely at the charges the banks impose when changing money. Bank Blue might charge a single flat rate for changing currency, regardless of the quantity of dollars you choose to "sell." With Bank Blue, it pays to exchange large amounts each time. Bank Orange might charge a percent of the total number of dollars exchanged. It pays to exchange small amounts at Bank Orange.

applies when you use a debit card or credit card to make purchases.

The Best Ways of Making Payment

When the time comes to pay for your program, you have two types of payment to consider: payment in dollars or payment in the currency of the country where you are going. You should pay in dollars only if the program requests payment in dollars and if the money is going somewhere in the United States.

Payments to a U.S. Office

Some U.S. colleges and universities require all their students going abroad to pay regular tuition to the college. The college then pays all the study abroad programs their fees. If this is the case at your institution, your payment arrangements will be simple. Your parents can simply arrange to pay your tuition in the usual manner, and your home institution will take care of the rest for you. If you usually receive financial aid from your college or university, this is quite convenient for you and your family. However, if you usually pay full tuition to your home institution, this might be an expensive alternative.

The majority of sponsored study abroad programs have U.S. offices to administer the program and collect the program fees. This is convenient for you. For students who pay out-of-state tuition or private university tuition, program fees might be less than the tuition they usually pay to their home institution. Regardless of the amount you owe, you can send your payment in U.S. dollars to the designated U.S. address in the usual manner for paying a bill. Several American universities based in other countries, and even some island programs based in other countries, have administrative offices in the United

Timesaver
Before you leave, find a guide to the currency of the country you are going to. Familiarize yourself with different denominations of bills and coins in the currency you will be using at your destination. Before making small purchases, count out the approximate sum of money. This will save time, and you will have more confidence when you first arrive.

States and can accept payment in dollars sent to those addresses.

Paying in Foreign Currency

If you are enrolling directly in a university or program in another country and receive a bill in the currency of the host country, there are two good ways to send the payment. For paying large amounts in a foreign currency, these methods are by far the most convenient, reliable, and economical. Paying by credit card is actually cheaper and more convenient than either method, but most program fees exceed the credit limit on the average person's credit card.

Cashiers Checks

When you receive the bill from the program, contact your bank and ask it to purchase the amount of foreign currency for which the program billed you. Allow the bank several days to arrange for this. Ask your bank to prepare a cashier's check payable to the program for the amount billed in the foreign currency. When the check is ready, simply mail it to the program by express or registered mail. Your bank imposes a service charge for the exchange rate. In addition, the bank charges a small amount (probably under $10) for the service of writing a cashier's check. These charges are modest, and they are not deducted from the amount to be sent to the program. If your parents take care of this transaction after you arrive overseas, they can mail a cashier's check in the local currency to you so that you can pay the program.

Wire Transfers

The second procedure is almost as economical and even more reliable. Obtain instructions from the program for wiring the funds directly to their bank account. Again, ask your bank to purchase the amount you need in the foreign currency, but tell it that you want to *wire* the funds to the program's account. There is a service charge for purchasing the currency and a wire transfer charge of approximately $25. If your parents take care of this transaction after you arrive overseas and open a bank account there, you can send them instructions to wire the funds to your account so that you can pay the program.

Getting Your Money There with You

The next part of your planning is to get the money overseas to meet your other expenses. There are two methods for handling your money. One is very reliable but sometimes inconvenient to use. The second is extremely convenient and economical, but some slight risks are involved.

Take Some Foreign Currency with You

Plan to have about $100 worth of the host country currency with you when you depart from the United States. To arrange for this, contact your bank at least one week before your departure and order the currency. There is a small service charge for the exchange. Big city banks can provide you with the currency in one or two days. Small town banks might require more time. Carrying a small amount of currency with you means that you will be able to handle initial expenses without changing money the moment you arrive in a new country. With some cash on hand, you can avoid getting cash at very expensive locations such as the airport's international arrival area. You need some cash right away for a train, bus, or cab from the airport to your first

Moneysaver
Whichever method you choose for paying program fees in foreign currencies, buy the foreign currency first and then send the money. If you send a check in dollars, or wire dollars, service charges are higher. There might be unexpected taxes or commissions, and it might take weeks to credit the money to your account. You could miscalculate the charges and have to send more money.

night's lodging, and it will take you some time to get your bearings and locate bank machines and currency exchanges. If you are traveling with a group that is being met at the plane, you might not have a chance to get to a bank to change money until the group reaches its destination. Be prepared! Have some currency on hand.

Use Traveler's Checks as a Safeguard

If you are visiting several countries, traveler's checks are the safest and most reliable way of carrying funds. They are replaceable and therefore protect you against theft. They are not subject to breakdowns in the international computerized banking system. They are good protection against any breakdowns resulting from Y2K problems in the international bank network. They are accepted in most parts of the world, except in the very smallest stores. When you purchase an item using a traveler's check, you receive your change in the currency of the country. You should carry at least half your funds in this form.

It is true, however, that it is beginning to be difficult to cash traveler's checks in some countries. Visitors to Argentina are advised to carry bank cards and dollars rather than traveler's checks. However, hotels cash them during banking hours, banks cash them, and the traveler's check company office cashes them as well. Travelers in Italy find it hard to cash the checks unless they do so at their hotel, which might not give them the best rate, or go directly to American Express or the office of their traveler's check company. Currency exchanges might charge high commissions, and small stores might refuse to honor the checks.

It is wisest to get your traveler's checks in dollars if you plan to visit a number of countries. With an

American passport, you will find it easier to use checks in dollars to purchase other currencies. For example, if you have traveler's checks in French francs and try to buy some British pounds before going to England, you will not be allowed to purchase them if you don't have a French passport. Similarly, if you have checks in pounds and try to buy European currencies in the U.K., you encounter the same difficulty in reverse. Therefore, it's best to have them in your own country's currency. Having traveler's checks in the local currency does not necessarily make it easier to cash a traveler's check. If a bank or currency exchange assesses a service charge or commission to cash a traveler's check, it will do so whether the check is in dollars or in the local currency.

The primary advantage of the checks is to protect your money against theft while allowing access to it at any time. You can cash traveler's checks at American Express offices, hotels, banks, and exchange bureaus. To cash them, you must present your passport for identification. You can also pay for items with traveler's checks and get change in the local currency. If you use a traveler's check to pay for an item at a store or restaurant, the provider might not give you the best exchange rate. Check the posted exchange rates at exchange bureaus and banks to get the best rate. Watch out for any commissions the bank or exchange bureau might charge.

Due to potential computer problems as a result of the year 2000, many study abroad experts advise students to have traveler's checks as a protection. Breakdowns in computer networks might prevent the use of bank machines, at least for a few days. Traveler's checks can be used at any time, even if

Unofficially...
"Traveler's checks are a pain and bancomats are easy," a student writes from Florence. It was difficult for her to exchange traveler's checks. She had to hunt for a place that wouldn't charge too high a commission or give her an unfavorable rate. She found that she got a much better exchange rate using her U.S. bank card at an ATM (a "bancomat" in Florence).

the bank computers are down. Y2K might not be the only reason for a bank computer network to fail. They might break down because of power failures, heavy use of the system, political crises, and so on. If you decide to rely on a bank card, be sure that you carry at least a few hundred dollars in traveler's checks as a safeguard.

At the end of your trip, you can redeposit unused traveler's checks to your home bank account. You just handle them as regular checks. Write your name as the payee on the front of the check and sign the check in the usual way. Turn it over and write "for deposit only" on the left end of the check as you do any other check that you deposit to your account. Then, endorse it and deposit it.

Bank Cards and Credit Cards

Bank cards are increasingly convenient and economical ways of transferring, carrying, and accessing funds. In some European countries, there are bank machines everywhere. Credit cards are accepted in most parts of the world. Visa is the most widely recognized and universally accepted. Ask about the use of other credit cards in the countries you plan to visit.

If you have a checking account in the United States, it is easy to have money deposited into that account at home, without changing the money to a foreign currency. You can withdraw the money directly from your bank account, wherever you happen to be, at any automatic teller machine that displays the logo for the network to which your bank belongs. You get the funds in the local currency at the best exchange rate of the day. This is far and away the most economical and speediest way to transfer small amounts of money overseas.

If your bank card is a debit card, it can be a great convenience. A debit card withdraws payments for purchases directly from your checking account at home. In this way, you avoid service charges that you would owe for a balance due on a credit card account. You can use either a debit card or a regular credit card to make purchases at any participating store, hotel, restaurant, or other business. In addition, you can obtain cash advances at banks. Use of a credit or debit card ensures you a better exchange rate than you get with traveler's checks. They allow a great deal of flexibility in handling your funds. You can even purchase a few traveler's checks with a cash advance to safeguard your cash.

Using your card as a credit card to make purchases does not give you quite as good a rate as you get with a cash withdrawal from a bank machine. It is a convenient way to keep records of your expenditures. However, if your parents receive the statement, don't be surprised if they ask questions about some of the items you charge to the account!

On the other hand, there are significant risks to relying completely on a debit card or a bank card:

- The card can be lost or stolen.

- The magnetic strip can be neutralized or malfunction.

- The computer system can malfunction and the bank machine will refuse your card.

- You cannot count on this method to withdraw large sums of money to pay bills.

- If you use a bank machine in an unsafe area, especially at night, you risk being robbed.

- It is easy to overdraw your account. Or, if you are using a regular credit card instead of a

Unofficially...
I am careful. When my son went to France, I got his Visa bill and saw charges to a company named FNAC. I called the program office to find out what that child was buying. I learned that it is a department store where you can get clothing, books, music, or electronic equipment!

Unofficially...
Many bank
machines in
other countries
are in secure
lobbies that you
cannot enter
without swiping
your bank card
in the lock to
open the door.
This is reassuring
if you are alone
and need access
to cash. Look
around carefully
before using
unprotected
machines on the
street. Don't use
machines in
crowded areas or
after dark.

debit card, you could easily run up a big credit card bill.

- In some parts of Europe and Asia, bank machines for the international bank networks are rare or nonexistent.

- Bank machines near you might be closed or out of service.

For these reasons, it is always prudent to have some traveler's checks on hand for safety and security. If you do not use them, you can easily deposit them to your checking account when you return home or use them as checks to pay other bills.

Estimating How Much You Will Need

Your program should give you information about the cost of living while you're there. Each program has to provide a budget to any student applying for financial aid. Therefore, the information should be available to you. If you need help developing a budget for your weekly expenses, consult your study abroad advisor and refer to Chapter 7, "Figuring Out the Cost of Programs and How to Finance Them."

Cost of Living

It costs more to use utilities in other countries than in the United States. Fuel and water supplies cost more. When you consider your expenses for the year, you need to consider the high cost of utilities such as electricity, hot water, and heat. Because these services are expensive, you will find that people in other countries are very frugal with their hot water, heat, and electricity. The heat usually does not go on until a certain date in the fall (between October 15 and November 1), regardless of how cold it gets on some days in the early fall. People take fewer baths and showers and do not shampoo their hair as often. They do not launder their outer clothes as often. They are careful about the use of lights, turning them off when they are not needed. Your host family might expect you to bring your own towel with you and take responsibility for laundering it. The utility might offer special rate reductions if washing machines or dishwashers are run late in the evening. Therefore, some appliances might have a timer switch to turn them on after you go to bed. In addition, it costs more to install phone service in other countries. There is a charge for each call, in contrast to the United States, where we pay a flat rate for a certain number of local calls. You can protect your budget by being frugal in your use of all these services. If you are living with a family, discuss with them the best approaches to conserving heat, water, electricity, and telephone charges.

Entertainment can be a big item in your budget and will use up your cash if you are not careful to monitor your cash flow. Each time you go out with friends to a film, or stop for refreshments at a café or pub, the expense can be considerable. Remember to check the prices carefully before you order and keep your expenses within your budget.

Taxes, Special Fees, and Other Unexpected Charges

Review the section in Chapter 7 on hidden costs and service charges, and take along at least $200 per semester to cover unexpected taxes, fees, membership charges, and other unplanned administrative expenses.

Be sure to find out about excise taxes (sales taxes) in other countries. Sometimes, these charges are much higher than in the United States and constitute a significant part of your expenses for the

Moneysaver
Practice shopping and preparing food before leaving home. Stretch your food budget by avoiding expensive items and eating at expensive American-style fast food chains. Find out how to prepare low-cost produce in season. Learn recipes for some local dishes that are easy and economical and that take advantage of plentiful local ingredients.

**A Student
Speaks Up**
When we first
arrived, we had a
month when our
housing was cov-
ered and meals
at the student
cafeteria were
very cheap. Some
of us spent too
much on eating
out and used up
funds we should
have saved for
later, when rent-
ing our own
apartments and
preparing our
own meals.
Budget carefully
for the whole
semester or year!

year. In the European Union, the sales tax is called the Value Added Tax (VAT). It usually runs about 17.5 percent but ranges from 4.8 to 24.2 percent, depending on the item. Read guidebooks carefully to see what sorts of taxes you might incur in the country you are going to. Under certain circumstances, you might be able to obtain a refund for the taxes you pay when you do a lot of shopping at a single store.

If you are going to a non-EU country, check guidebooks well in advance to find out how to obtain refunds in those countries. Expect to deal with a lot of paperwork and to receive your refund many months later. Have your passport with you when you go to shop. You must purchase more than a specified amount (usually the equivalent of $200) at the store, usually on a single day. The store will give you a stamped receipt showing the amount of VAT you paid. Keep all the receipts in a safe place for use when you leave the country. When you leave the country, you must allow extra time (allow at least an extra hour to be safe) at the airport or international train station to turn in all your stamped receipts. If you drive across a border in the EU, you might not find anyone on hand to take your paperwork. Customs officials in some countries might ask to see the purchases. In a few months' time, you will receive your refund at your permanent address in your home country.

If you follow these procedures, many large department stores will give you a discount on the day you shop so that you do not need to apply later for the tax refund.

The following countries offer VAT refunds to persons doing business with them: Austria, Belgium, Canada, Denmark, Finland, France, Germany,

Greece, Iceland, Ireland, Italy, Liechtenstein, Luxembourg, Monaco, Netherlands, Norway, Portugal, Spain, Sweden, Switzerland, and the United Kingdom. In theory, any non-citizen of these countries purchasing their merchandise or services is eligible for the refund. In practice, you must make a large purchase at a single company that is willing to help you do the paperwork to get the refund. You cannot get the refund for small purchases.

Some services help persons doing business in these countries obtain refunds in return for 18 percent of the amount refunded. For information about one of them, the International Sales Tax Refund Corporation, see www.insatax.com/ english.html.

For information on VAT in the U.K., see www. hmce.gov.uk/bus/vat/index.htm.

An online refund arrangement is on trial in the U.K. at the Web site indicated. Although the form is geared to businesses, especially those doing business with the U.K. by Internet, the resultant savings might eventually result in savings for consumers.

In an article on the *U.S. News and World Report* Web site, Katherine T. Beddingfield recommends Europe Tax-free Shopping, the largest company assisting travelers with VAT refund arrangements. Call 800-566-9828 for a wallet-size guide. On the Internet, see the Global Refund Web site for information about current rates and procedures for obtaining refunds (www.taxfree.se). The current rate chart appears at www.taxfree.se/index.html. Global Refund provides a complete table of current VAT rates for all countries.

In theory, a nonprofit agency such as a school is not liable for these taxes on educational activities, and citizens of other countries are also exempt from

Moneysaver
You can save money by fixing your own lunch. Pack an insulated lunch sack. Use it to store refrigerated items purchased at the market or supermarket, such as cheese, yogurt, and fruit. Perishable items should be kept as cool as possible.

the taxes. In practice, it is only possible to avoid paying the tax in certain circumstances with careful planning. Your school or program can avoid paying VAT on housing and meals if it gets clearance in advance. This is one of the ways that a program can sometimes save you money on services that it includes in the program fee.

Program directors should contact service providers well in advance of the date of service to find out whether they will accept the documents to waive payment of the VAT. Provide documentation proving that your institution is a not-for-profit organization. Most colleges, universities, schools, and other nonprofit organizations have an administrative office that knows what sort of documentation to provide. The provider might not be able to agree to waive the tax; however, institutions should inquire before sending payment for any large expense. Nonprofit organizations such as universities, the YMCA, and museums might have a way of implementing this. Other services might be able to offer an educational discount instead.

For the most part, however, you should just plan to add the tax to the amounts you pay and budget accordingly. The good news is that every country will probably have some tax-free items, such as books and food. Although the big department stores claim to save you money by helping you get the tax refunds, you might actually save more by purchasing equivalent items at smaller shops or discount stores.

Students who pay rent directly to a landlord or private company might find that they are eligible for a refund of the portion of their rent that goes to taxes. For example, in France, this refund is called the *Allocation Familiale*. To qualify for it, you have to

> **66**
>
> In Ireland, we bought some beautiful sweaters and the store gave us the receipts to refund the VAT. We crossed the border to Northern Ireland, parked our car, and went into the customs house. No one was around. Between two EU countries, customs offices no longer need to monitor travelers. We didn't get a refund but enjoyed the sweaters just the same.
>
> **99**

provide an additional official copy of your birth certificate to prove that you are an international student. Other documentation might be required but is usually available locally from your program or landlord. In a few weeks, you might receive a refund of some of your rent!

Banking Arrangements

Your program might assist you in setting up a bank account at a local bank. Because the program has its own accounts there, this might be intended as a convenience for you. The program can vouch for you and make it easier for you to get an account for the short period of time that you are in the country. You usually need proof of residency and a letter or some other document confirming your registration in the program. Be sure to ask about taxes and other service charges. Foreign banks have different systems for handling accounts.

Keep in mind that you do not have to use the bank the program selects for you. If you prefer, take the time to check around and compare services. Like American banks, those in other countries offer a variety of services. Some pay interest on the bank balance. Others might charge high service charges for short-term accounts. Some banks might charge lower service fees for cashing traveler's checks and other services. Some are mutual associations, with account holders actually owning a share of the enterprise, much like a credit union in the United States. Again, you should inquire carefully about service charges, taxes, and other costs. The program-approved bank might have agreed to exempt you from charges that you will incur elsewhere.

Check whether your bank in the United States has an overseas branch or an affiliation with a bank

Watch Out!
There is a positive and a negative side to getting the government refund on rent in France. Students who get the refund might then have to pay *other* taxes almost a year later, after returning to the United States. Before applying for any tax refunds on housing for which you might qualify as an international student, be sure to inquire about later liability.

Unofficially...
A professor maintains a U.K. bank account by depositing small amounts so the bank won't close the account. The bank pays a little interest, which covers the few pennies of tax that the U.K. assesses on the account and reports it on his U.S. income tax return.

in your host country. Inquire about the advantages of opening an account through a big U.S. bank. Ask whether you can wire funds (remember to change them to the local currency first!) to the account in advance to have money on hand when you arrive or to pay bills in the local currency before you arrive.

If you can access your U.S. bank account through a bank card, you might not need a local bank account to transact business. However, you might need your own bank account in the country to get certain refunds or other payments you are expecting. If you must arrange for a bank account, shop around carefully for various options. Ask about the following issues.

Does the bank cash traveler's checks without service charges to customers? Do you get any other discounts or free services? If you get an account through your program, is there an arbitrary date at which it closes automatically? How much tax is charged to the account balance? Can you get an international student exemption? What other service charges are imposed?

Safeguarding Your Money, Yourself, and Your Belongings While You Travel

Every year, students traveling abroad report petty thefts and sometimes upsetting losses of valuable and important belongings. In almost every case, they broke one of the basic safety rules for protecting their possessions. It is extremely important to observe some practical pointers to ensure that you are not one of the unlucky ones.

Plan ahead when you pack for the trip. As an international traveler, you are probably going to be noticed and observed. Avoid packing and wearing college T-shirts or hats, backpacks, or other gear with conspicuously American logos. Agree ahead of time to be careful about speaking English loudly with your companions in public. Otherwise, you may very well be watched and followed by someone who notices that you are a newcomer and that you might not be "street wise" about safeguarding your money and belongings. Agree not to discuss your plans for the day loudly in public and not to give any clues about the place where you are staying or times when you will be out of your room.

When changing money or stowing your change after buying something, put your wallet away in an inside pocket or pouch. Don't carry valuables in your backpack or in a purse with a shoulder strap. Skilled pickpockets can easily come up behind you in a crowded place and cut the strap or slit the pack to remove what they want, having observed where you placed your wallet and passport.

Lock your door whenever you leave your room, even to go down the hall to a friend's room. Also, be sure to lock the door whenever you are asleep in the room. This applies to napping during the day as well as at night. A person wearing what appears to be a hotel uniform might slip in and out unobserved to take a wallet or other item of value. Many travel stores feature lockable pouches or containers that make it difficult for an intruder or pickpocket to get at your belongings quickly and silently. Consider taking one along to lock up your camera or other valuables if your plans include swimming, camping, staying in a hostel, or other such activities.

If you plan to rent or purchase a bike, do not leave it overnight in unguarded areas, even if it is locked. If possible, bring it indoors or into a protected area and be sure that it is secured with a sturdy lock. Register your bicycle to help the police

A Student Speaks Up
. . .On a train, someone stole my bag, so I had to head home. Oh, well, I had my wallet and passport with me in a safe place. . . . Wear a money belt and have fun!

Unofficially...
One student went swimming alone on Hainan Island, leaving her backpack with her passport, money, and clothes on the beach. When she got out of the water, everything was gone except the bathing suit she was wearing. The local police had to lend her clothes and money to get back to Beijing. Her passport was later mailed to her, but she never got her belongings back.

Watch Out!
Coming home
alone, I was
assaulted. I
fought back and
wasn't hurt, but
I lost my wallet
and keys in the
struggle. The
police tried to
take me to a
friend's house,
but I couldn't
remember the
exact street
address and
phone number.
Memorize
addresses and
phone numbers
so that you have
them if you lose
your wallet or
book bag.

trace it if it disappears. Be careful about leaving your bag or pack in any place where someone else can pick it up and run off before you can stop them. Avoid any of the following: leaving a purse out on the table in an outdoor café, placing your backpack under your seat at the movies, leaving your pack in an overhead compartment while you snooze on the train, and leaving any valuables unguarded on the beach while you swim.

Always insist on a receipt for any purchase, watch when the charges are being rung up, avoid using large bills for the purchase of small items, and count your change with care. By displaying alertness when you are dealing with money, you will probably discourage anyone from short-changing or over-charging you. Avoid being out alone at night. Be especially careful about using bank machines when you are alone, after dark, or in areas that are not secure.

Just the Facts

- To minimize service charges, purchase foreign currency before you send payments and money overseas.

- Save money and time using a bank card or debit card, but take traveler's checks as a pre-caution.

- Budget enough funds for incidentals and entertainment, two items that can disrupt your budget.

- Plan ahead to protect your valuables and your money when you are traveling or out in public.

Getting There: Study Abroad Travel and Travel Arrangements

GET THE SCOOP ON...
How to arrange international travel ▪ Getting
information about other travel ▪ Super-saver
deals to plan for ▪ Finding and booking travel
to your destination

PART IV

Travel Options

Travel arrangements are one of the most important parts of the study abroad experience for many students. Many programs arrange for you to travel overseas with the faculty director and a group of program participants. In other cases, you must make your own arrangements. Regardless of the options each program offers, you will consider which arrangements offer the best value for the money. You also want the option giving you the most flexibility in selecting your return date, your point of departure, and the city you return to in the United States. Another factor about which you want information is the safety record of the airline.

Book your travel as early as possible. In today's travel market, the best fares are based on the amount of advance notice you give the agent who is booking your flight and the length of your stay. Because the length of your study abroad experience could range from under 30 days to almost a full year, advance notice is very important.

Watch Out!
Ask about the possibility of changing your arrangements well in advance. Put your request in writing so that it is not overlooked or forgotten by busy program staff. Be specific about preferred travel dates, the departure city, and your preferred final U.S. destination.

Most academic programs put the academic program and the in-country experience above the flexibility of travel plans. Their first objective is to get you to the location where the program begins by the starting date, to get you home on the date the program ends, and to offer the group the lowest possible price for making safe, reliable arrangements. If the program schedules the flight for you, you might regard it as inconvenient if you do not have much flexibility in changing your travel dates and plans.

You might prefer a return flight to another city, or you might want to change your return date because of a summer job opportunity or some recent developments in your family's summer travel plans. The lower the airfares that the program arranges for you, the less flexibility you have. The airline might charge you a service fee to change your travel dates and itinerary. In some cases, it might not be possible to reschedule without buying another ticket.

Review your travel options carefully and try to set your return dates as early as possible, no later than the program deadline. Changing plans might involve a penalty of $75 to $450. It depends on the restrictions on the original ticket and the types of changes requested.

After weighing all the factors in selecting your return date and flight, you might want to ask the program whether it can discount your program fees and let you make your own travel plans. The program might be willing to do this.

Finding Super Economy Fares

If you are making your own travel arrangements, there are a number of ways that you can save money on your travel. The first is, once again, to book your tickets as early as possible. As the date of the flight approaches, the airline charges more to sell the remaining seats.

Consolidators are discount travel services offering low fares on unsold tickets that airlines release at the last minute. They do a high volume of business and save money by cutting corners on services. To find consolidators offering the lowest fares, begin by purchasing several weekend editions of the largest city newspapers. Select the newspaper for your area, ideally the city from which your international flight will probably depart, but buy newspapers for other large cities as well (Atlanta, Washington, New York, Boston, Chicago, Seattle, San Francisco, Los Angeles, or Houston). Look in the travel section for ads placed by the largest consolidators. They publicize their services by listing good fares from their city to major destinations—from Johannesburg to Reykjavik and from Tokyo to Tel Aviv.

Some of the largest consolidators advertise in papers around the country and list their Web sites and 800 numbers for more information. Several consolidators advertise on the Web. Compare their prices with those who advertise in the newspapers. Next, contact several consolidators and start comparing fares. There can be considerable differences in the prices they offer. A few good ones are:

Uniglobe
www.uniglobe.com/default.cfm

Cross Ocean Travels, Inc.
347 5th Ave., Suite 1400
New York, NY 10016
Phone: 212-696-0101

Watch Out!
If a travel agent contacts you, make sure the agent is authorized by the program. One student who did not read the printed materials carefully booked a flight by mistake with a travel agent representing another program. She ended up paying $700 for a plane ticked she did not need.

Watch Out!
Be careful about getting an electronic ticket through a consolidator. If there is an error in an electronic ticket, it is harder to correct. You might have to pay a $75 penalty and arrange an adjustment later through the consolidator. Avoid this inconvenience by insisting on a paper ticket.

Payless Travel
265 Madison Ave., 4th Floor
New York, NY 10016
Phone: 800-892-0027 or 212-682-3111
Fax: 212-681-9834
www.paylesstickets.com

An index to consolidators is available for $53.25 from:

Travel Publishing, Inc.,
Norwest Center Skyway #402
56 E. 6th St.
St. Paul, MN 55101
Phone: 612-292-0325
Fax: 612-292-8642

When looking for the ticket source offering you the lowest fare, you should consider other factors that could make it worthwhile to purchase your ticket from a regular travel agent at a slightly higher price. You get the best results from a consolidator when you have firm travel dates and relatively simple arrangements to make. Because they do high volume business with a minimum of staff, consolidators are not able to provide the same service and follow-through that a travel agent can. Discount tickets are usually non-refundable and can be changed or canceled only with high penalties. Immediate payment with a credit card or with a check sent by express mail is required to hold the ticket. Other services, such as ground transportation or tour packages, are not included. The consolidator does not call back to help refine your travel plans.

Student travel services are agencies that specialize in serving students. To qualify for student fares, you need an International Student Identity Card

(ISIC), available from Council Travel or from one of its authorized representatives, or the Teacher Identity Card issued by the same service. Council also issues a Go25 card for travelers under the age of 25 to help them get similar deals.

You might also want to consider getting a membership in an international youth hostel group. Before you decide to invest in a hostel card, however, study reports in guidebooks such as the *Let's Go* and *Lonely Planet* series to decide whether you want such spare accommodations. Find out more about security issues at hostels in the countries where you plan to travel. There are two hosteling service centers in the Washington, D.C. area.

Below are some discount and student travel services:

> Discount Air Finders
> A service of the Potomac Area Council of
> Hosteling International
> 17 West Mulberry St.
> Baltimore, MD 21201
> Phone: 410-576-8880
> E-mail: baltimore.hostel@juno.com
> or in Washington D.C.:
> 11 K. St., NW
> Washington, DC 20005
> Phone: 202-783-4943
> E-mail: hostelling.travel@juno.com

> Academic Travel Service
> 26060 Salme Rd., Suite B
> Huntington Woods, MI 48070
> Phone: 888-332-2687
> E-mail: ats@mail.msen.com

Moneysaver
If you plan to do any travel on your own and want to buy Flexipasses or other discount travel fares on trains and buses, order them before you leave. Some student fare deals must be purchased in advance.

Council Travel
(Council has offices in many U.S. cities and abroad. For a list of addresses, see their Web site) www.counciltravel.com/

STA Travel
(Specializes in student travel; has offices in 15 cities).
Phone: 800-925-4777
www.sta-travel.com

Study Abroad Travel
8011 S. 34th Ave., Suite 150
Minneapolis, MN 55425-1637
Phone: 800-282-8212 or 612-854-3321
E-mail: Kitt@mn.uswest.net

Travac (advertises through *Transitions Abroad*)
989 Sixth Ave.
New York, NY 10018
Phone: 212-563-3303
or in Florida:
2601 E. Jefferson St.
Orlando, FL 32803
Phone: 407-896-0014 or 800-TRAV-800

Also check discount and student travel services that advertise on www.studyabroad.com. You can contact the major air carriers directly for information about special fares:

American Airlines
www.americanair.com/

Northwest Airlines
www.nwa.com

US Airways
www.usairways.com/

Delta
www.delta-air.com/

**A Student
Speaks Up**
My mother and I got a terrific deal from our U.S. travel agent on a travel package for summer vacation in Australia. We visited national parks, famous sights such as Ayers Rock, and the Great Barrier Reef for half the price of tickets purchased in Australia.

TWA

www.twa.com/

United

www.ual.com/home/default.asp

Japan Air

www.japanair.com/

Air France

www.airfrance.fr/

Separating Good Deals from Bad Deals

There are many stories about special opportunities for extra savings. You need to consider these options carefully and decide whether the savings are worthwhile.

Courier flights are a legitimate bargain. They offer you the possibility of traveling for a greatly reduced fare in return for carrying time-sensitive documents that cannot be trusted to the mail. To participate in this money-saving option, you must join an Air Courier Association.

The bargain rates are offset by the fact that the flyer must be ready to go at a moment's notice and the dates of travel are not predictable. For further information about this travel option, contact:

Air Courier Association, Denver, Colorado
Phone: 800-822-0888 or 303-215-9000
www.aircourier.org

Some international airport Web sites are:

Frankfurt
www.frankfurt-airport.de/

Florence
www.safnet.it/

Rome
www.adr.it/en/fiumic/mappa-fco.html

Unofficially...
Don't forget to order any special meals when you book your ticket. When ordering vegetarian, specify whether dairy products are acceptable. Other options are low calorie, kosher, Hindu, non-fat, and so on. Get your meal request in two days or more before you travel.

Bright Idea
Maps of most
major U.S. air-
ports are on
the Web (www.
atlastravel.ca/map.
htm). This helps
you plan ahead
for parking, find-
ing the departure
terminal, and
checking conces-
sions and shuttle
service. If you
have a connect-
ing flight, a ter-
minal map will
save you time,
point out avail-
able services,
and show
whether you
have enough
time to get to
your connecting
flight.

(Train schedules for connections to the city)
www.adr.it/en/fiumic/fiumic-treni.html

The opportunity to cruise on a freighter is available, but it is primarily a vacation opportunity, not a
money saver. Freighters usually embark on leisurely
trips, calling at many ports along the way. A trip
might include a number of ports in the Baltic like
Scandinavia, Russia, and Eastern Europe, Mediter-
ranean ports such as Europe and North Africa, or
stops in the Caribbean. Persons interested in a
cruise find the trips reasonably priced in comparison with regular luxury cruises, but the prices reflect
housing and meals for an extended period. They
cost considerably more than airfare and are not a
speedy way of getting to a study abroad destination.
They provide a unique travel opportunity to people
who are willing to spend many hours by themselves
on board a ship and to spend days on end at sea with
no land visible.

The Cruise People Ltd. is one of the travel
agencies handling freighter travel. As its Web site
(member.aol.com/CruiseAZ/freighters.htm)
points out, "All itineraries are contingent on cargo.
No two sailings are identical and ports of call and
length of voyage are never guaranteed."

"Freighter Travel Review" is a newsletter providing information about travel by freighter. The
subscription rate is 36 pounds sterling to a U.S.
address (about $60 U.S.):

Murphy Media Ltd.
14 Egremont Way
Colchester, Essex
CO3 5NJ, UK

Phone/fax: 01206-503798 (dial 011-44 first from the U.S.)

www.maxho.com/~frman/newsupdate.html

The Cruise & Freighter Travel Association is an organization with a newsletter and information about travel by freighter. It lists cruises on its Web site:

P.O. Box 580188

Flushing, NY 11358

Phone: 800-872-8584

E-mail: info@travltips.com

www.travltips.com/freighterdirectory.html

"Freighter Travel News" is a monthly newsletter by the Freighter Travel Club:

3524 Harts Lake Rd.

Roy, WA 98580

"Around the World by Freighter" is a Web site report on freighter travel. The reviewer lays out the pros and cons very well. Not for the person focussed on a destination, travel by freighter is a great experience in itself for the self-sufficient person who can handle long sea voyages (www.atwtraveler.com/freightr.htm).

Freighter World Cruises publishes a monthly newsletter that lists all the latest freighter shipping routes available for passengers:

180 South Lake Ave.

Suite 3335

Pasadena, CA 91101

Phone: 800-531-7774 USA outside California,

818-449-3106 outside USA

Another U.S.-based information source is Ford's Freighter Travel Guide & Waterways of the World, by Judith Howard (updated quarterly). This listing

Bright Idea
The higher up in a ship your room is, the more costly it is. However, the lower it is, the more smooth and stable your ride will be. Avoid seasickness and save money, too, by requesting a room on a lower level of the ship.

comes from travel agents who specialize in freighter travel:

> 19448 Londelius St.
> Northridge, CA 91324
> Phone: 818-701-7414

For more readings on off-beat travel possibilities, contact:

> Adventurous Traveler Bookstore
> Phone: 800-282-3963 (USA and Canada)
> Fax: 800-677-1821 (USA and Canada)
> E-mail: books@atbook.com

Moneysaver
The longer your stay, the higher the fare is likely to be. It might be cheaper to buy one round-trip ticket for fall semester and a second one for the spring semester. Compare different flight options.

Many students ask about using frequent flyer miles to book their international travel. There is a slight disadvantage to using certain frequent flyer plans. With some plans, you might have difficulty getting seats on flights that correspond to the dates when you must travel. If you need to meet up with your group at a specific location on a certain date, you might have to go a day early and book a hotel for an extra night. You might have to arrive late or change planes several times to get seats. Investigate the limitations of your frequent flyer plan well in advance if you are considering this option.

Booking Your Flight

After weighing your choices, be sure that you book your flights as early as possible. Good fares might disappear quickly, especially if an international event is scheduled close to the time you intend to travel. Be prepared to pay by credit card or to send your payment immediately to confirm your travel arrangements.

Be sure the agent repeats back to you the name of the airline, flight number, times, airports of departure and arrival, and terminals. This is especially important if you have discussed several options. Be sure that you and the agent end up with the same understanding about what is being booked. Make sure all the arrangements are satisfactory and the information is specific.

Ask specifically about the airport and the terminal for each departure and arrival on your itinerary. This can be important for flights arriving at or departing from airports in a large city such as Washington, D.C., London, New York, Tokyo, or Paris. Large cities have multiple airports and some of the biggest airports have multiple terminals. In some cases (as at JFK), it is not possible to get from one of the airport's terminals to another by walking because the terminals are separated by freeways. You must take a shuttle bus, which can be delayed by traffic. This might be a problem when you are trying to make a connection after weather has delayed your arriving flight. It might be an even more serious problem if you inadvertently book a flight arriving at one airport and have to connect to a departing flight leaving from a completely different airport. If you have to change airports, you should investigate the connections thoroughly. You might need to spend the night in the city before catching your connecting flight.

In Tokyo, most international flights come into Narita Airport, with flights from the U.S. arriving in the middle of the afternoon. It is evening by the time the connecting express train takes you from the airport to downtown Tokyo. From the central station, you must take a cab across town to the station for the monorail, which in turn takes you to Haneda Airport. Local flights within Japan leave

Moneysaver
Airfares climb steeply when a major international event is scheduled, such as the World Cup or the Olympics, or when the dollar is especially strong. Check with your travel agent at least six months before you travel. Book early if demand is high.

from this airport. An overnight stay in Tokyo is almost inevitable.

Your parents might wonder about the safety record of the airline, if the carrier is not an American company. Here are some factors to consider in trying to determine this. In recent years, many American companies established affiliations with air carriers in other countries so their domestic customers can book all of their arrangements through the same company and benefit from frequent flyer miles and other services. Lately, some major airlines have terminated some of these arrangements. A publication of the airline pilots union reported recently that the connections came to an end because of American concerns about the training programs and safety procedures that their partners were using. Therefore, you might want to find out whether an airline was formerly partnered with an American airline and what happened to that partnership.

Some fellowships and scholarships require the recipients to book all their travel with American carriers. Ordinarily, they provide extra funds to the scholar to cover the cost of a special ticket if the group is traveling with a carrier based in another country. Mention this requirement when booking your ticket or registering for a study abroad program.

Getting to Your Final Destination in the Country

As soon as you know your travel plans, be sure to notify your program. They need this information to arrange to meet you.

If you need to travel independently to your program destination, carefully review the travel arrangements you need to make using a guidebook to the country and the host university instruction packet. You can also get detailed information from the Web about connections from many important international airports. Search for the city's public transportation network, and you will probably find connecting rail and bus links from the airport to the downtown area. Ask your study abroad advisor for help if you encounter any uncertainties. The faculty who helped you select the program might also be of help in putting together an itinerary to get you from the international arrival point to the program site.

In Europe, there are connecting public buses or trains from the airports to the railway stations, most of which are located in the city centers. There is enough time involved in getting from one to the other that it is wise to plan an overnight stay if you know that you will be taking the train to any destination that is four hours or more from the capital city. Ask your travel agent in the United States to make a reservation for the next day on a long-distance train connecting the capital city with your final destination. A Europass covers the basic train fare, but you need to pay additional for the reserved seat on the day you plan to travel. Long-distance buses are available to connect many airports with cities within one or two hours' drive of the capital.

If you plan to make connecting flight arrangements, you should investigate the connections thoroughly as described earlier. Again, domestic flights might leave from a different airport, necessitating a cross-town trip that consumes enough time to make an overnight stay necessary.

Purchase a guidebook for the country well in advance of your travel, and read all the details of getting across town from the airport to the train stations and from the train to the bus stations in smaller towns. The connections are usually quite clear, with trains from the airport taking you directly to the major connecting points in the city.

As you investigate the arrangements for getting to your program site after your international flight, you will gather information that is also useful if you plan optional travel during a vacation period. If you are planning optional travel during a vacation period, you will probably use the train to travel within the country or to countries nearby.

If you are planning to travel by train, there are a number of options to consider. There is some advantage to purchasing a Europass for travel in Europe, a Britrail pass for travel in the U.K., or the equivalent passes for other countries. These must be purchased in advance in the United States through your travel agent. They offer a certain number of days of travel within a specific period of time. You choose the time frame and number of trips you prefer. If you do not expect to travel again for some time after you reach your program site, it is probably more cost effective to buy a single ticket for your connecting travel. Save the option of a rail pass for a vacation period when you expect to spend several days traveling by train within a specific time frame such as two weeks or one month. The best way to take advantage of the rail passes is to use them for fairly long trips every few days. Using a pass for a short trip is not a real savings.

Planning Your Travel Budget

The best way to figure out your daily costs for travel in another country is to buy one of the budget travel guides such as *Let's Go,* the *Rough Guides,* or *The*

Lonely Planet guides. Create a grid showing all the days you want to travel. The guides list the cost of various ways of traveling between locations. Alternatively, you might prefer to start with a rail pass allowing you a fixed number of days of travel in a month. Here are some options for savings on travel in various parts of the world:

- Rail travel all over Europe can be arranged directly through the French railway system (SNCF). You can book online and pick up and pay for your tickets in the country you designate (www.sncf.fr/voy/indexe.htm).

- This Web site has links to arrange connections between the rail systems of different countries (www.thetravelsite.com/Europe/RailCountries. htm).

- To book and pay in the U.S., you can get information at www.raileurope.com, or contact your local travel agent.

- Rail Pass Express, Inc. (www.railpass.com) is another online booking option.

- Eurolines Pass offers 30- and 60-day passes for $249 to $449 depending on the season, the age of the traveler, and the length of the pass. The service includes 43 cities in 22 countries from the former Soviet Union to the U.K. Call 800-688-9577 or visit www.brtravelgear.com/ euroline.html.

- Asia Budget tours offers information about travel to and throughout Asia. Call 800-642-2742 or visit www.southeastasia.com.

- Asia Transpacific Journeys is another service (e-mail: travel@southeastasia.com).

- A newsletter with tips for travel in New Zealand is available from KIWIphile File, 2715 Altura Ave., La Crescenta, CA 91214.

- For information about places to stay, try Worldhotel (www.worldhotel.com).

In France, you can choose between express trains (TGV) that cover great distances rapidly with few stops or regular trains that stop more frequently. If you know that you want to travel on an express train on a certain day, you should probably reserve a seat for an extra charge. In most of Europe, you can go to the Europass information center in the train station and ask for assistance in planning your itinerary. An attendant will use a computer to look up one or more itineraries, with all the connections marked, and print it out for you.

A Britrail pass is the British equivalent of the continental Europass. Type Britrail on the Web and you will find four or five travel services offering Britrail passes. Eurostar is the "chunnel" train that links the U.K. to Europe. Most of the Britrail and Europass sites offer links between the two systems, as well as information about Eurostar.

One of the best kept secrets for a money-saving and flexible way of touring Europe during your vacation is Eurobus. This service offers passes for linked charter bus circuits through Northern, Central, and Southern Europe. You can board at any city and get off at the city you want to visit. The Web site provides a complete list of the destinations and the times the bus arrives and departs from each city. You can stay as long as you like in any city along the way and then board the bus and proceed to your next destination. You can purchase a monthly pass or select another period of time. The Web site includes the scheduled departures from all the cities on the routes, a complete list of the cities served, and prices for passes of varying duration. Prices range from $195 for one month to $529 for four months for a non-ISIC card holder (www.frugaltraveler.com).

Another convenient bus travel package, the Eurolines, offers 30- and 60-day passes for $249 and $449, depending on the age of the traveler and the length of the pass. The service links 43 cities in 22 countries from the former Soviet Union to the U.K. (www.brtravelgear.com/euroline.html).

Japan offers a combination of high-speed trains, air travel (especially convenient in getting over the central mountains), and bus. You will find train travel expensive, but there are discount passes available. Air travel might appear more convenient, but bus travel is much less expensive.

Several students recommend Beijing Longmen International Tours Corporation (Beijing longmen guoji luxingshe). The manager of the "foreigners office," Ms. Helen Zheng Hui, can speak fairly good English. Also, the students really love Ms. Grace Wang. They are able to book domestic as well as international travel and hotels.

> No. A9 Daqudeng Lane, Meishuguan Houjie
> East District
> Beijing 100010.
> Phone: 86-10-84010086
> Fax: 86-10-64012180
> E-mail: blts@public.bta.net.cn
> www.chinablts.com

In China, Americans can almost always book air travel between certain destinations. Make air travel reservations at hotel travel service desks and at the Chinese Travel Agency (CITS).

Unofficially...
The best way to get things done in China is through the "back door" system of performing mutual favors for your acquaintances. Someone influential at your host university might be able to get you the tickets in return for some favor such as giving him a chance to practice his English, translating something, or helping a relative apply to a U.S. college or university.

Train tickets are far more economical. You can save money by going to the train station and purchasing tickets in advance to travel by train. If you are lucky, you can get soft seat or soft sleeper reservations. The soft seat cars have upholstered seats, arranged in individual compartments that seat up to eight people. Thermos bottles of hot water are provided for your convenience in making your own tea and ramen noodles along the way. The soft seats make up into soft bunk beds for overnight travel. Because train travel is slow, often lasting several days because of the great distances to be covered, the soft seat and sleeper options assure you a comfortable trip. The next level down in accommodation is called hard sleepers. These are padded boards arranged in bunk fashion so that the voyagers can stretch out and sleep at night. The most rugged way to travel is by hard seat. The seats are thinly padded in leather and arranged like booths in a soda shop in pairs with a table between them.

It can be difficult to get a reservation for travel between certain popular points. A black market in soft sleeper tickets exists in certain cities. The most influential workers have connections to get the soft sleeper (bunk) reservations. Plan ahead and make your reservations early.

Check into student bus rates for the municipal bus system in the city where you will be living. You might find that student bus fares apply only until riders are 21 years old. However, it is worth exploring. You need your passport and your letter of admission to the university. A photo is probably necessary to issue an ID.

Car rentals are expensive in other countries. In addition, gas outside the United States is much more costly than it is at home. Expect to pay at least

Bright Idea
Using your search engine, type "[name of city] bus map," (Florence bus map, Münster bus map, Manchester bus map, and so on), and you get convenient transportation information. (An experimental new service called Lorenzo offers information about the shortest distance between two points by bus in Florence at soarisc.comune. fi.it/ataf/index. html.) Use the maps for advance planning.

as much for a liter of gas as you would for a gallon at home. To rent a car, you must be at least 25 years of age and present a valid passport and driver's license (it does not need to be an international driver's license) and a major credit card.

Many university student organizations organize low-cost tours during vacation periods. Local tourist agencies might offer special packages for European weekend travelers. These are not available through American travel agents. Try a little surfing on the Web to see what sorts of package deals for a weekend train trip might be listed for the region near where you plan to study. The railway companies often offer a discount for a circuit of 3 to 10 days, returning to your starting point.

Stop into the city tourist office for information about locally organized tours of the region where you live. These offer a great opportunity to visit that castle about 20 miles away or a regional park famous for its natural beauty. For your free weekends, you will find numerous low-cost bus outings to choose from.

Just the Facts

- Consider your international travel options carefully and research the many savings available.

- Verify all arrangements before you book.

- Some money savers might be exciting trips but won't get you to a certain place by a certain time.

- For in-country travel, many money savers and time savers are available.

A Student Speaks Up
My advice to students going abroad is just to travel as much as you can. You may never have another opportunity to see the country and meet the people. Save your money for vacation travel and explore everywhere.

GET THE SCOOP ON...
Clothing to take with you ▪ Packing light ▪ A
checklist of things to take ▪ What not to take

What to Pack

Chapter 15

It's a general rule of savvy travelers to take twice as much money and half as much clothing as you think you will need. When you start packing, think about making the most out of the limited space you have, the weight of everything you have to take with you, the length of time you will be overseas, and how to create the lightest possible load. You have two basic questions to ask yourself. "What do I need for the country I am going to?" "Can I manage my luggage alone?"

You really can get by on much less than you usually take with you on family vacations or when traveling to college each fall. If you are an experienced back-packer, you probably are already thinking along the right lines when you start packing for your overseas adventure.

Clothing

As you consider what clothing to take, your first task is to put completely out of your mind the type of weather that prevails where you live or go to school.

66
We tell students:
Pack your bag
and then see if
you can carry it
around the house
three times. If
you can't do
that, keep taking
things out until
you can!
99

Research the prevailing weather at your destination carefully.

Check an encyclopedia for information about your country's climate. Take note of high and low temperatures in different seasons of the year as well as the amount of rain, snow, or heat to expect in your host country during the months you plan to be there. Take note of the latitude at which your destination is located. It is never too soon to start checking the world weather reports to watch the fluctuations of temperature, rainfall, and other weather conditions at your destination. Big city newspapers provide this information every day. You can also get it on the Web. For example, try the *Washington Post* (www.washingtonpost.com). From here, click the World Weather button to receive recent forecasts for any part of the world or use the Historical Weather button to find information about the climate of another country.

USA Today's "Traveler's Guide to World Weather" provides an overview of the average weather conditions throughout the year in cities all over the world. You can click on the letter corresponding to a city and get the average high, average low, records, precipitation, and dew points for every month of the year. You can view the data by country and select the cities you want to view, or you can select an alphabetical list of world cities and choose from those. The Web site includes tips for travelers and the current weather forecast for cities and countries of interest (www.usatoday.com/weather/climate/wcntry.htm).

For a more scientific approach to world climatic conditions for students of meteorology or environmental science, the National Climatic Data Center has detailed data and maps for regions of the world.

A list of publications is available on the Web site. The data must be ordered at $30 for a set (www. ncdc.noaa.gov/ol/climate/climateresources.html).

Nothing is worse than boarding a flight in Los Angeles in cut-offs and a tank shirt, arriving in London in a driving rainstorm with a wind-chill factor of 28°, and realizing that you asked your mother to mail your sweater and raincoat instead of taking them with you.

Keep firmly in mind that the seasons are reversed in the Northern and Southern hemispheres and that they also differ greatly from continent to continent and from latitude to latitude. When it is hot in Midwestern America in July, it is winter in the Southern hemisphere, so expect the coldest weather to occur when you first arrive at destinations south of the Equator. February in South Australia is the beginning of autumn; think fall colors and back-to-school clothes. November in Buenos Aires is spring; jacaranda trees are flowering and the first hints of summer heat are on the way. On the other hand, even summer weather can be surprisingly cold if you are traveling to northern Europe. June in London, Amsterdam, or Berlin can be cool and rainy. Take note of peak rainy season months if you're headed for Ghana, Indonesia, Costa Rica, or any other country near the equator.

If you have a stop-over along the way, be sure you won't be caught by surprise contrasts in the weather when you have to walk outside to board a small plane for your connecting flight. If you don't usually bother with a coat when you dash between heated buildings or between your car and the mall, get used to the idea that you're going to be doing a lot of outdoor walking. The buildings in other countries won't be air-conditioned or heated to the same

A Student Speaks Up
Steve was the best packer in our group. He packed everything he needed for one month in France into a wheeled carry-on bag that fit under the seat in front of him on the airplane. He had nothing heavy to lift and no checked luggage at all!

A Student Speaks Up

Each fall, our friend in Paris buys a suit jacket, skirt, or slacks in the latest fashion. She wears the same clothes, in various combinations, every day. She looks chic for her job at the Louvre and balances her budget. Her daughters, both university students, wear the same black sweaters and jeans almost every day.

degree as in the United States. Think about the outdoor weather, not the controlled climates we have in our cars and buildings, and pack the type of clothes you need for your destination. In China, south of the Yangtze River, buildings are not heated in the winter time. Locals do much of their cooking and laundry outdoors in their courtyards. The stone buildings are built to stay cool in the hot summer weather. On mild winter days, people often warm up their rooms by opening the windows to bring in the warmest air of the day. In the coldest weather, people wear outerwear all day long, indoors and outside.

If you are studying abroad in the fall, Southern Europe should be relatively warm when you arrive. Japan will be quite warm. South America, Africa, and Australia will be experiencing their coldest months of the year, warmer close to the equator and colder in the south. In Northern Europe, warm weather will already be alternating with cool, rainy days and autumn will be on its way. You might want to pack swimwear, but fall temperatures might drop sharply after your arrival. Pack some changes of comfortable, lightweight washable clothing for the month of September, but be ready with at least one heavy sweater and waterproof windbreaker or anorak with removable lining. Take long sleeved shirts, raincoats, and sweaters.

If you are going to a country with a long rainy season, pack a raincoat and shoes that can handle the rain. If the average winter temperatures will be below 32°, be sure to pack a heavy winter coat. Tall men, if you wear a size 11 or larger shoe and are going anywhere but Western Europe or Scandinavia, take along several pairs of walking shoes. It is difficult to buy large men's shoe sizes off the rack in the rest of the world. In Asia, it is impossible to buy

TABLE 15.1   AVERAGE WEATHER CONDITIONS IN CITIES WHERE STUDENTS FREQUENTLY STUDY

City	Average High in °F Hottest Months	Average Low in °F Coldest Months	Average Precipitation in Inches Except Where Noted
Beijing	86 Jul.	17 Jan.	.01 Dec.–8.8 Jul.
Berlin	73 Jul., Aug.	26 Jan.	15 days May–23 days Dec., Jan.
London	72 Jul., Aug;	36 Jan., Feb.	2.9 Oct.–1.4 Feb.
Madrid	90 Jul., Aug.	32 Jan.	2.5 Nov.–.04 Jul., Aug.
Mexico City	79 May	45 Dec., Jan.	4.8 Aug.–.2 Feb.
Montreal	79 July	7 Jan.	2.6 Feb.–3.6 Aug.
Moscow	71 July	11 Jan.	1.1 Feb.–2.8 Aug.
Oslo, Norway	71 July	19 Feb.	18 days Feb., May–21 Jan.
Paris	75 Jul., Aug.	34 Jan., Feb.	12 days Aug.–20 days Jan.
Quito	68 Sept.	49 June–Nov.	1 Aug.–6.9 April
Rome	83 Jul., Aug.	39 Jan.	1.0 Aug.–4.4 Nov.
Sydney	79 Jan., Feb.	50 Sept.	2.2 Sept.–5.2 March
Tel Aviv	88 Aug.	46 Jan., Feb.	0 days Jul., Aug.–15 days Jan.
Tokyo	86 Aug.	35 Jan.	2 Jan.–8.5 Sept.
Vienna	77 Jul., Aug.	27 Jan.	15 days Sept., Oct.–22 days Dec.

A Student Speaks Up
I am a French student who studied in the United States for a year and visited Mexico while I was there. I have also traveled around Europe a lot. Personally, I prefer to wear a long skirt rather than jeans when I am traveling. I just feel more comfortable, and the skirt is cooler in hot weather.

ready-to-wear men's shoes. Tall men have shoemakers make shoes to fit them.

In addition to contrasting weather conditions, another thing to remember is that people in other countries do not change their outfits as often as in the United States. All over the world, whether they work or go to school in Beijing, Rome, Tokyo, or Buenos Aires, people take this approach to dressing. Clothing is expensive outside the United States. People manage with only a few outfits. The good news for you is that you can get by for a semester, or even a year, with just a few changes of clothing.

In general, it is best to pack only *half* the amount of clothing you think you will need for the year. Some items can be shipped after you receive your permanent address, but overseas shipping is expensive, so it is best to travel light. Pack mostly casual clothes if you plan to be in a university environment. You probably won't need more than one dressy outfit for a theater performance, a special banquet, and so on. Waterproof, warm outerwear and a heavy sweater are much more important, even in the early fall, and you will need a heavy winter coat later. Again, however, you should not bring too much of anything. If you coordinate your clothing, you really can "make do" on a lot less than you may think. Bring some basic accessories, such as scarves, clips, and "scrunchies" to restyle your outfits or your hair. You might prefer to buy some new accessories at your destination to fit in with the local women.

If you are going to Southern Europe, ask the program coordinator or returning students about accepted clothing for women in the areas you plan to visit. In general, women are expected to have their arms covered when they enter churches, both as a matter of respect and for comfort (large stone buildings can be cool on the warmest days). Women generally do not wear shorts in downtown areas in Southern Europe.

For men: Pack the sort of clothing you wear to classes in the United States, adjusted to compensate for any differences in climate. Be sure to include some rain gear. Avoid bringing expensive jewelry or sports equipment.

Medicine and Personal Supplies

Carry all prescription medications with you. Pack them in the containers in which they were dispensed (don't transfer them to unmarked containers), and carry a copy of the prescription with you. Be aware that doctors in other countries might not prescribe certain medications that are common in the United States. Therefore, it could be difficult to get additional supplies of medication if you run out. You can buy every type of cosmetic, shampoo, or over-the-counter medication you use at home, although you will find that American brands cost much more than the European counterparts and that the best approach is to be willing to try some new items.

Unless you can confirm that your U.S. product is available in the host country and at an optometry shop near your study site, take enough contact lenses and cleaner or solution with you to last the entire time you are away. It is possible but expensive to express ship additional contact lenses from the United States.

You can arrange for repair or reproduction of damaged eyeglasses or frames if you bring the prescription with you. However, it might be easier to bring a backup pair of glasses with you.

Watch Out!
Before you pack an expensive mountain bike or other favorite sports gear, make sure conditions in the host country are appropriate for their use. One student went to great expense to take his racing bike to China, only to find the streets too crowded for him to enjoy using a bike constructed for high speeds and wide open spaces.

Other Essentials

Take a course catalog from your home institution. It will help you in the selection of your courses and in registering for classes for the year of your return. If you were provided with a record of the courses pre-approved for you to take abroad, bring a copy with you.

Be sure to pack ID photos. You need numerous passport photos after you arrive. You might be able to purchase them inexpensively at photo machines there, but it is probably much more convenient to take them with you.

Travel towelettes are useful for washing your hands, or the rest of you, while traveling. Have them ready to clean cuts, broken blisters, or scrapes, especially if you are traveling in the developing world. They are useful for quickly cleaning or disinfecting eating utensils such as chopsticks, glasses, or cups if you are suspicious about the cleanliness of the place where you are eating.

Take disinfectants and treat skin abrasions quickly when you are traveling in parts of the world where the tap water is not sterile. We take for granted the ease with which we can disinfect cuts by washing them in the Western world. Elsewhere, abrasions might get infected more easily.

Place identification labels inside each of your bags and make a list of your traveler's check numbers. We suggest making a photocopy of the inside of your passport so that you have a record of the number, date, and place of issue. This information will help you obtain a quick replacement if your passport is lost or stolen. Leave complete copies of this information with your study abroad office or your family before your departure.

Most standard film sizes, instamatic cartridges, and flash cubes are available wherever you go. Slide film is often recommended for best results as well as savings on film and developing. The new disposable cameras available around the world provide excellent prints. If you are wondering whether to get film developed locally or to wait until you get home, try out a test roll to see what kind of results you get locally before deciding.

If your saxophone, guitar, or other musical instrument is a part of your life back home, it would be a great comfort to you if you are going to be abroad for several months or an entire academic year. It will add pleasure to group gatherings. In addition, music offers a great way of making friends in your new surroundings. Consider bringing your instrument, or inquire about renting one in the host country if your own instrument is too large, valuable, or fragile to bring with you. If you do choose to bring your instrument, keep in mind that you have to carry and safeguard it during your travels. Depending on the size of the instrument, you might have to forego one piece of luggage to keep a hand free to carry it during travel.

Watch Out!
A camera is another valuable item that you need to safeguard. Remember not to let it hang from a strap around your neck when you are in a crowded bus or subway. Pickpockets can slit the strap and get away with your camera before you can stop them.

How Much Luggage to Take

For your international flight, you are allowed two pieces of checked luggage and one carry-on. This amount of luggage might be difficult for you to manage by yourself when you reach the country of your destination. If you are going abroad for a semester or year, ask whether you will be met at your destination and how much assistance will be provided to help you get your luggage to your final destination. If you have to manage the luggage by yourself, you should plan on taking only what you can handle. Wheeled bags or duffel bags are ideal. You should make sure all bags are lockable during travel and at any time when they are in a hotel or hostel.

Many students arrive at an international airport in a major city and then have to make connections by bus or train or by a different airline to get to their final destinations. Sometimes, you might have to go from the airport to a hotel in the city where your international flight arrives to stay overnight before making connections to travel to your final destination. Some programs plan a study tour with many stops before you reach your destination. Study tours might be on the move throughout the program, transferring from one city to another every few days! These realities of study abroad travel mean that you might have to transfer luggage repeatedly—in and out of buses and taxis, as well as on and off trains and planes—until you finally reach a point where you can unpack and settle in for a month, semester, or year.

The bottom line is that you should travel with no more baggage than you can manage by yourself. If you know that you will travel part of the way by train, keep in mind that you will have to walk down very long station platforms—sometimes as long as a mile. When changing trains, you will have to go up or down stairs, through tunnels, or over bridges to get from one platform to another. On the train, there is not much space for stowing luggage. Usually, the space provided is at the end of the car, not above your seat. This is much easier to manage with a light piece of luggage than a large, heavy one. This is why the advice to make sure you can carry your suitcase three times around your house is so practical. Again, make sure you can lock all of your bags.

> 66
> You will see more and remember more by keeping a journal or sketchbook instead of taking photos or videos. While you are adjusting your camera, you might miss something interesting. Be open to the moment rather than try to record it for the future. After all, there are many commercial shots of the same famous monuments and scenery.
> —A program hostess
> 99

Students coming from Europe to the United States often arrive with one manageable piece of checked luggage and a carry-on. They are used to traveling light, and they get by for an entire year with the items they bring to the U.S. with them and the few items they purchase after arriving! You can do the same heading in the other direction. Wheeled bags or luggage wheels are an absolute must to help you manage your baggage prior to departure and during luggage transfers.

Carry-On Luggage

Organize your luggage so that you have everything you need for the long international flight and your arrival in your carry-on baggage:

- Valuables, medication, contact lens fluid, or other items that you need each day.

- Brush, comb, towelettes, and toothbrush so that you can freshen up after a long flight.

- Your passport and traveler's checks or credit cards.

- The letter of admission to the program and important phone numbers and addresses.

- You might be asked to display your return ticket when you go through immigration upon arrival. Have it available so that you can present it if asked to do so (and when you stow it again, make sure you remember where you are keeping it so that you can find it at the end of a long stay abroad).

- In case one of your checked bags gets lost or delayed, put a change of clothing or at least a change of underwear in your carry-on as a precaution. If you know that the weather at your destination is radically different from that at

Watch Out!
Do not leave your bags unattended in any crowded public place, including airports, on the bus or train, or on the street during your arrival and departure. As an additional precaution: During your travels, do not display your name and address or talk loudly about your hotel address, travel, or weekend plans when in public places.

your departure point, you might include something to change into or an extra layer to put on as soon as you arrive.

▪ Reading material for the plane.

Checked Luggage

Be sure that all your checked luggage can be securely locked and that your name and destination address are on the luggage tag and inside the bag. Be sure you do not pack any valuables, money, or items you need each day (medication, contact lens care items, and so on) in luggage to be checked during your flight. The airline terminals are large and nobody is available to carry bags for you. Be sure your checked luggage has wheels so that you can manage them on your own if luggage carts are not available.

Your First Stop

Pack everything necessary for the first stop in one bag. Because most programs offer an introductory tour, stop-over in a major city, or one-month orientation session in a special location, it makes sense to review the schedule and organize your luggage so that the things you need at first are all in the same bag. Clothing that washes easily and dries quickly is ideal for the first phase of your overseas stay.

Throughout the year, be careful never to leave your luggage unattended while traveling, in any public area, or in an unlocked room. In recent years, several vacationing students have been robbed of passports, wallets, and other valuables left in unattended backpacks or purses. Do not leave a bicycle overnight (even if it is locked up) in a downtown city location. Always lock the door of a hotel or dormitory room, whether you are inside asleep or just down the hall. When traveling, keep your passport, money, and documents inside your clothing or beneath you while napping on the train.

Appliances

Don't take appliances if you can possibly avoid it. To operate American appliances abroad, you need an adapter and usually a converter (both available in hardware and luggage stores). The adapter fits U.S. plugs into the sockets used in other countries. At travel stores and hardware stores, you can buy sets of adapters, including one to fit three-pin round sockets in the EU, another for two-pin sockets in Britain, and a slant-pinned version for other locations. If you think you will have time to shop after you get to your destination, you can buy an adapter there that is sure to fit.

Converters adjust American appliances to work with the electric current in other countries. Most laptop computers come with them. Check a guidebook to find the voltage in your destination country. The voltage in China and in most of Europe is 220 volts (AC). American appliances run on 110 volt AC current. Japan uses 100 volt current. Appliances that run on 110 volt AC current will burn out if plugged directly into an outlet with 200 current. Some travel appliances have a converter built in. However, converters add weight to your luggage, as do the appliances themselves. Moreover, if the converter switch does not work properly, the surge of 220 current will burn out the appliance. The fewer of these heavy items you take, the lighter your luggage will be. Substitute a spray bottle for your iron, hair dryer, and curling iron.

If you must take an electric appliance, consider a battery-driven model. It won't need adapters or

Moneysaver
Instead of a travel iron, get a tiny plastic spray bottle. When you arrive, hang up the clothes you need, lightly mist the wrinkles, and watch them disappear. If you won't need the item immediately, hang it in the bathroom while you shower and let hot water vapor smooth out the wrinkles. Mist your hair with the spray bottle and quickly style it without shampooing and blow-drying.

converters and will be even lighter if you pack it without the batteries and buy them when you arrive. Alternatively, bring rechargeable batteries and purchase a battery charger for the local current when you arrive.

The appliance you will probably want the most while you are away from home is a portable cassette/CD player so that you can listen to familiar music when you are feeling homesick or when you want to share your favorites with new friends. Again, batteries help you avoid the problem of different currents. If your stay will be longer, you can buy a local cassette/CD player that you can sell or pass along to another student when you leave.

Computers

Students today want access to a computer to check e-mail, complete assignments, and access the Internet. If you like to use a computer for all your writing, data storage, and other academic work, it is convenient to have one with you. Taking a computer abroad is a big decision, however. Here are some factors to consider.

First, the negatives: Because a computer is both valuable and delicate, you cannot pack it in your luggage. You need to carry it on the plane with you and pass it through airport security. Once in the country, you have to carry and safeguard the computer throughout your travels. The small room safes you find in some hotels, especially in Spain, might not hold a laptop. With a combination lock, you might be able to fasten it to an immovable object in the room. Hotel phones usually have intricate long-distance access codes to make it difficult to place long-distance calls from the room without a credit card. This makes it difficult to access e-mail or Internet providers from your room even if you have a calling card or list of worldwide access numbers. Full service hotels usually have a business service center where these services and others, such as printing or faxing, are available for a charge.

Although service is not as extensive as in the U.S., universities in other countries increasingly provide computer labs where you can access e-mail and the Internet. You probably will not need to submit typed papers as you do in the United States. Written assignments are still handwritten in most countries, especially for short-term summer programs and intensive language programs. In fact, you might have to adopt a specific handwritten format, using composition books or special exercise paper, for written assignments (keep carbons or photocopies). American professors who assign research papers in the format that is customary at American universities usually set a deadline that allows students to prepare and submit the paper after they return to the States.

Dormitory rooms will not have telephones, or if they do, you have to solve the problem of access codes and credit card numbers to use your computer's modem. It might be necessary to purchase a telephone adapter to use your modem in the host country. You can access the Internet at cyber cafes, public and university libraries, and other centers in the host country. Plan ahead to find out where these are. If you rent your own apartment, installing a telephone line is very expensive. Payment of security deposits, installation charges, and taxes must come before the line is put in. In most countries, callers are charged for all calls. There is no flat rate for a certain number of local calls. These considerations might make a host family reluctant to allow a

Watch Out!
I shipped my computer, and even though I could prove that it was only for academic use and not for sale in Europe, I had to pay a 26 percent duty in order to claim it from customs. Another student shipped a printer that arrived with severe discoloration and damage, probably from heat damage to the plastic parts during shipment.

student to use a modem on their phone line and might make a separate installation prohibitively expensive.

On the positive side, if you do take along a computer, a portable notebook or laptop with a rechargeable battery is most convenient. Shipping a PC involves high cost and risk. It is more practical to buy one in the country and sell it at the end of the year than to take one from the United States.

In France, the telephone company (Poste, Téléphone, Télégraphique, or PTT) provides an entirely different information network with its own terminal (Minitel), which many people prefer and use. Unfortunately, it is not compatible with the Internet. You can purchase a telephone adapter in your host country that will let you use the modem in your laptop for e-mailing from your apartment. Dorm residents, who will not have access to a personal phone, will not require this adapter. You might be able to obtain an e-mail account at the university and access e-mail and the Internet through a local phone call to the university computer center.

If your computer does not have a converter, you need to purchase one to allow it to function on the local current and to allow the battery to recharge. In addition, you need to purchase a power cord or an adapter that will fit the local electric outlets. If you do a lot of computer work on unfamiliar equipment or work with new power sources, back up your work frequently. Take a lot of extra disks and keep copies.

Shipping Information

If you are going abroad for a semester or year, you might want to have your family ship items that you need later on (such as summer clothes if your term begins in the winter or winter clothes if your term begins in autumn). This way, you will not have to pack them in your luggage for the international flight and you will not have to carry them with you during any preliminary travel.

Families will have the most success shipping small, lightweight items via airmail. There are several factors to consider.

Shipping Costs

It costs about $50 to ship a box containing the equivalent of a dozen books to Europe, depending on the size of the box and the weight of the contents.

A box shipped by surface freight might wait on a loading dock in extreme weather conditions (heat, rain, and freezing temperatures). It might receive rough handling and arrive damaged. Airmail provides swifter, safer handling but is much more expensive.

Put clothing in plastic bags to protect it if the package gets wet. Leather mildews easily and the odor permeates the entire package. Wrap leather items separately.

Delivery Arrangements

Packages do not normally come to the residence in other countries. Most students live in dormitories or apartment buildings with small mailboxes for letters. Packages cannot be left safely in the entry halls where most buildings have their mailboxes. Instead, a delivery slip is placed in the recipient's mailbox and the package is held at a central post office or parcel delivery depot. Depending on the size and weight of the package and the location of the delivery depot, the student might need to arrange for a cab, car, or bicycle to pick up the package and get it home.

Watch Out!
A friend of mine completed her doctoral dissertation in Ecuador without a computer. On the way to photocopy it, she got out of the cab, paid the driver, and then turned to pick up the box from the seat. Before she could, the cab took off, carrying away the one and only copy of all her work. She could not trace the cab or recover the material.

Customs

Although the shipper can label the items as books or used clothing without monetary value, customs officials might open the box for inspection and charge duty on the items. In some countries, attractive or valuable items have disappeared from boxes between the point of shipment and the delivery point.

Food

Although it is tempting to send Christmas cookies or some other homemade food item to a son or daughter overseas, families should keep in mind that the package might be delayed and could attract pests or deteriorate while it is waiting. Vibration might cause fragile items such as cookies to disintegrate, or the package might become moldy. Some types of foods might not be allowed into certain countries. Ask questions at your post office about methods of shipment and types of foods that travel successfully.

A Student Speaks Up
Pack light and bring a lot of film! If you can't carry it, don't bring it. Wear a money belt and get out and enjoy yourself. Be ready for a lot of walking. Bring plenty of clothing that you can layer.

An Unofficial Guide to Packing Light

- Pick items that can be mixed and matched.

- Pack clothing that will wash and dry easily.

- Be willing to live with one or two basic colors. Black is versatile and stylish.

- Adopt a wash-and-wear hairstyle and leave heavy hairdryers and curlers at home.

- Take clothing that washes and dries quickly. Jeans are slow (and expensive) to dry in Laundromats or on the line.

- Test your luggage to see whether you are taking too much by carrying it around the block or three times around the house.

- Plan around one or two basic outfits and layers to put over them.

- If you know the schedule will be quite full, with little free time for shopping, take all the toiletries, batteries, healthcare products, film, and other small items you might need.

- Bring at least one month's supply of cosmetics and health products, even if you plan to buy local products eventually. This will give you time to get your bearings and find the best deals and places to shop.

- The longer your stay, the more time you'll have at your destination to shop for local products such as film, toiletries, and so on.

- Whatever products you use up, or worn-out clothing you leave behind, will make space in your luggage on the return journey for gifts and souvenirs.

- A collapsible bag that fits inside your luggage is useful for short trips, day outings, and carry-on for the return trip. (See other tips for shipping things home in Chapter 19, "Finishing Up.")

Six Things You Really Must Take

- Photocopies of your documents.

- Contact information from your home university.

- Connections to home (photos, small mementos) to stave off homesickness.

- Rain gear.

- Towel and soap for home stays, dormitory stays, and staying at youth hostels or YMCAs.

- Dictionary for the language you're studying.

Watch Out!
In Latin America, women should avoid wearing skirts or shorts. Wear slacks. In many countries, there is still an attitude that women who wear tight, revealing clothing expect to be touched. Ask about local attitudes before you pack and bring loose fitting clothing if people have had problems in the past.

Five Things You Should Leave at Home

- Expensive jewelry items.

- Valuable sports equipment or other items that mark you as a likely target for thieves. If sports are a major part of your life, consider renting equipment while you are abroad.

- U.S.-made notebooks and paper unless advised to do so. You need to purchase notebooks and paper of local style and dimension for your work. Purchase carbon paper, too, and make copies of your work.

- Appliances: Do without them or buy a local version and sell it or give it away at the end of the year.

- Because U.S. brands are more expensive than local brands, consider adopting some local brands if you have time to shop when your supplies run out. If in doubt, ask a returning student.

The Unofficial Packing Checklist

- [ ] Traveling alarm clock (with batteries) and a light (optional) so that you can read at night

- [ ] Tiny plastic spray bottle

- [ ] Insulated lunch sack (optional)

- [ ] Toothbrush, floss, toothpaste

- [ ] Pocket knife

- [ ] Pocket flash light

- [ ] Picnic set for eating while traveling or for lighter meals in the dorm

- [ ] Laundry bag

- [ ] Cord and clothespins (can be bought on arrival)

- [ ] Toilet paper
- [ ] Travel towelettes
- [ ] Jeans (one or two pair)
- [ ] Luggage locks
- [ ] Comb, hair brush
- [ ] Back-up disks to protect against loss of computer work
- [ ] Warm shirts (depending on climate)
- [ ] T-shirts
- [ ] Underwear (five sets)
- [ ] Heavy sweater
- [ ] Towel and soap
- [ ] Raingear
- [ ] Nail clippers
- [ ] Nail file
- [ ] Bathing suit
- [ ] Plastic sandals (for shower)
- [ ] Bathrobe
- [ ] Antiseptic cream
- [ ] Decongestants
- [ ] Cold care products
- [ ] Vitamins (optional)
- [ ] Extra ID photos
- [ ] Dress slacks (one pair)
- [ ] Walking shoes (two pair, one can do for dress)
- [ ] Jacket (one—not needed for short summer programs)
- [ ] Warm tops (two or three, depending on prevailing climate)
- [ ] Sunglasses

- ☐ Camera
- ☐ Film
- ☐ Pictures of home and family
- ☐ Favorite music from home
- ☐ Copies of your passport, traveler's checks, and other documents
- ☐ Men: dress shirts (one)
- ☐ Women: jeans or slacks (two pair)

For Your Carry-on Luggage

- ☐ Important phone numbers and addresses
- ☐ An extra layer in case the plane is chilly or the weather is colder where you're going
- ☐ Reading material
- ☐ Passport
- ☐ Letter of admission to program
- ☐ Traveler's checks
- ☐ Bank or credit cards
- ☐ Emergency contact address and phone in host country
- ☐ Mosquito repellent, bug spray
- ☐ Brush, comb, towelettes, and toothbrush
- ☐ Valuables, medication, contact lens fluid
- ☐ A dictionary for the language you are studying
- ☐ A change of clothes

Just the Facts

- Do your homework and be ready for local weather conditions.

- Take only what you can manage by yourself.

- Review your travel schedule; pack to have what you need when you need it.

- Be sure you can lock your luggage and protect your possessions.

- Leave valuables at home.

GET THE SCOOP ON...
Traveling safely when you're traveling for the
first time ▪ The basics of overseas travel ▪
Dealing with travel snafus ▪ Coping with arrival
and jet lag

Making the Trip

Chapter 16

If this is one of your first trips, you might feel a mixture of excitement and apprehension. There are many things you need to keep track of when you travel internationally. You might be worried about who will meet you and how you will get to your destination. Your parents might be concerned about your safety while traveling and when you arrive in a new country. There are several things to keep in mind and to plan in order to make your trip a safe, comfortable one.

Traveling Safely When You're Traveling for the First Time

Here are some safety tips for your international flight and first days in the country.

Your Luggage

- Don't accept any package, or put anything in your luggage, that is given to you by a person you don't know.

- Keep valuable items such as your passport, computer, traveler's checks, and camera to a

317

minimum, and carry them with you on the airplane. Don't put them in your checked luggage.

- Don't leave your luggage unattended. Besides being stolen, your suitcase could be suspected of containing a bomb. Officials might destroy harmless luggage when the fear of bomb threats is high.

- Never pack money in your suitcase.

- Leave valuable jewelry and sports equipment at home.

- Lock your luggage and be sure the luggage tags have a contact address and phone number (preferably a business address).

- Don't expect to find lockers in train stations and airports where you can leave your luggage. You might find these in some countries (Spain and Germany still have them), but other countries such as the U.K. have eliminated them because of bomb scares.

- Never make joking comments or any other remarks about carrying harmful items in your luggage. Airport officials are required to investigate and might even arrest persons who make chance remarks.

- During the flight, keep track of your portable tape deck, if you have one with you, and your other possessions. Don't leave your return ticket on the plane!

- Dress in a way that blends in with thousands of other international travelers. Avoid wearing T-shirts, sweatshirts, or hats with logos proclaiming your college affiliation or any other U.S. city or team connection.

- In public, be as discrete as possible about who you are and where you are headed.

- Be careful about discussing your travel plans loudly in public. This includes talking about your destination, valuable items, the amount of money you are carrying, and your travel schedule.

The Basics of Overseas Travel

Call the airline about two days before your date of travel and confirm your flight. Give your frequent flyer number and request a special meal if you want one. If you are traveling with a group on a student flight, don't expect your registration to be in the computer by name before the week of the flight. Your registration will probably be held in the name of the travel agent until the week you travel.

Be at the airport in the terminal building two hours ahead of time. Have your passport ready with your ticket at the check-in counter. Your visa will be checked, and you will need the right credentials to board the plane.

Allow plenty of time to get to the boarding gate. In some airports, the international check-in can be crowded at certain times and so can the security check-ins. It might take some time to get to the gate by rail, van, or underground walkways. Your family can go with you to the gate. There are usually restaurants and shops where you can have a last snack with them. Be prepared for boarding to start earlier than with domestic flights and for the final call to come earlier.

Be alert when you go through the airport security system. It is safest to wait with your computer until the gate is clear or until a friend has gone

Watch Out!
Before I went abroad, I talked on a public phone about having a scholarship check for my semester of study. Right afterwards, I met a guy who looked like a student. He talked about how short of cash he was. He began borrowing money from me, and before I knew it, he got my whole scholarship. He was a con artist. Fortunately, he was later caught.

Timesaver
I always put lit-
tle, important
things such as
receipts, pass-
ports, or keys in
a "little impor-
tant place." I
never proceed
until I have
stored these
items carefully,
remembering
where I put them
so I can get
them out again
when I need
them. This tech-
nique helps me
keep track of
tickets, parking
meter slips, and
any of those
easy-to-lose but
essential pieces
of paper.

through the security check-in ahead of you. Place your laptop on the conveyer belt and walk through the security gate when there is nobody ahead of you holding up the line. There have been a few incidents in which a supposed traveler deliberately sets off the alarm at the security gate. Then, the other passengers are forced to wait while security personnel check this person for metallic items. In the meantime, a partner picks up a laptop that had just gone through the x-ray machine and makes off with it.

On the Plane

As soon as you get settled in your seat, find a good place to store your plane ticket. Remember, you need the rest of the ticket to get home again!

Early in the flight, you are given a landing card to fill out. This is a very important document. Few people realize that this card determines your status when you enter the country. It is stamped by immigration officials when you deplane, indicating your status (tourist, temporary worker, student, medical worker, and so on). They mark the card to show how long you can remain in the country. The card asks you for an address in the country. Have a hotel or other contact address handy to enter on the card. You might want to put the address of your university from your letter of admission.

They also ask you some questions for customs inspection. You are asked to declare any valuable items you are bringing into the country, such as cameras, computers, and so on. If you have nothing brand new, you should not declare anything. You might be charged import taxes on a brand new item of value unless you can prove that it is for your personal use and not for sale.

After the immigration inspector stamps the card and your passport, you should keep the card in your passport until you leave the country. For students who plan to be in the country for a semester or year, this is particularly important. Keep with the landing card any papers associated with your visa application and do not misplace them during your stay in the country. These papers might be necessary to confirm your student status in your destination country.

Have something warm to wear when the plane cools off. Take along an eye mask so that you can sleep without being bothered by the movie or by light and activity in the plane's cabin. Plan to use something as a roll to support your back and be sure to get a pillow from the flight attendants so that you can rest.

Avoid eating salty things and drink as much plain, fresh water as you can. Eat fresh fruits and vegetables and limit your use of alcohol and sodium-based drinks (sodas). These strategies will prevent you from becoming dehydrated during the flight. The combination of inactivity and dehydration on a long plane trip can leave you constipated and very uncomfortable during your first day or two in the country. Leave your seat and move around, or stand up and stretch frequently.

This is a good time to store your dollars, especially your U.S. coins, and to look over the currency of the destination country so that you can become familiar with the size, shape, and denomination of the different bills and coins.

Read any material that the program planners gave you to study on the plane. It might contain important information about the arrangements for meeting your flight and precautions or tips for your first day in the host country.

Be very sure of any flight connections you have along the way and the name of the airport at which you will finally disembark. More than one traveler has gotten off the plane or train at the wrong stop. When you arrive at your final international air destination, proceed to the immigration desk. Have your passport, landing card, and the letter of admission to your university available to show the immigration inspectors. They might ask to see your return ticket.

Next, you proceed to baggage claim. If you haven't already done so, you might want to step into a washroom and clean up a little before claiming your bags, but don't delay too long because another traveler might mistakenly pick up your bag. After you get your bags, you exit through the door marked "Nothing to Declare" and enter the international arrival hall of the airport. This is the first point at which waiting people can greet international travelers. Here, you might be met by the driver or guide who is waiting to take your group to the hotel or program site.

If you are traveling from one country to another on the train, the conductor asks to see your passport as well as your ticket. Sometimes, the conductor keeps your passport until you are close to your destination. Again, be very sure of the name of the train station where you get off. Many big cities have several major train stations, and your train might stop at more than one of them.

If you plan to travel on a sleeper train, it might be worth the money to get a single room or a double to share with a friend. The cost does not include the basic train fare (which might be covered by your Europass, if you have one). It is usually about the same as a three-star hotel room in a major European city (about $100). A double, of course, is cheaper.

You can get a good night's sleep on the train and save the whole following day for sightseeing at your destination. You can often take a shower, change clothes, and arrive ready for the day's activities.

If you choose a sleeper with four or more people, the arrangements are less convenient. You can request a compartment with all women or all men. However, you still might not have much privacy to clean up and change clothes completely. Secondly, you must be extremely careful with your belongings. There is not much physical danger or risk that another passenger will steal anything because the conductor takes the tickets, watches the passengers carefully, and does not give back the tickets until it is time for each passenger to get off. The risk is that you might have to get off the train in the dark while others in the compartment are still asleep. It is easy to leave something behind in total darkness. People have left keys, hotel reservations, or even plane tickets on the train in a tote they were carrying with their suitcase and left behind in the dark. Furthermore, it is not possible to clean up properly until you get to your destination.

Dealing with Travel Snafus

The most serious travel snafu that can occur is to enter a country without the proper visa for the purpose and length of your stay. The United States has visa waiver agreements with an increasing number of countries. This makes it easy to enter for 90 days, either for business or pleasure, without needing any kind of visa. However, if you plan to stay a longer time, you must have a visa. It is usually impossible to enter a country with a visa waiver and then change to the status you need. The immigration inspectors might require you to go back home and apply for the right type of visa, which would be upsetting, inconvenient, and very expensive. Therefore, you should be sure to read Chapter 12, "Applying for Your Visa."

Replacing Lost or Defective Tickets

If you lose your ticket, contact your travel agent. The agent can fax you a photocopy of the original ticket. Take the photocopy to the airport on the day of your departure and explain the circumstances of the loss. The airline can usually replace a ticket for approximately $75. If there is a problem with the ticket, the airline can usually replace it, also for $75. Keep your receipts. If any changes have to be made as a result of errors by the agent who sold you the ticket, you can request a refund of some part of your expenses.

If you make hotel reservations through a reservation service, either in the United States or in the country where you are traveling, the agent has a record of the reservations and can provide you with the information if you lose your receipt.

Train tickets and passes can also be replaced if you have records of your reservations. Most other difficulties can be resolved if you know how to reach your destination.

City Smarts

Here are some helpful travel safety tips:

- When you reach your destination, be alert in crowded areas and in cities.

- Be careful with your belongings when you are out in public. See Chapter 15, "What to Pack," for suggestions of ways to carry your belongings and safeguard them.

- Do not leave purses or other valuables in any place where someone could easily grab them

Bright Idea
Memorize as much of your itinerary as you can. Learn useful addresses and phone numbers by heart. If your wallet or backpack is stolen, you might not have the numbers that you need to call. If you are upset by a robbery or any other emergency, you might find it difficult to find your emergency contact's street or house by sight. Know the numbers you need.

and run away. People have lost valuable items on the pew in a church, under the seat in a movie theater, on a table or chair in an outdoor café, and in the overhead compartment of a train.

- Avoid carrying your camera or purse on a strap over your shoulder in crowded areas. Someone could cut the strap, grab the camera, and run off into the crowd.

- Carry your money in an inside pocket or use a money belt that is difficult for pickpockets to reach.

- Lock your hotel room door whenever you leave it, even for a moment, and when you are asleep inside.

- In public, don't discuss where you are staying, especially when you will be *away* from your room. It is easy to assume that people talking other languages all around you don't understand you when you speak English. However, many people do understand and might be paying more attention than you think they are.

Some Special Precautions for Women

In some parts of the world, particularly in Southern Europe and parts of Latin America, young women might be bothered and even harassed in public if their dress and behavior set them apart from local women. Men might follow you, whistle, make comments, and try to strike up a conversation. They might assume that you do not speak the language as well as they do and that you might feel somewhat at a disadvantage. Or they might simply make assumptions based on your clothing and behavior. In general, this attention is annoying but not threatening.

A Student Speaks Up
My Japanese host family talked openly about the size of my breasts and the women would walk up and take hold of them. They treated the differences in my body shape as a curiosity and talked about them as if I didn't have any feelings. After a while, I began dressing to conceal my body shape.

Local women usually ignore them or vehemently tell them to get lost. Ask your resident director to teach you what to say to get across the idea that you are annoyed and want them to go away. Take note of the colors of clothing that people wear locally. You might observe that European women dress in more subdued colors than Americans do.

If you smile and act friendly, men could become more aggressive. Don't make eye contact while out in the street, but walk briskly and look busy. It is always better not to engage by responding to remarks or to anyone trying to flirt with you. Avoid appearing frightened or helpless by keeping a distinction in your mind between an effort to pick you up and a real threat. If you find it necessary to say something to frighten off a pest, use the language of the country. Learn some aggressive expressions that mean. "Go away," "Leave me alone," "I'm not interested," and "I'll call the police."

Try to go out in groups. Avoid standing alone on the street to meet a friend. Arrange to meet in a café or store where you can be busy and mingle with a crowd. Never go out alone after dark. Be observant of local clothing and behavior patterns. If local women are not wearing skirts, shorts, or sleeveless tops, don't wear them yourself. If local students don't carry backpacks, arrange to carry your books and gear in another, less conspicuous fashion. In time, as you become used to the strategies for minimizing this attention, it will probably decrease.

Women should not go out alone at night. If you think you are being followed on a bus or subway, get off the subway quickly and simply change cars. Try to get off the subway or bus quickly without giving out any signals ahead of time that you are coming to your stop. These tricks make it difficult to be followed.

Strikes

In the event of a strike involving American carriers or carriers serving the United States, there are several different ways in which other airlines assist travelers. During the first few days of the strike, other carriers do their best to accommodate travelers on a space available basis, especially those trying to get home.

If the airline is unable to resolve the strike immediately and you have tickets for a departure date that is fast approaching, it is the carrier's responsibility to help passengers. If you are traveling on a group flight arranged through your program, the program sponsor is usually not responsible for booking you on a carrier that is experiencing a strike. However, the program will probably make every effort to help you by working with the carrier or travel agency to find alternatives. Its goal is to have the program start on time. If necessary, the program might choose to postpone or reschedule some program events in the event of a longer strike.

In some countries, strikes are a customary way of exerting pressure on the government. Strikes of government employees might make it unsafe for airlines to fly into the country for a period of time. Fortunately for you, a general strike affects not only students planning to study abroad, but also all the service industries supporting tourism in that country. For this reason, airlines are usually under pressure from hotels, resorts, restaurants, and all the other service industries to resolve labor disputes quickly, especially if the carrier serves a country that relies heavily on tourism at certain times of the year.

> **"**
> If you are out at night (preferably not alone), visualize, before anyone approaches, what you could do to protect yourself. Hold an object like a key and imagine using it to defend yourself, or work out what you would say. Use the language of the country. Imagine shouting loudly to help you overcome any sense of timidity. Keep to well-lighted streets.
> **"**

It is probably safe to say that threats of an airline strike during a peak period of tourist and student travel to a popular destination, such as Europe, are going to see a quick resolution.

Know How to Reach Your Destination

Although 90 percent of all travelers get to their destination without incident, there can be delays or other problems in communication. If you are traveling to your international point of departure on a connecting flight, be sure that you have a plan in case your flight is delayed by weather or by other factors. It is usually best to have one travel agent or airline book the entire flight so that you have guaranteed connections. Go to the Web and get a map of the terminal at each point in your trip. Know in advance how to get from your arrival gate or terminal to the terminal where you will check in for your next flight. Make sure your airline can put you up overnight if you miss your international flight because of a weather delay. Have the study abroad program's U.S. office number to call in case of a problem. It will alert the people who are supposed to meet you at the other end of your international flight.

It is not unusual for someone's bag to be missing when the group arrives at its destination. Many times, this happens because another traveler mistakenly took your bag and failed to claim his own. These mistakes usually get sorted out in one or two days. Similarly, if the bag was placed on the wrong flight or missed the flight, it is usually recovered within several days. Be sure that you have all the addresses where you will stay in the first few days after you arrive. If your bag happens to be lost, you can give the addresses to the airline and have it delivered to you when it is found. Have several copies of your itinerary with names, addresses, phone numbers, and reservation numbers. Having photocopies of your tickets, passport, and other information makes it easier to replace anything lost along the way.

If your faculty director is not traveling with you, be sure you and your group have a back-up plan in case the director or guide does not meet you. Everyone in the group should have a map and the address and phone number of your hotel so that you can get to the hotel on your own if necessary. Find out how the bus will be marked and where it will be located so that you can find it outside the airport if necessary.

If you are traveling on your own to meet a group, it is especially important to have a map and the address and phone number of the place where you will meet the group. You should carry an extra set of instructions and emergency contact information in your luggage so that you can connect with your group in the event of any problems along the way.

Finding Transportation to Your Study Site

There are several ways in which programs can arrange for you to get from your international arrival point to the program site. If you are being met, have a back-up plan in case of problems.

If you need to arrange your own transportation to your final destination, purchase a student guide well in advance of your trip. Plan to pack light so that you can manage your luggage when you make your connections. Read carefully the descriptions of various travel options for getting to your destination. Calculate the costs, and plan to have currency on hand to cover the costs of your bus or subway

Watch Out!
I got off the train at 3 a.m. I left the folder with my hotel reservations, itinerary, and plane on the train. Fortunately, I had copied the entire itinerary into my computer. Its battery allowed me to turn the computer on and find the name and address of our hotel. Later, I was able to replace my ticket and reservations.

ride and cab fare on the first day. If you plan to carry a lot of luggage, consider spending your first night in the city where your international flight arrives and taking the train to your final destination on the following day. You can take a cab, bus, or subway to the city center and take a second cab to the train station (usually located in the city center) on the following day. You will find that cabs vary greatly in price from one city to another. If you can manage your bags easily and arrive during the daytime, you can probably use public transportation. Good, reasonably priced connections are usually available to whisk you from the airport to the city center. From your downtown arrival point, it is much cheaper to take a cab to your hotel. Again, read your guidebooks carefully and ask your study abroad advisor or teachers for advice about getting around the city where your flight arrives.

Arrange to have at least $100 worth of the host country currency available when you arrive. (See Chapter 13, "Sending Money and Making Payments.") Find out how the airport is laid out (again, try the Web for this information or consult the travel guides), and know where to get ground transportation. At the airport, follow the signs for buses, cabs, or trains to the point of departure for your connecting trip.

There will probably be two options for you. The first is to take public transportation into the city center to catch a train or an inter-city bus. The second is to catch a bus or train-bus linkage directly from the airport to your final destination. Most major airports in other countries have convenient train or bus connections to town as well as linkages to other cities. If you need to, talk to someone who has used the airport and made the same connections. Find out more about where to buy tickets, what sign to look for, and how much money to have out and ready.

Preparing For and Recovering from Jet Lag

Jet lag is the name for the fatigue and disorientation your body feels when it is transported by jet plane from its normal daily routine to a new location. When it is suddenly forced to live by a schedule 5 to 12 hours different from the one it is accustomed to, it rebels in several ways.

These are some of the signs of jet lag:

- Sudden extreme sleepiness in the middle of the day.

- Feeling wide awake in the middle of the night.

- Not feeling hungry at meal times or feeling hungry soon after eating.

- Temporary memory loss and irritability.

- Constipation or other digestive upsets.

- Dizziness or a mild sensation that the ground is moving beneath you.

These symptoms might occur for a day or two, gradually diminishing over a week. Most people say they have more trouble going from West to East than from East to West. You can do several things to minimize the effects of jet lag.

Some business travelers, knowing that they have to be ready to function at their best when they arrive at a location around the globe, have made a science of preparing in advance for jet lag. For several days before their departure, they adjust their meals and sleep times to correspond to the ones in the country

> **66**
> It's an interesting cultural experience to observe how people handle themselves in public. You might notice in certain countries that people don't smile as much or look one another in the eye (an urban phenomenon). An easy friendliness might be met with suspicion in some countries; a non-motivated smile can mean that you want something or are just hypocritical.
> **99**

they are going to. When they arrive, the shift to a new routine is not as abrupt. This method of adjusting your meal habits in advance is a surprisingly effective way of minimizing jet lag, but it is too much bother for most people, who simply adjust after they arrive. Most people find that the best way to overcome jet lag is to adopt the routine of the new location as completely as possible right from the start. Sleep on the plane so that you won't be excessively tired when you arrive. Avoid drinking alcohol on the plane and when you first arrive. Alcohol makes you sleepy at first, but when it wears off a few hours later, you will find it difficult to sleep. Drink as much water as you can on the plane and avoid salty foods that dehydrate you.

If it is evening in the new country when you arrive, eat dinner without any coffee or tea and go to bed, even if you are too excited to sleep. If it is daytime, stay up for the rest of the day and eat meals at the normal times for your new location. Try not to take a nap during the day. You will probably feel very sleepy by dinnertime, but try to keep busy, eat dinner, and stay up as late as you can. During the night, if you wake up, resist the temptation to get up and read, to write letters, or to watch television. Stay in bed, relax, breathe deeply, and help your body adjust to a new sleeping schedule. Get up early the next morning, eat a light breakfast, and keep physically active during the entire day. Continue to drink as much water as possible (you might need to buy bottled water to have on hand during a long day of touring). This helps your digestive system to adjust to its new schedule.

Eating plenty of fresh vegetables and fruits also helps your digestive system readjust. If you are in an area where it is best not to eat certain kinds of fresh produce from local vendors, buy fruits you can peel. Order plenty of cooked or fresh fruits and vegetables in a hotel or restaurant where your guide tells you it is safe to do so. A light evening meal that includes pasta, bread, or other starches will help you sleep better. In theory, you should continue to avoid coffee and other stimulants, alcohol, and spicy foods. All of these can disrupt your body's routine. On the other hand, you will be excited about being in a new place and trying the country's specialties. Just do your best to be moderate during the first few days because it will help you get over jet lag more quickly.

Think of the process as training your body to a new schedule for eating, sleeping, and activity. As hard as it is to stay awake and busy during those sleepy times, or to remain in bed when you feel wide awake, the more completely you observe the schedule of your new surroundings, the quicker you will get over your jet lag.

Getting Rested and Ready for the First Few Days

The first few days in your new country will be very exciting and tiring in many ways. In addition to getting used to new surroundings and finding your way around, you will be adjusting to a whole new way of doing things.

The water, the phones, the transportation system, the regulations, the way people respond to you in public, and the attitudes of people in charge will all be unfamiliar to you. You will be looking for places to change your money, worried about how much things cost. You might be participating in orientation tours that keep you moving at a tiring pace. You might need to buy some small medical item—perhaps a bandage for that blister you are getting from your new walking shoes; however, there isn't

Unofficially...
Traveling alone in Europe, I started feeling homesick. I had trouble getting the film out of my camera, ruined a whole roll, and burst into tears. Eventually, the moment of culture shock passed and I began to enjoy the Amsterdam scene: boats passing, ducks calling, and warmly lighted homes on the other side of the canal.

time to find a pharmacy or the guide does not seem concerned about helping you.

Like many students, you may have promised to call your parents as soon as you arrived. You were thinking of the easy access to telephones you usually have in American hotels and in American homes. However, it is different on a student tour. You might not have a telephone in your room. Your host family might not have a working telephone. The busy schedule of the orientation might not leave you a free moment to find a phone and learn how to use it, or perhaps you're having trouble using your calling card. You take several days to write a letter and finally have an opportunity to buy stamps for it, but your tour schedule doesn't give you time to find a mailbox before crossing the border into another country. Now, you have to start all over again to buy new stamps and your first letter home is getting badly out of date. Most programs anticipate these difficulties and send a reassuring fax or e-mail to alert the program office and families that the group has arrived safely, but as a student, you feel frustrated when you can't contact your family and friends right away.

All travelers experience some of these irritations when they get out of their familiar territories and routines. The frustrations are aggravated by the newness of the countries you are visiting, the strange accents or wholly new languages you hear all around you, and the differences you encounter in all of the basic ways of taking care of things. The stores are organized differently and are open for business on different schedules. You might arrive in some towns late in the evening after many of the retail shops and services are closed. On the one hand, you are excited to be in the places that you have come such a long way to see. You are eager to meet the people you will be with for the semester or year. On the other hand, you are experiencing a lot of stress as you try to deal with so many unexpected new situations that you cannot control. This stress will come on top of the physical adjustment to jet lag.

It is not surprising that many people display unusual irritability during the first few days. On top of all the newness of the country, perhaps you have to cope with something that really goes wrong, such as having the airlines lose your suitcase temporarily or having the hotel lose your reservation. It might seem to you at times that the whole group wants to do one thing and you would rather do something very different. Suddenly, a little thing takes on enormous importance. There are outbursts of temper over various frustrating bits of red tape, such as getting a bus pass or paying a security deposit for a key. You are furious with your program administrators, or the host university, or your roommates, or the landlady. You feel that somebody must be to blame for all the problems you are having.

The best strategy for coping with the first few days is to get plenty of rest. Wise program administrators give students time to relax and have a little privacy. Take advantage of these moments to slow down whenever you can. Your body needs time to get used to the new routine. It can be reassuring to take the time for some small activity over which you have complete control, such as reorganizing your suitcase, putting your feet up for a few minutes, taking a short nap, or getting some refreshments. Little by little, the areas of your life over which you have control will increase as you get acclimated to your new surroundings.

**A Student
Speaks Up**
My landlady was
wonderful. She
did everything
for us and her
meals were fabu-
lous. People who
spent all their
time with
Americans should
just ask them-
selves why they
came in the
first place.

Settling In: Meeting Your Fellow Students and Hosts

If you want to get the most out of your program, the sooner you can begin meeting people, the better.

The people you meet will be the most important part of your study abroad experience. They determine whether you come home feeling you had an experience that was not quite up to the standard of life at your home university or feeling that you have a new home in the country you lived in for a time.

You can choose either to spend most of your time with the Americans who came with your group, some of whom you may not have met before, or to spend as much time as possible with people from the country. American students who get to know people from the host country are almost always the ones who enjoy their experience the most, improve their language skills the most, and make contact with the country a part of their careers. Those who stay with Americans might do well in their classes and enjoy what they see of the history of the country and its monuments, but they are also likely to be the ones who complain the most about the differences between the cultures. They might come home feeling that the program did not meet their expectations for the quality of the housing, the teaching, and the excursions.

Do not expect housing, meals, university facilities, and services to equal those in the United States. The cost of providing comparable services in other countries is much higher than students can usually afford. Tourists who travel in American-style comfort are often isolated in a bubble from which they can look out at what is picturesque in the country, but they can never understand it.

There are two ways to benefit from a host family. The first is to enroll in a program that offers home stays. It is important to have realistic expectations about home stays and to know what type of opportunity it will be. In some home stays, the families expect to offer most or all meals to the students and to make them as much as possible a part of the family. The hostess takes a lively interest in her guests and makes every effort to make them feel at home. In other cases, the arrangement might simply offer a room and certain kitchen privileges. When you choose your program, you should make sure which type of arrangement to expect.

The second type of host family arrangement is a social rather than a living arrangement. Families from the community who are interested in getting to know American students sign up to host them once or twice a month. They might invite the students to a family meal, take them on an excursion, or include them in an outing to meet their extended family. The people who become involved in these host family arrangements are sincerely interested in getting to know you. Give yourself a chance to become acquainted. Don't place your expectations too high. You might not hit it off immediately or find them like the families you know from the United States. Continue to spend time with them anyway. You might find the relationship warming up as time goes on, particularly if your language skills are improving. Whatever the connection turns out to be, you will undoubtedly learn a great deal about the culture from these contacts and they will be excellent for your language learning.

If there are many American students at your program site, it might be more difficult at first to meet

**A Student
Speaks Up**
I didn't live with
a family in Paris,
but I joined the
Chorale de La
Sorbonne. I met
some profes-
sional musicians
and met with
them every
Sunday to have
dinner and sight
read madrigals.
Soon, I made
other friends
who were orga-
nizing a choir
and orchestra
tour. We traveled
all over France
during spring
vacation, staying
in people's
homes and per-
forming in
cathedrals and
châteaux.

the degree-seeking students. However, you should take every opportunity your program offers to get to know them. Some of the best opportunities for doing this come in community activities and events planned by student groups from the university. Take stock of your interests and find out whether any groups would help you meet students with similar interests. Join a choir, sign up for yoga lessons, get involved in a sport, join a film discussion group, or find a service organization through which you might volunteer for a community project. One student joined the town bridge club. Another signed up for early morning tai chi lessons. The wife of a Fulbright scholar joined the women's basketball team at the University of Heidelberg and traveled all over Europe with them, improving her German all the while.

In some countries, the residence halls organize much of the social life of the university. In other countries, there is little formal activity in the residence halls, but they still might offer you an excellent way of making friends. In Paris, the international university city located in the southern part of the city offers an excellent opportunity for students from all over the world to meet and share common interests. The residents organize concerts, art exhibits, lectures, and other events. Each of the halls is supported by sponsors from a single country (Mexico, Denmark, Brazil, Canada, the United States), but students from many other countries and from France are welcome to live in each hall. In other towns where there is no university city, American students get to know other students by taking swimming lessons, joining a drama group at the local recreation center or cultural center, or joining a cycling or skiing club.

Just the Facts

- Good planning ensures a safe trip.
- Keep good records of your documents and travel arrangements.
- Give yourself time to rest and get used to the new routine.
- Take opportunities to get to know your host family and students from the host country.

Being There: Having a Successful Study Abroad Experience

PART V

GET THE SCOOP ON...
Coping with culture shock ▪ Getting along with
your host family ▪ Dealing with red tape ▪ What
to do if you get sick

First Things First: Getting Settled

Chapter 17

What is culture shock? This term refers to the feeling of confusion that often occurs when a person leaves a familiar place and moves to an unfamiliar one. You are learning a great deal very quickly. Everything is different, down to the ways of solving the most basic problems. It is tiring to have to learn everything from scratch. It leaves you feeling helpless and out of control. Different people react differently to culture shock, although almost everyone must cope with it to some degree.

Whatever the length of the study abroad experience you have chosen, many of you will experience similar emotions as you adjust to life abroad. At first, you will probably be delighted with your new surroundings. Later, you might begin to feel frustrated because people do not respond as you expect when you request assistance. Learning where to find supplies and how to take care of basic needs will occupy

343

> I would like to prepare you for culture shock and the [country's] mentality, but I think you will discover that on your own. It is the fear and anxiety of living in a completely alien society without the ability to articulate your feelings fully. Eventually, you will enjoy your experience or at least look back on those times fondly and just reminisce.

much of your time. If you do not make allowances for this adjustment, you can easily become tired, which can make you more susceptible to illness or feelings of sadness, discouragement, and irritation.

Students have several suggestions for getting through difficult periods:

- Get plenty of rest at the beginning and try not to do everything at once.

- At the same time, don't give up. Take a break if you need to, but keep trying.

- Try to be flexible; expect surprises.

- Try to understand the differences you encounter from the perspective of the host culture or to "see yourself as the host culture sees you."

- Keep your sense of humor.

- Don't be too hard on yourself; other people are going through the same thing.

- Try not to let your expectations get too high so that you won't feel disappointed.

Things will get better, but you can expect difficult times to come along periodically. Although people are willing to help, neither the host institution nor your home college or university can guarantee that your experience will always go as smoothly as if you were back at home. Leaving college life in the United States for life in another country, you might find some differences overwhelming at times. The food is not what you are accustomed to, and the people look, speak, and act differently from people at home. Taking care of many simple daily tasks can be more tiring and stressful in a new location because there are so many new things to learn. You might be farther away from family and friends than you have ever been before.

If you are prepared for this adjustment, however, you might find that you are able to settle into your new surroundings with relative ease. Here are some traits that students find particularly helpful in adapting to new situations:

- A sense of humor
- Ability to fail and keep going
- Willingness to expect the unexpected
- A desire to understand the internal logic of the culture in which you find yourself

Feelings of discouragement are usually the strongest at about the midpoint of your stay abroad, no matter how long you stay. Those of you who are abroad for the entire year might feel that you have reached a temporary low point as winter weather drags on and the rapid pace of learning that you experience earlier in the year begins to slow down.

As the end of your stay abroad approaches, however, these feelings will disappear. Instead, you will be in a hurry to do all the sightseeing, try all the unique foods, and attend all the cultural events you haven't yet tried. You will want to spend as much time as possible with new friends and you might even begin to plan for a return trip to the host country. By the time you get back to your home campus, you will find yourself missing all those wonderful foods and good times from your semester or year abroad. If that happens to you, you'll know that you are experiencing "reverse culture shock!" For more about the process of getting used to being home again, see Chapter 20, "The Unofficial Guide to Re-Entry."

A Student Speaks Up
A word about attitude: Keep an open mind, a willingness to learn, and a sense of adventure. [A developing country] will be hard on you, physically and emotionally. Don't become negative, complain, or give in. Instead, be open to meeting as many [local] people, from all walks of life, as you can, and be open to learning their ways.

Unofficially...
As a French person teaching Americans, I found that it is difficult for Americans to open up and talk about their feelings. They think something is terribly wrong if you discuss sharing the bathroom or using the kitchen or anything like that.

Getting Along with Your Host Family

Many people have excellent relations with their host families. Some students do not find the arrangements compatible. If you are having trouble with your host family for any reason, alert the program administrators as soon as possible so that the situation can be investigated. Usually, some discussion and a solution can be worked out if the situation is mentioned early in your stay. As an earlier chapter stated, the first thing you need to do is to get a clear sense of the host family's priorities in offering you a place to live. If they have a genuine interest in providing a cultural experience for you, you can look forward to a rewarding experience. If their primary purpose is financial, then you know in advance to look for your cultural enrichment elsewhere. However, you should be aware that you cannot make any assumptions, and the more you can learn about what the host family expects, the friendlier your relations with them will be.

Even if the arrangement is primarily a financial one, you are a guest in the family's home. It is your responsibility to be as considerate as possible and to make sure you understand the family's "ground rules." Assume that the family is genuinely concerned about your well-being and comfort. Do your best to keep them informed about your plans and to get their permission before you use anything.

Find an appropriate time to ask tactfully about some of the arrangements. If your language skills make it difficult for you to converse, arrange for someone who is more fluent to help you clarify things with your host family. Explain that some habits are very different in your home country, so you want to make sure that you don't use too much hot water and electricity and that you know about meal times and the time to come home in the evening. They will appreciate your concern.

Supplies and Laundry

Electricity and hot water are very expensive in other countries, so be sure that you understand how the family wants you to take care of your laundry. Offer to wash your sheets and towel as well as your other laundry yourself, and ask how often they want you to use the machine (if there is one in the home). If the host mother expects to take care of these for you, she will probably let you know right away. Find out whether there is a time of day to do the washing because the rates are lower. If the family prefers for you to do your personal laundry at a Laundromat, they will let you know.

Telephone

Use of the telephone is another item that is much more expensive in other countries than in the United States. Your host family, landlord, or program is charged for each local call you make from their telephones, as well as for long-distance calls. Expect to pay for any use of the telephone. Because of the high cost of phone service, there may or may not be a working telephone in the household. If you live with a family, tell them you are aware of the cost and ask whether you can use the telephone and reimburse the family for calls. This might be difficult if your stay is short because telephone bills come one or two months after the call is made. If you think your use of the phone might be a problem for the family, make every effort to place international calls at a public telephone booth through a calling card or find out how to make those calls from a public phone or from the central post office.

Moneysaver
As mentioned earlier, you might find it more comfortable, and also less expensive, to live in a residence hall or apartment and get to know a host country family through regular social contact.

Although your program's administrative office might have e-mail and a fax machine, a long-distance call might be involved in connecting to the e-mail service, as well as in sending international faxes. Therefore, even these services are apt to be more expensive than in the United States. Be prepared to cover the expense and to be moderate in the use of any services involving the telephone.

Electricity

Ask about the use of electricity after dark. Electricity is very costly in most parts of the world. The family needs for you to turn out all lights whenever you leave a room. Be very careful about this. If you are used to studying in your room in the evening, discuss your usual study patterns and see whether this is all right with the family. If they use the space for other purposes during waking hours or if they prefer to have lights out by a certain time, you might have to adjust your study schedule. Are they looking forward to having you visit with the family after dinner rather than studying? If you sense that it will be awkward for you to study in your room in the evening, plan to do more studying at the library, in the park, or at the university during daylight hours.

Meal Times

Find out what the usual meal times are. Lunch and dinner might come several hours later than in the United States. If the program has not already determined the number of meals you will have with the family each week, this is a good time to work out a meal schedule. Offer to help fix meals and be useful in the kitchen. (This is a great way to learn some delicious recipes!) Find out whether you can use a little space in the refrigerator to store a few items for your lunch. If not, ask whether you can keep food in your room. (If insects are a problem, the family might prefer that you not do this.) If you are expected to fix some of your own meals, find out what sort of schedule is possible. Assume that you must provide your own staples (oil, flour, salt, coffee, and so on), and don't use any of the family's supplies unless they invite you to do so.

Bathing Schedules

Because of the cost of hot water, be sensitive to the family's bath schedule and don't take a shower every day unless they indicate that this is acceptable. Always assume that you must provide your own soap, shampoo, and other toiletries, and don't use theirs unless specifically invited to do so.

Adjusting to New Time Schedules

Discuss the time when the family would like for you to return at night. Most families, especially in the city, want the doors safely locked, everyone at home, and lights out by a certain time. If the family is used to a more flexible schedule, they will probably give you a key and let you know their preferences. Be considerate and let your landlady know when you will be back. Even if she seems rather brusque and businesslike, she will probably worry about you.

The host family might not recognize that you want to sleep at hours different from theirs or that you want quiet in order to study in the evening. In some countries such as Japan, space is limited. You might be expected to share sleeping quarters with family members at night, and during the day, the family might have other uses for that space. Because privacy is at a premium, respect the family rules. In Europe, you are expected to keep doors shut, even the door to the WC. (Bathrooms are sometimes called water closets in England.)

You might need to adjust to the mid-day rest period that many cultures observe. In some of the hottest parts of the world, people actually go to bed and sleep for several hours at mid-day. South of the Yangtze River in China, for example, a two-hour rest period occurs all year in the middle of the day. In the extreme heat of a tropical summer, this period is extended to three hours. As the day cools down, activity resumes and might last long into the evening. In Spain and the rest of southern Europe, shops and businesses close at mid-day for the same reason, to avoid the hottest hours of the day. Air conditioning is changing this pattern somewhat, but it remains a tradition in many parts of the world.

Dealing with Roommates

Unofficially...
Agnes got engaged and spent a lot of time with her fiancé while she was spending her junior year in his country. When she caught a cold, she decided to stay downtown with her boyfriend's family and did not tell her host mother about it. The host mother was very hurt by this.

If you make arrangements to room with a student from the host culture, it is also important to work things out as clearly as possible. Many questions about the use of electricity, hot water, the phone, the kitchen, and locking the door at night will come up as you adjust to one another and to living together. The American way is to be as positive as possible and not discuss any problems that come up. Some Eastern cultures are more reserved than Americans about discussing problems or misunderstandings. If your roommate is from China or Japan, you might find it difficult to begin a discussion to resolve any problem. On the other hand, some European cultures are much more open. Their feeling is that you should talk out all the problems (sometimes quite loudly), and then you can resolve them. To the French, for example, an interesting conversation is one in which everyone expresses their opinion and describes in detail just how different their point of view is. Ideally, everybody comes out respecting the uniqueness of the other person's observations.

To the French, the American's effort to find common ground with everyone else in the room might seem bland at best or repressed at worst. To Americans, a French discussion (called in French "an explanation") often feels like criticism. If you embarrass Japanese or Chinese people by putting them in the wrong, they might feel that they have lost face. With all these differences, there are many challenges in learning to communicate across cultures.

The basic rule for getting along with people from another culture is that you should never make any assumptions. If you can discuss the differences in your expectations without allowing it to hurt either person's feelings, you might be able to work things out and understand each other better.

Dealing with Bureaucracy

You will face a lot of paperwork and a lot of new regulations. Remember that you are subject to the laws of the host country and must conform to its regulations, even if you do not know all of them. Finding out what is required of you is important. In the modern world, people travel quickly from their home country to another country. They often find themselves in a situation in which they do not understand a great deal of what is being said around them and rely on a knowledgeable resident director to help them out of difficulties. In situations such as this, they tend to feel a little isolated and somewhat immune to the normal regulations of human conduct. Beware of this feeling!

You are subject to the laws of the country you are in. The United States Department of State is there to assist Americans traveling around the world, but it cannot help you if you have broken a law or tried to side-step a regulation. Although your program will try to help you with as many things as possible, it might not anticipate everything.

In many countries, you have another step to complete in order to remain in the country for the term of your study program. Your visa gives you permission to cross the border and apply for permission to remain in the country. Once there, you might have to get a residency card.

Expect to need a lot of photos for various residency cards and identification cards. You might feel that you really need certain identity cards in order to save money on bus transportation and other expenses. However, you might not qualify for some of them. Even with your international student identity card, you could be too old to get a discounted bus pass, for example. You might experience many frustrating situations in which you trudge back and forth from one office to another in hopes of resolving some administrative tangle. For example, you might spend several hours trying to obtain a student bus pass to help your budget. At the end of the line, a final wrinkle in the regulations might materialize to defeat the entire effort.

Sometimes, a regulation gives foreign students an unexpected break. In Europe, international students are exempted from paying the portion of their rent that is tax, for example. Check whether your landlord or landlady has already included a deduction in your rent because you do not have to pay taxes. Filing for the refund might put you in line for other types of taxes.

In principle, you do not have to pay excise (sales) taxes on items you buy in many countries. In practice, you are allowed the rebate only under certain strictly defined conditions of purchase, and there is a lot of paperwork involved in claiming your refund (see Chapter 7, "Figuring Out the Cost of Programs and How to Finance Them").

Housing Costs in Other Countries

Housing in European communities is at a premium. It is also extremely expensive in Japan, where the majority of the population must live in big cities along the coast because the interior of the country is so mountainous. Student-priced quarters are apt to be small, dark, and less comfortable than you are accustomed to. Renting something equal to the facilities at your college or in your community might be extremely expensive. Remember that many people use their bedrooms at night just to sleep in, not to study in.

Signing a Lease

After you have selected a place to live, you might have to sign a contract or lease. Be sure to read the terms very carefully. You will probably be in the country for 9 or 10 months at the most. Most landlords want a 12-month lease. Check whether you need to find someone to sublet the apartment from you to complete the terms of the lease. If you bring your family with you for an extended period of study abroad, you have a good reason for renting an apartment for 12 months at a time.

Students staying abroad for less than 12 months should avoid the complications of a lease if other options are available. Rent from a landlord who is willing to agree to rent to students for 6 or 10 months. It is better not to have to find someone to sublet the apartment for the final portion of a 12-month lease. You could end up being liable for cleaning or telephone costs incurred by the person who sublet from you.

Damage Deposits

Expect to pay a damage deposit in cash equal to one month's rent prior to moving in. Normally, study abroad programs do not cover this through the fees you paid to them but expect you to assume responsibility for this amount when you arrive.

Sharing Financial Responsibilities with Roommates

Many students arrange to share an apartment or a room with students whom they meet at the university rather than with participants in their program. They prefer not to room with other Americans because they would rather practice their language skills. Getting to know someone from the host country or a neighboring country has many advantages.

However, it is important to agree at the beginning what the financial obligations will be at the end of the school year. If you assume responsibility for signing the lease and collecting rent from the other students, you could also bear full responsibility for any damage done. If the other students leave before you do, you might end up losing your damage deposit to repair something done by another person. Conversely, if other people are still living in the apartment after you go back to the United States, you might be held liable for damage done after your departure. You might have difficulty getting your deposit back. If the housing arrangement was made for you by the program, it might hold up your transcript until you pay the cleaning or repair bill.

There are no universal solutions to these difficulties. Sometimes, the program offers options that eliminate many of these problems. It is important to be aware of the problems that can occur so that you can find a way around them if possible.

If You Get Sick

Be sure to do your homework many months in advance about health precautions to take before and during your time abroad. The Centers for Disease Control has an extensive Web site with several publications for travelers, a list of precautions to take for specific diseases (especially insect-borne diseases) and specific recommendations concerning immunizations and health precautions for travelers to take in each country of the world. For further information, you should consult the Web sites of the U.S. State Department (www.state.gov) and the Centers for Disease Control (www.cdc.gov).

If you are not going abroad through a sponsored program that has provided you with health information, it is critical that you thoroughly read the information available at the CDC Web site. In some instances, travelers are advised to get additional information about health risks in certain regions. Discuss the information with your physician and arrange for all the immunizations recommended for your destination.

You can download a free pamphlet, *Medical Information for Americans Traveling Abroad,* from the U.S. Department of State Bureau of Consular Affairs Web site, along with tips for travelers going to specific regions and several other booklets.

The document "Health Information for International Travel" is available for $20 from the U.S. Government Printing Office, from local physicians and health centers, and from the Centers for Disease Control:

Watch Out!
A booklet for senior travelers is available at the State Department Web site. Many of the travel information sheets for specific countries alert senior citizens to the fact that Social Security Medicare is not available outside the United States. Evacuation information is available at the site. Insurance information is provided elsewhere in this book.

Phone: 877-FYI-TRIP

Fax: 888-CDC-FAXX

www.cdc.gov

The CDC Web site provides extensive information about specific diseases, health precautions to take in specific world locations, and immunization requirements for travel between nations. In addition, the site is linked to other sources of health information provided by medical associations and other professional associations.

As soon as you arrive in a new location, it is a good idea to find out as much as possible about how to handle illness. Ask your program director, if this information is not included in the orientation. If there is no program director, ask the international office to advise you. If you are participating in a host family program, there is usually an understood procedure. Normally, the host family is responsible for getting a doctor for any student who gets sick. Check this procedure before you get sick because you might not feel well enough to make a lot of inquiries after something goes wrong! Remember that you probably need to pay for any medical care when you receive it and keep the receipts for your insurance to pay upon your return.

If you are in a country where the diet is quite different from the one you are accustomed to, you can expect some stomach ailments. Some foods will not settle well with your stomach, especially when you are recovering from jet lag during the first days after your arrival. During the first few weeks of acclimatization, diarrhea and constipation are common. This is why it is called "traveler's diarrhea." Trips to hospitals when you are new in a country can be expensive and confusing. It is best to be careful at first and work your way up gradually to trying some of the

Unofficially...
In the hospital in Kunming, we met an American who had been there for six months, recovering from a reaction to the malaria medication with which he dosed himself on two occasions because he had a fever and thought he might have malaria. The second time produced a nearly fatal reaction.

more exotic foods. Be wary about eating at outdoor food stalls that blossom in the summer in many countries. The warm temperatures and unsanitary practices of some sidewalk vendors provide excellent breeding grounds for a host of bacteria, and you can be certain the tables you eat off, as some students have said, "probably haven't been clean since they left the production plant."

You might also keep in mind that people in some countries are not susceptible to *giardia*, an intestinal parasite that is uncomfortable and difficult to treat and that Americans often get. Therefore, you should take particular care about eating at small food stalls. See the guidebooks particularly geared to students, travelers who backpack, and others who are likely to go off the beaten path for particular precautions that Westerners should take in certain countries. *The Lonely Planet* guides are often recommended for this purpose.

In many parts of the world, heavy smoking is much more the norm in public places than it is in the United States. You might find it difficult to get a restaurant table away from people smoking very strong cigarettes or cigarillos. If you are sensitive to smoke, you might have difficulty with allergies. Take antihistamines and decongestants along as a precaution. You might also spend more time in cities or dusty areas than you are accustomed to. Sitting at an outdoor café on a busy city street might expose you to car fumes and dust as well as the picturesque views you came for.

Throat irritations easily lead to respiratory infections. If you begin to have difficulties with colds and sore throats, limit your exposure to dust from the street. Some students who like to jog on campuses at home have been advised not to jog in city parks

A Student Speaks Up
Jogging in the park in Beijing, I inhaled a lot of dust and developed an infection of the larynx. The doctor advised me not to jog outdoors. I began to go to a hotel swimming pool instead, but I missed outdoor exercise.

after developing severe irritations. This is a problem in Beijing, for example, because the prevailing winds bring dust from the Gobi Desert. Because jogging causes you to breathe heavily (that's one of the reasons you do it, of course!), you might be causing more irritation to your throat and lungs than you would by simply walking around a city. If you notice the early signs of irritation, find a location that is less windy or dusty, or consider wearing a mask. In some countries, it is quite common to see people wearing masks to protect other people from colds or to keep from getting one.

If you get sick, do not hesitate to consult the clinic on your university campus or contact your program director or the person designated to help you. Don't wait. You might have some very ordinary ailment or you could be experiencing something more serious.

Some people have a severe reaction to Mefloquine (Larium), the anti-malaria medication most often prescribed for people going to the tropics. The reaction can be quite severe, but it is usually quickly remedied by switching to another medication. Among the medications given to persons actually stricken with malaria, some might produce extremely dangerous reactions. If you think you have contracted malaria, see a physician and do not try to dose yourself.

If you are not traveling with a student group, see the hotel doctor. Do not underestimate the training physicians have received. One teacher walked out of a hospital in China, against the wishes of the physicians, after a severe stomach ailment began to abate. He did not know that he had chronic appendicitis. It returned under dangerous circumstances later.

Think Clean

Read this section before going out to travel, explore, and eat on your own. If you are not staying in hotels or traveling under the supervision of an experienced guide, bring your own chopsticks or utensils when eating out or traveling in developing countries, if it is convenient. Plastic utensils are relatively easy to keep clean. If you stop to buy a drink at a vending stand, accept only bottled or canned beverages, not drinks in glasses. However, be aware that street vendors might combine the contents of half empty soft drink bottles and recap them for sale. If you have any reason to wonder about this, canned soft drinks or bottled water sold in stores are a safer option.

Wash your hands before meals. The leading cause of food poisoning is staphylococcus, a bacteria found on the skin. It is also vital to protect against Hepatitis. Be sure your hands, chopsticks or utensils, and bowls are clean. Carrying disposable wipes is a convenient way to clean up at any time. Remember to carry toilet paper with you whenever you are out in public. Most public restrooms do not supply paper. Restrooms in cafes, hotels, museums, fine department stores, and restaurants are usually better supplied, but be prepared.

A Few Additional Precautions

Bring rubber shower shoes or sandals to wear in the shower at the dormitory and do not go barefoot anywhere. Some parasitic diseases causing significant public health problems in tropical countries are transmitted through tiny wounds in the feet. Others are airborne and absorbed by inhalation. Although these parasites are usually picked up by those who work out of doors, it is best to be careful.

Watch Out!
Be very careful about trying to medicate yourself, as some Americans think they should do in developing countries. Potentially fatal reactions can occur if people start adjusting blood pressure medicine, anti-malaria medicine, and so on, without medical supervision. See a doctor. Even in developing countries, physicians are sufficiently trained to handle an emergency.

Because tap water in many parts of the developing world is not chlorinated or sterilized, you should check to be sure you can drink the tap water. In addition, you will find that cuts and abrasions get infected more easily than they do at home and are harder to keep clean. Take any cut or scrape seriously, and apply antiseptic ointment regularly until the injury is healed.

If you are sensitive to mosquitoes, bring plenty of mosquito repellent. In Southern Europe, windows do not have screens. Some Americans are troubled by mosquitoes in Southern France, Spain, and Italy in the summer time. If you are traveling in the tropics and expect to visit tropical rainforests in locations such as Costa Rica, bring a lot of insect repellent and read up on some of the insect-borne diseases that you might encounter.

The materials on the Web site of the Centers for Disease Control have some warnings about diseases transmitted by insects in tropical countries, but you should do further reading on the subject if you are traveling on your own.

A Word About Alcohol Consumption

Some countries have no minimum legal age for drinking or the minimum age is less than 21. Although young people from other countries might also drink excessively, Americans take the blame for it.

Drinking heavily increases your susceptibility to other illnesses. Because it affects your judgment, it also increases the risk of accidental injuries in a country that might have different traffic patterns from the ones you are accustomed to. Alcohol impairs your judgment and affects your ability to recover quickly from jet lag. Heavy drinking in public alienates people from you and your group. Have fun, but don't go to extremes.

"Let's be frank about this. If the drinking thing is new to you, one word of advice: Don't go out and get hammered your first night here. Americans are famous for their inability to drink, so whether it's your first time drinking or not, your drunken stupor will be blamed on your Americanness and on nothing else." This student was expressing her personal opinion, but she has a point. The use of alcohol is a complex subject. There is no single rule for advising students about its use except to say that the pattern of use in the United States is different from the norm in other countries. Many Americans restrict and frown upon the use of alcohol by minors. In return, many students consider it socially acceptable to drink to excess when they gain access (legitimately or otherwise) to liquor.

Unfortunately, Americans have developed a reputation around the world for drinking excessively and losing control. This is due to the behavior of a few highly visible individuals who have been unable to keep their consumption of alcohol to a level at which they could still exercise good judgment.

In many other countries, there are fewer regulations to restrict drinking. In Europe, families that use alcohol are expected to teach their children how to consume it in a responsible manner. Families might allow teenagers to drink a little wine diluted with water at dinner and gradually show them to respect the effects of alcohol. Few other countries have laws like those in the United States, limiting the sale of alcohol to individuals who are not of legal age.

Alcoholism is regarded as a serious problem in many countries where heavy drinking was once accepted as a manly thing to do. Public displays of drinking in large social groups are becoming less common in Europe. Health departments have launched public campaigns to encourage the responsible use of alcohol. In one example, signs were posted in the French metro a few years ago, showing a pair of children holding hands and the motto: "Sobriety and Health Go Together." Alcoholism is an increasing problem in China and some other countries where people have become affluent enough to afford liquor but feel discouraged about depressed economies and limited job opportunities. Nonetheless, those who are unable to control their drinking tend to be looked down upon or marginalized.

In Japan, alcohol is available everywhere, sold from vending machines. Drinking to excess is considered acceptable in certain situations, especially formal dinner parties where etiquette requires people to fill up each other's cups or glasses whenever they are empty. However, on closer inspection, you will observe that the Japanese, like people in many other societies, turn events involving heavy drinking into rituals that have some safeguards in them. For instance, the participants might be taken home in taxis from dinner parties where heavy drinking is expected so that they do not endanger themselves or others by driving while intoxicated. Become aware of the structured situations and unwritten rules that govern alcohol consumption where you are going.

Because the consumption of alcohol is prohibited by the Koran, some Muslim countries prohibit the possession, manufacture, or consumption of alcohol. Saudi Arabia prosecutes any American or other person who has or uses alcohol in the country. Check the State Department travel regulations for further information, but do not rely entirely on the State Department information because the advisory for some countries might not mention alcohol restrictions that exist. Check with your program sponsor or with the embassy of the country you intend to visit. For further information, contact:

> U.S. State Department
> Emergency Services
> travel.state.gov/acs.html/#emr

> Travel Information and Consular
> Information Sheets
> Travel.state.gov/index.html

> Canadian Department of Foreign Affairs and Trade
> www.dfait-maeci.gc.ca/travelreport/
> menu_e.htm

> British Foreign and Commonwealth Office
> www.fco.gov.uk

> Australian Foreign Affairs and Trade Office
> www.dfat.gov.au/consular/advice/

> Centers for Disease Control
> www.cdc.gov/travel/index.htm

A health and safety video is available for approximately $20 from the Institute for Shipboard Education:

> 811 William Pitt Union
> University of Pittsburgh
> Pittsburgh, PA 15260
> Phone: 412-648-7490
> Fax: 412-648-2298
> E-mail: Pwatson@sas.ise.pitt.edu

Just the Facts

- Preparing for culture shock minimizes the effect.

- Getting settled often involves considerable red tape.

- Life with your host family involves discussion and adjustments.

- Find out how your program wants you to handle health problems, and make sure that your insurance will cover treatment.

- Thorough research and prevention help avoid serious health problems, especially in developing countries.

- Review travel information and safety recommendations for the country where you are going.

GET THE SCOOP ON...
Coping with different teaching styles
▪ Preparing for final examinations ▪ Making
opportunities to improve your language skills
▪ Seeing what you came to see

Getting the Most Out of Your Study Abroad Experience

Chapter 18

W hen the academic year starts, be sure you maintain a balance in your life so that you can get the most out of the whole experience. Some students misunderstand the academic system and think it is very easy compared to university life in the United States. It is tempting to spend so much time getting out to see the country and making friends that you neglect your academic work. You might end up feeling that you didn't get the most out of your academic program. Other students throw themselves into the academic work. They might end up feeling frustrated because they didn't take advantage of the sights they came so many thousands of miles to see or befriend the people they came to meet.

Getting the Most from Your Academic Program

To get the most out of your academic program, if you enroll directly in a host university, you need to spend some time learning about the philosophy of education in the country. Don't assume the goals are the same as in the United States. Ask professors at your home university, before you go, to help you understand some of the important differences in the teaching approach for the country where you are going.

Adjusting to Different Teaching Styles and Course Format

Professors in other countries do not feel the same level of responsibility as in the United States for making sure that students master the material. The distance between students and professors can vary a great deal from country to country, but it is almost always a more formal and distant relationship than in the United States. In many places, the professor is a lofty, distant figure and a repository of great wisdom and knowledge. It is the student's job to extract the knowledge from this source. Professors are not as accessible as in the United States.

In many university systems, the students are expected to complete a general education in secondary school. When they come to the university, they must do all their study in one specialized field. When they first enroll at the university, the department gives them a program of study comprising almost all the courses they will take for the degree they hope to earn and a list of the materials they have to read in preparation for their degree examination.

Courses at many universities in other countries meet less often than classes do in the United States. Typical classes meet one and a half or two hours per week for a semester or a year. In some countries, students might attend a larger number of courses than in the United States. They might take fewer examinations and do fewer papers in each course. One partial examination and a final examination, sometimes an oral examination, could be sufficient to measure their work. In discussion sections, the students might be expected to participate in discussions and write seminar papers. The section leaders get to know the students better. After the professors see the work the students do at the end of the year, they might get to know some of the better students and recognize their potential for pursuing serious, advanced study of the subject.

You will probably find that the whole approach to knowledge is different in other parts of the world. In the United States, the usual purpose of a university course is to lead students toward mastery of a certain body of knowledge. Each course completed represents an important number of credits earned toward the degree. In many countries, students attend lectures by distinguished professors who present their point of view or the mode of analysis they have developed through their research. Often, the first few lectures of the semester are the most critical in laying out the method the professor intends to use. The rest of the lectures might be illustrations of the ways in which the approach is useful. The balance of the term's lectures might consist of the professor illustrating the way her method illuminates the subject. The research partnerships that develop between some American professors and undergraduate students are a unique feature of the American university system. Such arrangements are extremely rare in other countries.

The degree program requires students to attend a certain number of lecture classes just to learn some of the best scholarly methods. Students might not complete a great deal of written work in those courses. They apply much of what they learn to the degree examinations or to the work they do in seminars. In seminars or discussion sections, they do more written work under the supervision of those same professors or with less well-known, junior faculty whom they get to know better.

In many countries, all or most of the students' efforts go to preparing for degree examinations. The students take these examinations after one or two years of university study. If they complete their first degree, they can go on to earn one or two more diplomas. Part of the reason for the screening that happens in the degree examinations is that many public universities enroll huge numbers of students. The students must pass a certain number of courses and degree examinations to complete their degrees. However, the system is less strict than in the United States. Students can return and take the courses and examinations several times, if they want to do so. This partly depends on whether their families can afford for them to remain in school. Some students drop out and go to work if they are not successful at the university.

Some students might not be strongly motivated to complete their degree quickly when they first enroll in the university. Therefore, they might not work very hard during the first year or so. In some places, unemployment is high and university graduates have a great deal of difficulty finding jobs. Unless they want to drop out and go to work in relatively unskilled jobs, some young people have good reasons for wanting to remain students as long as possible.

The system varies considerably from one country to another. In the British system, a student can enroll in a college of the university and study with tutors who work more closely with him or her. The student might meet individually with the tutor to discuss readings and develop topics for research papers. At some British universities, therefore, the students might work closely with professors at an earlier phase of their studies. As in the United States, the students and faculty might get to know one another sooner in academic programs that enroll smaller numbers of students.

Understanding Foreign Grades

In a system where so much emphasis is placed on degree examinations, rather than course credit, it is a little complicated to convert the work you do into the equivalent of American university credits. For this reason, it is important to work closely with the international office or with your program director to make sure that all the work you do is properly recorded. There might be a separate enrollment system for you so that the international office can keep track of your work and convert it to a record that the sponsoring American university or your home university can use to transfer the credit.

The final examination and grade is based on the system used by the host university. Gather some information about the system for converting this to an American grade. If your program has a U.S. sponsor, the sponsor makes the conversion for you. If you enroll directly in a host university, the study abroad office or registrar at your home university makes the conversion to the American system when the credit is transferred. Although the grade usually does not appear on your transcript at your home university, you must earn a satisfactory grade for the credit to transfer.

A Student Speaks Up
I was horrified when I got a test marked with a D. I had worked extremely hard in the class. Then, I found out that D in Australia means Distinction, and I had done very well on the test.

TABLE 18.1   AUSTRALIAN GRADING

Letter Grade	Australian Significance	U.S. Grade Equivalent
HD	High Distinction	A+
D	Distinction	A
C	Credit	B
P	Pass	C+
CP or TP	Conceded, Conditional, or Temporary Pass	D
F	Failure	F

TABLE 18.2   FRENCH GRADING SYSTEM

French Numerical Score	Significance	U.S. Grade Equivalent
16–20	Très bien (very good)	A+
14–15.9	Bien (good)	A
12–13.9	Assez bien (rather good)	B
10–11.9	Passable (satisfactory)	C
8–9.9	Barely passing	D
0–7.9	Insuffisant (failure)	F

TABLE 18.3   BRITISH GRADING SYSTEM

Class	Numerical Mark	American Letter Grade
Class I	70–100%	A
Class II, Division I	65–69%	A
	60–64%	B
Class II, Division II	55–59%	B
	50–54%	C
Class III	45–49%	C
	40–44%	D
Fail	35–39%	D
Absolute Fail	0–34%	F

For further information about how the grades are converted for the program you choose, consult your study abroad advisor and the program sponsor. It is a good idea to check with your home university and make sure that it knows how to convert the grades you will receive to the American A, B, C, D, and F system. Even if the grade does not transfer to your American university transcript, the registrar's office might still take note of the grades to decide whether your credit transfers. The office of financial aid might take note of the grades to determine whether you will continue to receive financial aid from the college. A record of grades might be required to continue living in a specialized residence hall such as a sorority or special interest residence.

Next, you should consult with your host university academic advisor and ask that person to explain the grading scale and system to you. Ask about the grades they award for work that is outstanding, good, satisfactory, minimally acceptable, or unacceptable. Be sure whenever you receive a grade that you understand what sort of academic progress you are making.

Preparing Assignments and Examinations

As a student from another culture, you might have to do more preparation for the lectures to understand what the professor is talking about. Your classmates from the host country have been through rigorous training in secondary school. Some of them have followed it with two years of advanced study at a special "high school" or "college" designed to prepare students for the university. When they arrive in the university, they might already have a large body of knowledge to which

Unofficially...
Students in Japan must be careful to enroll for their classes through the international office and follow their instructions. They must keep complete records of all the work they do and ask the professor, the international office, or the American program director to validate it before they leave for home. The professors do not provide course descriptions or grades after the course is over.

they can apply the approaches the professor is suggesting in the lectures. If you are taking a history course, for example, and you are not as familiar with the history of the country, you might have to do more background reading than the other students in the class to follow the lectures.

When they begin their program of study, students are given a long list of possible readings and are expected to pursue a course of reading that accords with their particular academic interests. Therefore, many of them may already have read some of the material that you are encountering for the first time.

Don't be fooled by classmates who do not appear to be putting as much time as you are into reading prior to the examinations. Some of them might not be doing very much work. However, they might not expect to complete the course successfully, as you want to do. Others may already have completed a great deal of the reading over the summer before classes began, or they might already have a good background in the field. Still others might be going to the library or somewhere else to read and doing more work than they let on. In many cultures, it is permissible for students to share notes. Ask some of the other students in the class if you can review their notes after the lecture. They might consider it a compliment and be helpful to you.

American students are also struck by some differences in the way work is evaluated. In some courses, you are asked to write research papers. You might meet with a professor or a tutor and discuss a possible reading list. From this, you select a direction to pursue in your work.

On the final examination, you are asked to apply the method to a small body of material. In a literature class, you might be given a passage from one of the novels or even a short poem that you have read. You are asked to comment on it. The students then write for two or three hours. The idea is to bring out all the analytical "tools" that you have been given during the semester or year and show how they can be used to discuss the passage.

If you are in an intensive language program, the system might be somewhat more familiar, with frequent written exercises and examinations. However, you might be given a great deal more vocabulary and be expected to cover more material each week than you do in your American classes. If you are learning a writing system that is different from the alphabet used for Western languages, you might find that your teachers in the host country expect you to learn more and faster than your teachers did in the United States. Because they are surrounded with their own writing system, they might not realize that you have had less contact with the system and have become used to taking more time to learn new vocabulary. If you have classmates from other countries, you might find that their mastery of the writing system is more advanced. Do not be discouraged by this. Spend as much time reading as you can. Look for examples everywhere in the street signs, ads, and bookstores and on the products you buy. Just keep immersing yourself in the system and practicing it as much as you can.

While you are abroad, you do not need to miss out on preparing for the next phase of your studies in the United States. Alison Noyes of Smith College did some research on the examinations you can take in other countries to prepare for admission to American graduate schools. It is possible to take the qualifying examinations for graduate school at

A Student Speaks Up
I took careful notes every day in class. By the end of the semester, the other students were asking me if they could borrow my notes. The first lectures set up the system we used for everything else we talked about all term.

many centers worldwide. Citizens of the countries where the examinations take place can and do gain admission to American medical, law, graduate arts and sciences, and management programs. American students studying abroad can make arrangements to take the tests overseas. They should experience no problem doing well enough to meet graduate school admission standards in the United States.

The Medical College Admission Test (MCAT) is offered at testing sites in Australia, England, France, Germany, Israel, Japan, Lebanon, and Singapore. In England, MCATs are given at the University of Sussex in Brighton (about 55 minutes south of London by train) and the University of Lancaster (3 hours north of London and south of Edinburgh). These are the only MCAT sites in Britain to date (according to new information from Lancaster).

You can find additional information in the MCAT registration packet:

> MCAT Program Office
> P.O. Box 4056
> Iowa City, IA 52243-4056
> Phone: 319-337-1357

Graduate Record Examination (GRE) sites are available in the People's Republic of China, Egypt, England, France, Germany, Israel, Italy, Japan, Kenya, Korea, Philippines, Russia, South Africa, Spain, Taiwan, and Thailand. Additional information appears in the GRE registration packet (www.gre.org).

Law School Admission Test centers are available in almost 150 countries. Additional information appears in the registration packet. No test centers are currently available in the U.K., although this is being changed. For information about the test and many other aspects of law school admission and

career planning, see the Law School Admission
Council home page:

> Law School Admission Council
> Phone: 215-968-1001
> Fax: 215-968-1119
> E-mail: LSACinfo@LSAC.org
> www.LSAC.org

For information about MBA programs and international registration for the Graduate Management Admission Test (GMAT), go to the MBA explorer home page (www.gmat.org/).

Making the Most of Your Social Experiences

Your social contacts are the core of your experience when you study abroad. Not only are they valuable in themselves, but they also are the main route to improving your language skills and acquiring a deeper appreciation for the culture.

Improving Your Language Skills

In the film *Down By Law* (1986), the Italian comic Roberto Benigni plays a man who knows no English and starts trying to learn by writing down absolutely everything he hears in a ludicrously tiny little notebook. The effect is humorous because he obviously can't remember and use every expression he hears, much less cram the whole English language into his tiny notebook. Clearly his character has no idea, when he starts, how much there is to learn. People who have studied other languages enjoy this film because it conveys so well the feeling you have, after beginning the study of a language in an American classroom, when you go to the country for the first time. Suddenly, you realize what a vast amount there is to learn about the language you are studying. Trying to use what you have learned so far seems

Bright Idea
When we were offered various housing choices, including apartments to share with other Americans on the program, some of us rented large apartments with a couple of extra rooms and put up notices to find local students to share them with us. It was a great way to make friends with some local students.

Unofficially...
One of the measurements of intermediate language skill is the ability to compare things. It takes a lot of experience to handle the nuances of a comparison. If you ask other people to compare things such as two films, or two lectures, you can learn a lot of useful vocabulary.

like trying to use one of Benigni's tiny little notebooks.

In the United States, you expect to complete a certain body of material in each class and make steady progress each term. You move along with a group of other students, at approximately the same pace. Each semester, the entire class reaches approximately the same goals. The following semester, they pick up where they ended the previous term and continue, more or less as a group. The normal process in the beginning and early intermediate phases of language learning is much like studying any other subject. However, as you move to increasingly advanced levels, the learning process becomes more complicated. You begin to explore whole realms of language in which there are many phrases and expressions you have not learned before. In each class, you cover a large body of these phrases, but there is no longer a set order in which you learn various expressions or work on aspects of style and grammar. Instead, classes advance your skills in some areas of language use, leaving other areas relatively undeveloped. For example, you might become accustomed to discussing cuisine in class, but when it comes to medical terminology or scientific research, your vocabulary will probably remain rudimentary unless you have the opportunity to take a class at a university in the country of the language. Only over a period of many years will you explore enough different areas of language use to be comfortable talking about virtually any subject with any person and to achieve near native fluency.

Whether you are in a country that speaks your native language or you are perfecting your skills in another language, every one of you will sometimes find it difficult to communicate. At other times, things will go smoothly and you will feel more positive about your stay. If you are studying another language, your language skills might not always serve you as well as you expect, especially at first. You might not be able to convey your full personality in the language you are studying, or you might find yourself in many situations that require expressions or terminology that are new to you.

When you go abroad, you will probably know the fundamentals of grammar and structure for the language you are studying, but you will immediately discover that it is difficult to follow native speakers when they are speaking in a relaxed, slangy way. You will also find that your professors use expressions that you have not studied before, and it will be hard to follow them, particularly at first. In your daily life, you will find some people easy to talk with and others very difficult to follow. When you are chatting with just one person, you might be able to carry on a conversation easily, but when a group is speaking, you might feel lost.

At certain times of day, you will feel like a radio that has just turned itself off. You become fatigued and can no longer follow the conversations around you or contribute. The good news is that this fatigue will happen later and later in the day as time goes on. Your proficiency, and level of comfort with native speakers, will steadily improve. By the end of the year, you might be able to comfortably discuss the details of gardening with your landlady. When her daughter the veterinarian comes to dinner, however, you might find yourself feeling left out of large segments of the conversation. When you go into the computer store and look at the merchandise, you might see many English cognates on the displays, but the menu at a fine restaurant has many expressions you never found in the textbooks you used in the United States.

You might feel frustrated in your language classes. Instead of beginning the class as a group at approximately the point where you all stopped at the end of the previous term, you will be in a class with some very fluent speakers and some who have not covered the same material you have had. The instructor might launch into a discussion of a point you do not follow or might spend time on a point you know well. You might feel that the class "should" be better suited to the exact point in your own language development at which you enrolled. You might feel irritated at your American teachers because they obviously failed to introduce so many expressions that you hear and read all the time. The fact is that at the advanced level, there is no precise point at which all advanced students can start a class. There are still too many aspects of language usage to cover. Nobody in the class will be perfectly bilingual by the end of the semester. Everyone in the class will still have different strengths and different gaps in their abilities to use the language. Therefore, you might feel less in control of your own progress than you were in first- and second-year classes and very aware of all the things you still need to learn.

The only solution to this is to keep reading and writing as much as you can and to spend every possible moment using and listening to the language. If you can watch television or attend movies, take advantage of them to get a sense of contemporary language. Read the newspapers, even if the first paper you read plunges you into the middle of ongoing coverage of many local news stories you know nothing about. See whether you can subscribe

to an e-mail news service to follow a condensed
version of the local news in the language that you
are studying. Avoid watching the international CNN
channel, available in hotels all over the world, and
concentrate on getting your news through local
channels.

Although you arrived in the country with far
more language experience than Benigni's character, it might still feel a little bit as if your notebooks
are much too small and new expressions are coming
at you much too fast for you to remember and learn
what you hear. Still, it is helpful to look for and jot
down as many new expressions as you can every day
and to practice them. When you are not with speakers of the language, practice thinking in it. Whenever you are alone, practice describing to yourself,
in the language you are studying, everything you are
doing. This exercise will make you aware of useful
expressions you need to learn.

Above all, do not make yourself feel discouraged
by comparing your language skill level with others
in the group. Don't give up because you still have so
much to learn. Remind yourself that you are at the
appropriate level for the amount of time you have
spent learning the language. You will make a great
deal of progress over the semester or year that you
are in the country. Allow yourself to rest. Take
breaks when you need to, but don't give up.

It is important to converse with your host family.
No one will care if you make mistakes; the family is
eager to converse with you. You might suggest helping to set the table or other small services as a way
to break the ice and learn some vocabulary. Some
families might ask you along on excursions. It is a
good idea to ask in advance what costs are involved.
At that point, the family will make it clear whether

you are expected to pay (for concert tickets, for instance) or whether you are their guest.

These activities will deepen your connection with the family and help create lasting ties with your host country.

Enjoying an Active Social Life

Although it is important to understand and benefit from the academic program, one of the most important aspects of being in another country is getting to know people. Given the reserve of people in some countries when you first meet them, it can sometimes be a little intimidating, especially if you tend to be shy. In a country where people value life-long friendships, getting to know someone for one semester or one year might not seem worthwhile. You might need to create some excuses for getting to know people.

Set aside the idea that the people you meet must be your age, dating prospects, native speakers of the language, or any other restrictions you might place on your friendships without realizing it. Think of the conversations as a chance to learn something completely new about a person with whom you might not ordinarily spend time. Don't set too high a threshold for letting people get to know *you*. If you restrict your friendships to ones that help you meet goals such as finding a romantic partner, a business contact, or a language partner, you might feel frustrated. Without realizing it, you could pass up opportunities to meet some interesting people who might lead you to the very things you were hoping for. Be open to letting friendships develop with people of all ages and all walks of life.

Take advantage of every opportunity your program provides to get to know students and other

A Student Speaks Up
I would go out of my way to ask questions of everybody I saw regularly. After a while, people began to recognize and speak to me and I began to make friends. This was what I needed to improve my conversational skills.

people from the host country. Think up an idea or excuse for a party and put up a notice inviting everybody. Organize language-practicing partnerships in which you meet for an hour once a week with a native speaker of the language you are studying. Each person gets one-half hour to practice the language he or she is learning while the other offers ideas and suggestions.

A costume party for Halloween, Mardi Gras, New Year's, or some other occasion is a great way to break the ice and let people get to know one another better. You'll be amazed at some of the costumes. If the Americans invite the local students, expect some of them to come dressed to represent stereotypes of Americans! It's fun to see how Americans are perceived by others.

Join a choir, organize a band, volunteer to help one of the campus offices where you can meet students, or offer child care in return for an hour of language practice. One of the best ways of developing an active social life is to get to know international students. They are interesting and rewarding to know. Those who are completing their entire degree in the host country will have friends and will introduce you to other people. If some of the international students are cooking in your residence hall, ask them to show you how to prepare dishes from their country. Just ask a lot of questions. Tell people your clock stopped, and ask for the correct time.

Put up a note offering to share the price of a piano rental with some other students and organize a practice schedule. Suggest renting some other item, such as a ping pong table. Set up a volleyball or badminton net. Check with the local fitness center or community center and sign up for classes.

A Student Speaks Up
A Chinese student showed up at our Halloween party wearing a mask that was nothing but a huge, beautifully sculpted papier-mâché nose that he had made himself. Everyone enjoyed the reference to our large, European noses.

Find a class in yoga, tai chi, tai kwon do, modern dance, or ballroom dance. Find a craft shop that offers lessons (in knitting, ceramic painting, making cous-cous, Chinese calligraphy, or something else you've always wanted to learn). Sign up. You'll meet some people who have no connection with the university.

Offer to give lessons in a skill you have. It might be a craft such as woodcarving or lessons in music, tai chi, or poker. Alternatively, put up a note asking someone to give *you* lessons in something you want to learn about the host culture or about another culture that is well represented in the student body. Offer to do portraits or teach English.

Spend time talking with the workers. Whether it is the cleaning lady, the gate-keeper, the cook, or the groundskeeper, the person will probably enjoy a chance to chat with a student. You will get some good language practice and learn some vocabulary you might not otherwise hear. You never know what interesting stories you might hear or the contacts it might lead to. If nothing else, different people can give you advice about where to find shops or buses, how to get the telephones to work, or who's who in the institution. You might even get a fresh perspective on the political or economic scene.

Keep your expectations low. Some people might be a little reserved when they realize that you are only in the country for a short period of time. On the other hand, others will be interested in learning more about where you are from. Those who have been abroad themselves might be most interested in getting to know you.

Talk to as many people as you can. If they are older people, get them to tell about their youth and how they were educated. Find out how things differ

A Student Speaks Up
One cab driver we talked to said that people always judged a new leader by the quality of his calligraphy. To have any influence, the leader's characters had to have "chi" (vital life force). The cab drivers knew how many Mercedes the president owned and could predict the fortunes of other government officials by how many and what kinds of cars they had.

today from the former traditional education. Have them describe any major historical events they lived through or other conflicts in the country. Be tactful when you bring up moments in history when the U.S. was in conflict with the country you are visiting. Let others take the lead in describing their experiences from a personal standpoint. Remind yourself that you came to learn from other peoples. You might hear some rich stories of human courage and endurance.

If you are in the country to study the language, make friends among people who do not speak English so that you can work on the host country language together. That said, don't turn down the chance to get to know anybody.

If they are working people, ask them about the forms of entertainment they prefer. Ask them what they consider to be the best and worst kinds of entertainment in their country. If they watch television or go to movies, ask them what they enjoy.

Never turn down an invitation to go anywhere and try something new. If it's a concert and you hate classical music, go anyway. If it's a golf tournament and you hate golf, go anyway. Give everything at least one try, especially if it is something related to the host culture, such as the dragon boat festival on the Yangtze River, a Breton folk festival, or a national holiday.

Taking Time to Be a Tourist

Although it might be expensive to get out and do the tourist things in the country you came to see, be sure to do as many of them as you can. Sign up for tours organized by the city or the university. Reading about the monuments and visiting them outside of an American group provide a better

A Student Speaks Up

After the Kyoto earthquake, my friend's grandmother was pulled from the ruins of her home. At 82, she had still been practicing dentistry. She was most disturbed by the loss of her equipment, which forced her to retire before she was ready.

Unofficially...
For travel inside China, plane tickets are easier to purchase than train tickets. It is still difficult to purchase hard sleeper or soft sleeper train tickets, especially during peak travel seasons. Individuals can only purchase them a week in advance. Travel agencies can book round-trip travel for a 15 percent service charge.

chance to use your language skills and learn something more about what you will see. Local tourist offices can provide information about sightseeing destinations you might not hear about outside the country. For weekend travel or vacation travel to neighboring countries, you might find the best arrangements at agencies within the country. However, air travel between countries can be expensive. Advance reservations are still advisable.

Watch Videotapes Before You Go

Before you go, read about the historical sites of interest in the area you will be visiting. Guides might not always fill in the entire story. If you need suggestions, ask at the tourist center before you go on the tour. Usually, the guides are more than happy to provide a little more detail and suggest reading material, videotapes, and other information about the monuments in their city or the region.

For dramatic interpretations of the history of the country you are going to, browse your local library for videotaped series that bring to life important periods of history which are often associated with the monuments you will visit in the country. Two such examples in British history are films about the lives of Henry VIII and his daughter, Elizabeth I, produced by the BBC.

If you are going to Asia and you want to know more about the religion and philosophy of the country you are going to visit, you might want to view the great Indian epic, the *Mahabharata*. Filmed in English by Peter Brook, it is available in library video collections. For those interested in visiting the Buddhist countries of the Himalayas, viewing *Seven Years in Tibet* or *Little Buddha* might be helpful. The televised version of James Clavell's *Shogun* is also available on video and was used to teach a popular

class on Japanese culture at the University of
Oregon when it first appeared on television. A video
on the classical world, *The Seven Wonders of the Ancient
World*, is available through Audio-Forum (described
later). Depending on the country you are going to
visit, your reference librarian can help you find
other videos. Many dramatizations as well as docu-
mentaries provide background on the history and
culture of the country you are going to visit during
a period that is particularly important for those who
plan to tour the country and visit its monuments.

Audio-Forum is recommended for its comprehensive supply of all types of language instructional
materials. It has videos of many parts of the world,
including cities and regions within countries. Ask
for information about Audio-Forum's Travel Guides
on video (average price around $30):

> Audio-Forum
> Jeffrey Norton Publishers
> 96 Broad St.
> Guilford, CT 06437 USA
> Phone: 800-243-1234 or 203-453-9794
> Fax: 203-453-9774
> E-mail: info@audioforum.com
> www.audioforum.com/

Search the Web Before You Go

You can often prepare for a visit to a site by viewing
its Web site. Just to give you an idea of how specific
you can be when searching the Web for information
about cities and towns you intend to visit, here are
Web pages for a few frequently visited sites that students are often taken to see:

> Bath, a famous 18th century spa in Great
> Britain and site of several of Jane Austen's
> novels (www.hotbot.com/?MT=Bath+UK).

Pézenas, a popular tourist destination in the Languedoc region of Southern France, associated with the playwright Molière:

Office of Tourism & Culture
Bp 10- Boutique du Barbier Gely
34120 Pézenas
Phone: 33-4-67-98-35-45 or 33-4-67-98-36-40
www.logassist.fr/visite/pezenas/index_e.htm

A reading list about the city of Cairo posted by Boston University (pharos.bu.edu/Egypt/Cairo/reference.html).

Le Pont du Gard, a Roman aqueduct and famous landmark of Provence (www.eerie.fr/Nimes/pont_gard.html#REF_ENGLISH).

Home page of the China Education and Research Network (CERNET), with a map of China from which you can visit the provinces and get brief informational sketches about their history, cities, and famous landmarks—enough to guide you toward further readings about sites you plan to visit (www.cernet.edu.cn/china/index.html).

Read About the Places You Will Visit

The French love concise little books of information called précis. One famous series is called *Que sais-je*. You will find numerous summaries of interesting facts, topics such as the history of the French language, brief overviews of the lives of famous people (particularly writers), outlines of French history, and overviews of current, colloquial French.

A French high school student preparing to enter the university might purchase an outline of one of the centuries of French literature in the Lagarde and Michard series and use it as a guide to begin reading some of the works the guide discusses in preparation for her examinations. A student of French history can acquire a quick overview of the main events to serve as a guideline for following lectures or appreciating a tour of various monuments. Other précis are available on colloquial French expressions, art, and a variety of other subjects.

In other countries, you will find similar guides. For readings in English on the history of countries you intend to visit, many bookstores on the Web can be an excellent resource:

Blackwell's, based in Oxford, England, is one of the world's greatest bookstores (www.blackwell publishers.co.uk/). A popular summary of British history currently recommended by Blackwell's is *England and its Rulers: 1066–1272* (M.T. CLANCHY. Institute of Historical Research, University of London. Price: £14.99 net. $26.95).

Blackwell's further recommends the new History of the World series. Recent titles include *Latin America* by Peter Bakewell and *India* by the late Burton Stein.

Other book dealers that provide quick access to materials via the Internet are Amazon.com, Borders.com, and BarnesandNoble.com. The Internet book dealers often have lists of recommended titles in various subject areas such as reading lists for the country you intend to visit and guidebooks to museums, art history, and so on.

Contact the Embassy Cultural Services

To get additional information about places to visit and ways of learning more before you go, contact the cultural services of the country you are going to visit and request the address, phone number, and Web site of its tourist office in the United States. The addresses of the embassies of all the countries maintaining diplomatic relations with the United States are on the Web site www.embassy.org.

Following are cultural offices of countries frequently visited by Americans:

BRITAIN
British Tourist Authority (BTA)
551 Fifth Ave., Suite 701
New York, NY 10176-0799
Phone: 800-GO2
Fax: 212-986-1188
www.britain-info.org/
www.britcoun.org/usa/

ITALY
Embassy of Italy in the United States
1601 Fuller St. NW
Washington, DC 20009
Phone: 202-328-5500
Fax: 202-462-360
www.italyemb.org/

FRANCE
Embassy of France
101 Reservoir Rd., NW
Washington, DC 20007
Phone: 202-944-6000
Fax: 202-944-6072
www.info-france-usa.org/

GERMANY
Embassy of Germany
4645 Reservoir Rd., NW
Washington, DC 20007-1998
Phone: 202-298-4000
Fax: 202-298-4249 or
   333-2653
www.germany-info.org/

SPAIN
Embassy of Spain
2375 Pennsylvania Ave.,
   NW
Washington, DC 20037
Phone: 202-452-0100
Fax: 202-833-5670
www.spainemb.org/
   information/

JAPAN
Embassy of Japan
2520 Massachusetts Ave.,
   NW
Washington, DC 20008
Phone: 202-238-6700
Fax: 202-328-2187
www.embjapan.org/

CHINA

Embassy of the People's
Republic of China
2300 Connecticut Ave., NW
Washington, DC 20008
Phone: 202-328-2500
Fax: 202-588-0032
E-mail: webmaster@
china-embassy.org
www.china-embassy.org/

MEXICO

Embassy of Mexico
1911 Pennsylvania Ave.,
   NW
Washington, DC 20006
Phone: 202-728-1600
www.embassyofmex ico.org/
   english/main2htm

ARGENTINA

**Embassy of the Argentine
Republic**
1600 New Hampshire Ave.,
NW
Washington, DC 20009
Phone: 202-939-6400
Fax: 202-332-3171
athea.ar/cwash/
   homepage/

BRAZIL

Embassy of Brazil
3006 Massachusetts Ave.,
   NW
Washington, DC 20008
Phone: 202-238-2700
Fax: 202-238-2827
E-mail: scitech@brasil.emb.
   nw.dc.us
www.brasil.emb.nw.dc.us/

GHANA

Embassy of Ghana
3512 International Dr., NW
Washington, DC 20008
Phone: 202-686-4520
E-mail: hagan@cais.com
www.ghana-embassy.org/

GREECE

Embassy of Greece
2221 Massachusetts Ave.,
   NW
Washington, DC 20008
Phone: 202-939-5800
www.greekembassy.org/

EGYPT

**Embassy of the Arab
Republic of Egypt**
3521 International Ct., NW
Washington, DC 20008
Phone: 202-966-6342

ISRAEL

Embassy of Israel
3514 International Dr., NW
Washington, DC 20008
Phone: 202-364-5500
Fax: 202-364-5423
E-mail: ask@israelemb.org
www.israelemb.org/

NORWAY

Royal Embassy of Norway
2720 34th St., NW
Washington, DC 20008
Phone: 202-333-6000
www.norway.org/

Just the Facts

- Understanding host country educational goals helps you get the most out of your academic experience.

- Recognizing the purpose of examinations and papers ensures a more successful performance.

- While abroad, you can stay on your career course by taking graduate admission examinations or getting information at international centers on the Web.

- Getting to know people is the most important aspect of your study abroad experience.

- Engage people you meet casually and get the inside story on the situation in the country.

- Advance reading and viewing of videos and Web sites can help you get the most out of being a tourist.

Finishing Up

Chapter 19

A s the time for your return to the United States approaches, you have to take care of some final details to help you make a smooth transition to your home university. Knowing that you don't have much time left in the country, you will want to spend time with friends, travel, and sightsee. You will also be preparing for examinations in a university system that is unlike the American one. These matters will claim your attention until the last few days before you leave. Before you set your departure date, however, make sure that you allow enough time for final business. Allowing a few extra days for business matters could save you time and money in the long run.

Arranging for Transcripts of Work Completed

Throughout the world, many universities are modeled after the European system. This means that the mode of evaluating your work could be similar to the approach in a British or European university.

Timesaver
While you are at your host institution, it is hard to keep track of important deadlines at your home institution. Keep a special calendar of critical dates to ensure a smooth return. Write down housing deposit deadlines, course registration deadlines, deadlines for declaring your concentration, and other important dates, and allow plenty of time to send materials by international mail.

Before the final examinations of the term, confer with your resident director or international student advisor so that you know what type of examination to expect. Ask them to describe a typical examination question and the approach that the instructors expect. Written examinations are likely to last as long as three hours in some countries.

If your instructors are professors from the host country university, they will probably want you to explain or interpret fully the method of analysis that they presented in their introductory lectures. Expect the exam to include a brief text or statement to analyze. Plan your answer so that it becomes a dialog with the statement, analyzing both its strong and weak points. Bring in illustrations or comparisons with your readings for the course. Show how the method of analysis you learned about in lectures can be used to interpret the passage.

In many countries, the final examination is almost the entire basis for your grade. One or two written examinations or a mid-term may contribute to the grade as well. If the class is a seminar or small group discussion section, if the language of instruction is English, you will probably be graded on the same basis as all the other students in the class.

At some British universities, the entire spring term is devoted to preparation for examinations and to the actual examination weeks. American students are sometimes surprised to find that they must pay for examination term as well as for those in which they attended seminars and lectures. Preparation for the examinations constitutes an important part of the learning experience, although your study during the final term is not necessarily guided by a tutor or instructor. You are expected to learn a great deal from the way you organize your time and material and systematically review all the readings and assignments of the year.

Some institutions send all the examinations to impartial readers for evaluation. The students are identified by means of a code number. The readers, professors from other universities who are scholars in the relevant field of study, evaluate each paper on its merits, without knowing the national origin or academic background of the student. The London School of Economics is one institution that uses this impartial system of examination evaluation.

The British examination is so substantial a portion of the grade that an international student might receive only partial credit for the course if he or she requests permission to waive the final examination. Permission is given to waive the examination in only one or two of the courses the international student is taking. For those courses, the student might receive half the credit earned in the other courses.

At some French universities, international students who enroll directly in regular university classes are given an oral examination to supplement the written one. This is to compensate for the fact that their written language skills might not be as fully developed as those of the other students in the class. Your program director might ask the instructor to write some comments about your contributions to class discussion. This is especially likely if the language of instruction is not English. The instructors might be asked to comment on the amount of progress you made in speaking and writing the language and in understanding the class discussion. The program director or sponsoring university can take these comments into consideration in giving you a grade.

A Student Speaks Up
I studied all the material really hard and when I got to my first examination, they just asked me about the lectures from the first day of class. Until the resident director explained the culture, I felt as if there was no point to my studying.

**A Student
Speaks Up**
My Japanese
teacher didn't
give many tests
during the
semester. I was
really surprised
when he gave a
long dictation
requiring us to
write more than
40 of the charac-
ters that he had
assigned during
the semester.
The test was
very long and
exacting.

Be sure you know the host university's rules for taking final examinations. In France, you must arrive on time and present your student ID to enter the examination room. Late arrivals are locked out of the examination room. If you miss the examination, it might be difficult to arrange another examination before you leave the country. Check carefully in advance to make sure that you comply with your host institution's requirements.

If you are seriously ill and need to schedule a make-up examination, find out whether the examination can be mailed to you in the United States. Next, contact the study abroad office at your home university and find out which office at your home institution proctors special examinations. Usually, a dean's office handles such matters. Provide correct instructions so that the examination can be mailed to the proper office. It is your responsibility to contact that office and make an appointment to take the examination. The dean's office will mail the examination back to the instructor after you complete it.

Find out who issues the transcript—the U.S. sponsoring institution or the host university. Find out how to order duplicates if you ever need additional copies of the records.

Many students overlook the importance of a signed, written request for a transcript. Others assume that the transcript should be sent to an office at their host institution without checking to make sure.

Contact the study abroad office at your home institution and confirm procedures for transferring credit. Find out which office is supposed to receive the transcript for your study abroad credit. Do not assume that it is the registrar's office, the office of the department in which you are majoring, or the study abroad office. Check to be sure. If your home institution is a large university, a transcript might easily get delayed if it goes to the wrong place. Leave written instructions at the transcript-issuing office, stating the address to which your transcript should be sent.

Make sure your bills are paid in full. If your account is not completely clear, the sponsor or host institution will not issue the transcript promptly when grades are ready. Many students have to wait for credit until their final payments are complete.

Ask when the transcript will arrive at your home institution. Do not expect the grades to come in as quickly as at an American institution. For intensive language classes, the grades are usually available within a few days or within a week or so after the conclusion of the program. For semester or year-long programs, the evaluation can take longer.

Many European instructors expect to evaluate examinations during the summer break and to announce them before the students return the following autumn. The London School of Economics, for example, invites a board of faculty from other outstanding U.K. institutions to read and grade all examinations. (The identity of the students is protected during this process.) American students in the classes receive the same evaluation that regular degree-seeking students receive. All of this takes time, however. The official transcript arrives approximately six weeks after the end of examinations.

Although instructors often speed up the evaluation process for American students, it is not uncommon for the transcripts to arrive several months after the conclusion of a direct enrollment program. If you hope to graduate after your credit

Watch Out!
Although the language of instruction might be English, the standards might not be the same. Check carefully to find out what is expected. Get examples of the writing style the university prefers and practice composing in that style.

transfers, you should factor this time lag into your plans.

In Australia, grades for full-year courses are awarded at the conclusion of the full academic year in November. If you attended the first (February to June) semester at an Australian university and took a course that extends through two full semesters, you will not receive your grade until the course ends in November.

Closing Accounts and Leaving Forwarding Addresses

Watch Out!
I applied for the *allocation familiale*, a refund from the French government of the taxes I paid on my rent. As a foreign student, I was entitled to the refund, but it had to go to a bank account. My bank disregarded my instructions and closed my account too soon. Now, we cannot locate or retrieve the funds.

Be sure that your bank account is closed and has a zero balance. If any money is owed to you, make sure that the account remains open long enough to receive the funds or arrange for them to be deposited to a friend's account or the program account so that the money can eventually reach you. Get signed copies of any documents stating when the account will be closed.

Be careful if you apply for any special dispensations that you feel you might be entitled to as an international student. Sometimes, the privilege of avoiding one charge might make you liable for some other costly or time-consuming procedure.

Clear up all utilities, repairs, and other charges and get confirmation in writing that the account is closed. Leave forwarding addresses for all your correspondence. Any deposits that are paid in the host country currency might involve service charges that will consume a large portion of the deposits. You can plan ahead to get the money before you leave, arrange for it to be deposited to your bank account before you close it, or have the money left behind in cash and arrange for a student on the next program to use it.

Getting Deposits Back: Final Meeting with Landlord

If you expect to get a room damage deposit back, be sure that you clean your residence carefully. Carry out and dispose of trash; clean all sinks in your apartment or room as well as any bath or shower facilities in your room or apartment. Empty food out of the refrigerator. Don't leave anything wet that will cause mildew. You will be charged if it is necessary to pay maintenance personnel to clean your room.

It's a good idea to have your last contact with your landlord face to face. If possible, arrange to be there with someone who oversees your program or another responsible witness. Don't hesitate to take a camera along and make photos of the condition of the apartment at the time you vacate it. Make sure that all financial arrangements are final and agree that there will be no additional charges beyond the ones settled at that time. Turn in your key. If you shared with someone from another program, settle accounts with that person before you leave. Make sure your name is taken off the phone bill and the utilities bill.

If you leave while others are still living in the apartment, make doubly sure that your account with the landlord is settled. Reach an agreement about the condition of your room and, if possible, arrange to get your room damage deposit back before you leave. Otherwise, you will probably share responsibility for the condition of the apartment when the last person leaves and you might lose your deposit. If your apartment mates depart for other countries before the accounts are settled, it can be quite difficult to trace them and recover any portion of the deposit that they owe.

Moneysaver
For your own protection, do not allow friends to move into an apartment or room after you leave it, even if there is some more time left on the lease. The landlord will hold you responsible for any dirt, damage, and long-distance phone or utility charges. Leave messages in writing to close any accounts such as the gas.

Bright Idea
Instead of saving all my photos, postcards, and souvenirs until the end of the year, I made a point of shipping a little package every month or so. My family enjoyed the packages, especially the photos, and I avoided major packing hassles at the end.

Packing for Return

As the semester ends, you are probably thinking about your travel plans and trying to eliminate things from your luggage so that you can get around the country easily and economically. The best solution is to begin shipping some items home as far in advance as possible.

Don't try to ship packages to another address in the country where you hope to pick them up. The timing of shipments is unpredictable. Furthermore, you cannot be sure that the destination will have the facilities to accommodate your package.

Plan ahead and start shipping items home at regular intervals during the year. When the cold weather passes, box up your heavy winter clothes and send them home. In most countries, the post offices sell ready-made boxes for shipping home small quantities of clothing, books, souvenirs, and other items. It is best to ship used items and to label their value clearly to avoid paying customs duty. Shipping will not be inexpensive. Consider the postage the price you have to pay for the convenience of traveling extra light.

Give worn-out clothing to a charity or to someone who can use it. Ask the workers in your residence hall or apartment building to suggest a place where you can donate used clothing or other items.

Just before you leave, check for a place to leave any appliances you purchased that are wired for the local electrical current. Other students in the same study abroad program might be able to use them when they arrive. You might also have bedding sized to the dimensions of the local beds and other items that cannot be used in the United States. If there is no place to store them for the next students from your home institution, offer them to local students.

As you eliminate things you don't want to carry with you or ship home, you might wonder whether to keep your course notes, syllabi, examinations, and other materials from your courses. Be sure to keep at least a detailed summary of each course. Your course files constitute important sources of information about the academic program you followed.

If you study abroad for an entire year, get an early start during the second semester by compiling files on your coursework for the first semester and mailing them to your study abroad office or to your home. If appropriate, mail course descriptions directly to the professors to be evaluated and ask them to forward the results to the study abroad office when they are complete.

Use Table 19.1 to prepare a report on each course that still requires approval.

It is not a bad idea to prepare a similar report for each course that was already preapproved. When you return to the States, you might want to request a change in the course equivalency. If there is any question about the credit you earned, the report represents proof that you completed the course and that the academic content was substantial. If there is a problem getting the host university to issue a transcript, you might be able to appeal to the sponsor or to your home institution, provided you have a good, complete copy or report about the work you did.

Because you probably will not know the outcome of all your courses until after you return home, it is wise to mail home a file for each course. The expense is worth it if you need the file to prove that you earned the credit.

Don't be surprised if the grades take a long time to arrive. Some professors might be accustomed to

A Student Speaks Up
I waited almost a year for a grade in one course after mailing my final paper to the professor. Months went by without word. Fortunately, I kept a copy of the paper on disk, which the study abroad office printed and faxed to the program sponsor in the U.S. I finally got my grade and credit.

Watch Out!
Make sure that your home university knows how the course titles and numbers correspond to the courses you originally planned to take. Sometimes, the sponsor assigns different course numbers from the ones listed in the host university materials. Your study abroad advisor will need confirmation that the courses on the transcript are the ones you got approved.

TABLE 19.1 FINAL REPORT ON A COURSE TAKEN ABROAD (MAKE COPIES AS NECESSARY)

Name:

Program Attended: Dates:

Number and Title of Course: Department:

Professor:

Course length: Semester   Term   Academic Year

Attach a syllabus, reading list, schedule of lectures, and a list of graded assignments or other basis for grade.

If the course is not taught in English, provide a brief course description, telling in English what the course was about:

submitting grade reports after their summer vacations. Typically, the transcript reaches the study abroad office two or three months after the conclusion of the program, but longer delays are not uncommon. A delay longer than four months could mean that a professor has mislaid the record of your grade. Ask the study abroad office to follow up and obtain the records from the program sponsor or the responsible person at the host university.

Once the final business matters are complete at your host institution, you can look forward to something that many students hope for: a chance to relax with a vacation of travel before you return home. As you organize your travel, be sure you make an early decision about the date of your return flight. Students in some parts of Europe are advised to select the date at least six months in advance to ensure that seats are available in the price range of their student tickets.

As the day of an international flight approaches, the price of remaining seats will increase. If there is a major international event, or if travel is extremely popular because of a favorable exchange rate, the prices might shoot up rapidly. If you wait, you could find that no seats remain in the price range of student tickets. You might have to pay for an upgrade or, in some cases, for an entirely new ticket if you wait too long to select the date of your return trip.

Some students choose to work for up to six months after completing their study abroad programs. If this option interests you, you should arrange for a work visa before leaving the United States. Work abroad visas for work in certain countries are available through the Council on International Educational Exchange (CIEE),

If your host family invites you to go on an excursion with them, it's a good idea to ask what costs are involved. At that point, the family will make it clear whether you are expected to contribute or be their guest.

www.ciee.org, and through BUNAC (British University North American Clubs), www.bunac.org/. Read more about this in Chapter 21, "Marketing Your Study Abroad Experience."

Many students line up internships or opportunities to teach English for a short period of time before their departure. Other options include waiting on tables, serving as an *au pair* (child care provider) or language tutor, translating or editing, doing odd jobs, serving as a tour guide, or helping out in a small business. This is an excellent way to diversify your knowledge of the country and its culture by rubbing elbows with people from other walks of life.

66

From a journal: Carlisle, England has a very fine museum about Hadrian's Wall and the Romans in Britain. At Vindolanda, they have the only known examples of wooden writing tablets: personal letters. Imagine trying to write any amount of news on a thin piece of wood in Rome so that some courier could carry it all the way to the frontier!

99

If you choose to work or to extend your stay in some other manner, don't forget to keep up your journal. The observations will be memorable later. Many publications have grown from journals kept during study or work abroad experiences!

Be sure to get mailing addresses for all your friends before examinations begin. People will leave the university as they complete their final examinations. Don't wait until the last minute to get the address of a friend from another country; that student might depart before you get the chance.

As a matter of courtesy, pay a final visit to your host family. Take along some little memento and express your thanks for their hospitality over the year. This is your final opportunity to cement the friendship and perhaps ensure that it continues for many years to come.

All students abroad should check with home institutions to nail down housing for the semester of their return. Make sure your room reservation and roommate assignment are in order. Check on all other important matters, such as registration for the semester of your return. You should have received notification during your term abroad of any important deadlines on campus. You or your family should have received notification to make your housing deposit and to take care of other important matters such as course registration for the semester of your return. Provide the study abroad office with addresses and phone numbers where you can be contacted or where messages can be left for you during the vacation period prior to your return home.

Did you receive a scholarship or award that requires you to submit a final report on your study abroad experience? The best time to complete that assignment is just prior to your departure, when all your memories are still fresh and you can verify important addresses and other information as you prepare the report. Make copies of the report as soon as you complete it, and mail the original to the designated office before you leave the host country.

Next, complete your program evaluation and send it to the study abroad office. This is valuable information for the office that advises students who might be considering the same program. Give plenty of advice and suggestions for other students. Mention any important deadlines or documentation that the next students should know. The information might be circulated or included in program brochures. Other students using the files will appreciate any details or good advice that you provide.

> **66**
> I shipped a box of clothes to myself at American Express in Paris, intending to pick it up just before I flew home. However, it did not accept packages and shipped it back to [the city from which I mailed it]. It sat in the central post office until I could send written authorization and payment so that someone could claim it and mail it to me.
> **99**

Just the Facts

- Book your return flight early.
- Know how to prepare for final examinations.
- Get transcript and credit arrangements straight.

- Take time to clear up accounts and get your deposits back.
- Ship home your clothes, supplies, and course papers.
- Ship photos, souvenirs, and small gifts periodically instead of carrying them home.
- Travel light.
- Don't overlook short-term work abroad options.

After You Get Back

PART VI

GET THE SCOOP ON...
Coping with the shock of returning ▪ Assisting
outgoing students ▪ Reaping academic benefits
▪ Maintaining overseas ties

The Unofficial Guide to Re-Entry

Chapter 20

The challenge of returning to your home university, community, and family is greater than you might expect. You have enriched your perceptions of the role of your country and community in the global scheme of things. At home, some things have changed in ways that may surprise you. Your experiences have changed you, perhaps more than you realize. If you recognize the dimensions and complexity of the challenge that lies before you, you will probably find the process of re-entry enjoyable and rewarding.

Reverse Culture Shock

Returning home involves some surprises and some adjustments. You have grown independent and have broadened your sense of the academic opportunities awaiting you and the dimensions of your long-term goals. You might find it difficult to adjust to some of the restrictions that characterized your life before you went away. Coming back with fresh

A Student Speaks Up
In Africa, people went out of their way to meet us and help us. A well-known player from the national women's soccer team brought one of her uniforms for the women to try on. The children kept asking for our autographs. But when we got off the plane in New York again, it was the same old "get out of my way" world we had left behind.

perspectives and plans for your final year at college, you will not always feel comfortable to find that people are still doing the same old things in the same old way.

In your family and community, and on your campus, other people may have taken over some of the roles you filled before you left. At first, you might not feel as if you fit into the picture in the way that you did. You probably will come back brimming with plans for new projects, and you might not always find it easy to get people excited about your new ideas. It can take a while to find a group you feel comfortable with and to settle into a modified version of your former routine.

As the AIFS handbook points out, you will have an easier time returning to your campus if you have been in regular contact during your time abroad. If you have received a newsletter from your campus, and if you have been in touch with your campus, your friends, and family, you will feel more involved in events and changes in the world you left behind. This news will get you thinking about how you will integrate yourself into that community when you return. At the same time, if you have written regularly to friends and family, they are aware of your thoughts and experiences and some of the ways in which you have grown.

No one will be more eager than your family to read stories about all the amusing, exciting, or moving adventures you have during your stay. Your parents will probably save every one of your letters or e-mails. When you return, you might find a complete set of materials they have saved for you. Their involvement in your experiences over the year and their keen interest in your recollections will be a rewarding part of your return.

The material that your family saved for you, together with notes from your journal, might provide the nucleus of several articles or stories about your experience. Former students, teachers, and writers returning from a year in another country have written interesting books describing their experiences. *In the Circle of the Dance: Notes of an Outsider in Nepal*, by Katharine Bjork Guneratne, is a recent example. It describes the year she spent in Nepal in association with an anthropology research project. Many great writers have contributed to the collection of books on travel and living abroad. Readers are fascinated by the opportunity to experience another world through literature. Your notes may invite you to make a new, timely contribution to the field.

Adjusting to the Return to the States

Coming back to the United States will hold many surprises for you. Depending on where you arrive from, the world of freeways, shady suburbs, shopping malls, and busy cities will look very different to you. You may have forgotten how fast the traffic moves and how large the cars are. If you spent the year in a country of crowded marketplaces, you might wonder where all the people are. Whatever the crowds looked like and however they behaved in the place you lived, Americans will at first seem strange and different in comparison.

You will be glad to find some of the comforts and pastimes you used to enjoy, and at the same time, you will miss things that you grew to love about the country you lived in. Even after those first vivid impressions of strangeness pass, you will have mixed feelings about being back. You might feel irritated by policies and restrictions that never bothered you

❝
The streets of China were solidly packed with people, milling about in the marketplace, bargaining, carrying home their purchases, even carrying sofas and refrigerators on their backs. In contrast, my hometown seemed quiet and empty. I heard the sound of lawn mowers, cars, trains, and planes and knew that busy lives were all around me, but I couldn't see anybody anywhere.
❞

**A Student
Speaks Up**
The people in
Ghana were so
nice. They made
us feel like
superstars.
People shake
hands and con-
tinue to touch
one another as
they talk, and
everyone is help-
ful and kind.

before you left. On the other hand, you might find
that many of your reasons for going were valid, that
you have gained what you hoped from the experience, and that the future promises many opportunities to use knowledge you acquired.

Your experience abroad might make you appreciate being brought up in the United States with all
its opportunities. You took advantage of an opportunity to go to a developing country to study, teach,
or work and found that you could do it with relative
ease and, probably, at relatively low cost. On the
other hand, many of the friends you made in that
country can only dream of coming to the United
States to study. They counted themselves lucky even
to attend the university. You might return with
renewed appreciation for the many services available on your home campus and in your community.
Many students who return from study abroad
become interested in helping a student from their
host country to study in, or visit, the United States
and volunteer for community or campus programs
that promote international exchange.

At times, you might experience reverse culture
shock—depression for feeling your language skills
begin to fade and for missing the food and the cultural richness of the place you studied. However
much you may have missed "American know-how"
while you were away, getting back to the familiar
ways of doing things might sometimes aggravate
you. You got used to coping with another system and
probably took some pride in how well you understood it and learned to get things done. As you readjust, the type of control you had over your life will
once again seem to slip away from you, at least temporarily. Your family and the other people you first

see upon your return might not be able to recognize how much you miss the places and people you have left behind. They might not fully appreciate the improvement you made in your language skills, the significance of the knowledge you acquired in your classes, or the degree to which you matured and learned to take care of yourself while abroad. Although many people will be keenly interested in your experiences, some will not.

The good news is that recognition and appreciation will come with time. You will not only readjust to the system you grew up with and know well, but also you will gradually integrate many of your new skills into that world. Once you return to campus, your language teachers will notice your improved skills, and your papers will reflect the way your thinking has matured. You will find opportunities to make use of your ability to think and to find solutions outside of the conventional guidelines. Your friends will also grow and change while you are away, and some of them may no longer be as close to you as they used to be. On the other hand, you will have new interests and find people who share them.

Talk to Your Study Abroad Advisor

One of the people who will be most eager to hear about the experience is your study abroad advisor. Your careful, detailed evaluation of the program will be invaluable to the office that will prepare other students for study abroad experiences. Campus advisors cannot be present on every program, and when they do have an opportunity to visit program sites, they often get a rosy picture in the brief time they are there. Your report about your experience will be very helpful to the study abroad office.

If you have trouble getting some of your old friends to listen to all your anecdotes and descriptions, you will find willing ears among the students who are looking for information about study abroad opportunities. Volunteer to lead coffee hour discussions or informational meetings scheduled by the study abroad office, or arrange to come in at a regular time each week to help advise students who are selecting programs. If some of your professors particularly encouraged you to choose the program, let them know how much you appreciated their help and offer to help publicize the program.

Orientation programs for outgoing students are a valuable part of preparing for study abroad. The study abroad office will welcome your assistance in organizing information sessions for students going to the country where you sojourned. You will have the latest information about local transportation, dress, customs, slang, course offerings, and a variety of other things. Offer to attend the orientation sessions and bring along your photos and other materials to help prepare outgoing students. They can benefit from your first-hand knowledge of the country.

Sharing Your Experience

There are many opportunities on your campus to share your experience with students who are genuinely interested in the experience and who will ask many detailed questions. They are the students who are seriously considering study abroad in the near future. As a fellow student who has just returned from abroad, you will be their most important and credible source of information. Not only can you help them choose a program, but you can also prepare them to get the most out of their study abroad experience. You can confirm everything valid and helpful that the program administrators told you. You can add essential new tips and advice.

You will also enjoy talking with international students from the host country. They, too, will welcome your familiarity with their home country. They will appreciate your proficiency in their language and your interest in their food and customs. By participating in international clubs on campus and in the activities of international residence halls or language houses, you can recapture some of the excitement of your experience and make some important contributions to international awareness on your home campus.

Some new leadership roles may await you in conducting a discussion group on international relations in the region from which you have returned. If you find a club that promotes cultural awareness, you might become activities chair or run for office. Many campuses have clubs in which students from a region of the world share their interests with students who are studying the language and culture of that region. Is there a Latin American Club, an Indian Students Association, or a Russian, Japanese, or Chinese Studies Club? Why not start a group for the area in which you are interested? Contact your student activities organization with a plan to organize a Middle Eastern studies or African studies night with music, costumes, and food. Don't be discouraged if a single organization does not have the funds to cover all the costs of the event. Talk to several organizations and campus offices and persuade them to share the costs. Among the offices that might support your plan are the international

A Student Speaks Up
I think the most important information about this program comes from students who have been there. I'm not so interested in having someone from the study abroad office tell me about the program. I would like to meet the students who just got back and find out what it was like from them.

A Student Speaks Up
When I got back from Argentina, I could really speak Spanish! I joined the Hispanic Cultural Club and an international conflict resolution group that meets weekly to discuss international affairs. Recently, I obtained a grant to do research in Bolivia.

studies office, the dean of students office, the language department, the foreign students advisor, and the multicultural affairs office.

Did any of the students in your study abroad program discover new talents while you were abroad? Make use of these talents in creating a new band to play the latest Middle Eastern hits, a dance club where you can work on your tango, or a sports club where you can improve your rugby or tai chi skills. If you are a graduate student, you might offer to serve as international affairs editor for the graduate students' newsletter. Whatever the skills you acquired while abroad, you will benefit from the opportunity to relive your experience and exhibit your leadership skills. Your friends will appreciate the opportunity to express their new abilities and keep their interests alive.

There are a number of international organizations with a service focus that you might want to join if they are active on your campus. If they are not, consider establishing a chapter. For those concerned with global environmental issues, the Sierra Club or regional environmental groups will assist you in setting up a chapter on your campus:

Sierra Club
85 Second St.
Second Floor
San Francisco CA, 94105-3441
Phone: 415-977-5500
Fax: 415-977-5799
E-mail: information@sierraclub.org
www.sierraclub.org/

International service organizations include Rotary International, which might have a chapter in your home town or college community. Find the campus advisor or community chapter, or contact the international offices and click on Where Clubs Meet:

Rotary International
One Rotary Center
1560 Sherman Ave.
Evanston, IL 60201 USA
Phone: 847-866-3000
Fax: 847-328-8554
www.rotary.org/

There are many international humanitarian relief organizations. In addition to disaster relieve organizations such as the Red Cross (www.red cross.org) or Care (www.care.org/), they include organizations that provide relief for poverty-stricken communities. Among these are both sectarian and non-sectarian organizations:

Habitat for Humanity International
www.habitat.org/

Oxfam America—with links to Oxfam International
26 West St.
Boston, MA 02111 USA
Phone: 800-77-OXFAM
Fax: 617-728-2594
E-mail: info@oxfamamerica.org
www.oxfamamerica.org/

There are many others. If you attend a church or synagogue in your campus community, ask about ways in which you can participate in international service projects organized by your denomination, either at the regional or national level. Consider starting a project of interest to you.

Bright Idea
I studied at Oxford during my junior year and subsequently became a Presbyterian minister. I am currently organizing a church youth group for a summer home stay program in Morocco.

Describing Your Experience in Writing, Through Presentations, and in Person

One of the first ways in which you can build on your recent experience is to design a proposal for an internship in the study abroad office. This is a valuable way of gaining a grateful audience for your experiences and earning credit by performing important services for the study abroad office. You might be able to include some of the following:

- Develop web site information.

- Develop a slide presentation using your own photos or graphics.

- Revise the study abroad office FAQs.

- Revise the handbook for students preparing to study in the country.

- Participate in the orientation session for students getting ready to depart.

You could also offer to collect and analyze data for the study abroad office. This data can include market analysis (finding out which information sources and publicity materials had the most influence on students' choices of study abroad programs), tabulation of responses from program evaluations, charting demographic patterns in study abroad enrollment, and studying patterns in enrollment by concentration, year in school, or other useful information.

Prepare a paper on cultural adjustment for the country that could be used in a handbook, or prepare a paper on the historic or cultural sites you visited on program excursions to help future students get more from their visits.

Are you a member of one of the underrepresented groups in study abroad (discussed later)? Describe what persuaded you to participate and propose methods for encouraging more students from your group to study abroad. Give presentations or organize information sessions especially for organizations in which your group is strongly represented. Invite speakers from the study abroad office, faculty involved with the program, and students who participated in other programs.

In a book called *Missing the Boat*, Crauford Goodwin and Michael Nacht describe what they discovered when they decided to find out why students and faculty in some fields are not taking full advantage of the opportunities that international exchanges offer. Those who go abroad speak enthusiastically of their experiences, but the word is not getting around. You can make an important contribution by sharing your study abroad experience and the opportunities it will provide with students in your major, your field, and other groups that might not be aware of how study abroad can benefit them.

According to the IIE *Academic Year Abroad 1990–2000*, some groups that are underrepresented in study abroad programs are:

- Men (6 out of every 10 students abroad are women)
- Science majors
- Medical students and professionals
- Athletes
- Graduate students
- Minority students (8 out of 10 students abroad are of European origin)
- Double majors
- Math majors
- Computer science majors
- Agriculture and engineering students

Bright Idea
As a graduate student, I studied abroad one summer on a scholarship. That fall, I organized information sessions to tell other graduate students how to get financial aid for study abroad. The next summer, graduate students enrolled in several programs. The oldest was 53, and more than half were African American.

- Education students
- People who are timid and afraid of taking risks
- Law students

Like a student who organized an information session for graduate students in education, you might be instrumental in stimulating interest in study abroad in a student population that had not considered it before. The graduate student pointed out that education students can earn credit toward their academic specialty and collect valuable classroom materials during a summer of study abroad. Teachers already in the classroom can earn additional credits that are required for certification and "recharge their batteries" with new enthusiasm for the following year of teaching. Her enthusiasm for her experience prompted many others to consider the opportunity. You, too, might be able to convey your own excitement about international study to a group of students who would benefit from earning academic credit in another country.

Did you go to a region of the world where Americans are less likely to study abroad? *Academic Year Abroad* records that more than 64 percent of Americans who go abroad are likely to study in Europe. Latin America comes second with 15 percent of the students. Much smaller numbers go to Africa, Asia, Oceania, or the Middle East. Write a paper presenting reasons for students to study in the country you visited, explaining what attracted you and why you benefited. Use your paper to create a Web page, a flyer for the study abroad office, or an article for the campus newspaper.

Organize a campus awareness program to increase interest in areas of the world of critical importance. Invite students from the region to give presentations or display cultural achievements. Consider developing a scholarship for an incoming international student from the region or a study abroad scholarship for an outgoing student.

Some of the ways you can describe your experience can have a direct effect on other students considering study abroad. At the same time, you can use your experiences on your U.S. campus in many other ways. You might play a role in making some valuable improvements in study abroad opportunities at your institution.

Incorporating the Experience into Re-Entry Coursework

In research papers, you can build on the insights you gained overseas. You might be able to use the new perspective that it gave you on situations in the United States in courses on public policy, government, or sociology. You might have an opportunity to do research on the country that interests you in an anthropology, international relations, or language course. Management students might be able to do comparative studies of organizations in the United States and abroad. Economics students might be able to use what they observed about the functioning of the EU or NAFTA.

Your senior honors paper can build on some of the work you did abroad. With access to professors and materials via the Internet and interlibrary loan, you might be able to continue research begun during your study abroad year and build substantially on the preliminary work you began while abroad.

Did you start taking an interest in international relations while you were abroad? Perhaps you went abroad because you were already interested in this crucially important field and wanted to learn more about it. Now is the time to show what you've

> 66
> Last year, I had the opportunity to study at a Japanese university, where I had my first experience of international relations from a non-Western perspective. I was curious about Japan's relations with nations other than the U.S. From the material I gathered in Japan, I developed my senior thesis.
> 99

learned. Write some position papers for the student newspaper. Develop a class project involving a debate on an important issue in world affairs. If there is no Model UN chapter on your campus, consider inaugurating one. Successful chapters can go on to international competitions where they meet skilled teams from outstanding universities all over the world.

High school students can check out the International Model UN Association (IMUN), a nonprofit organization holding non-governmental organization status with the United Nations that promotes global awareness at the high school level (www.imuna.org/).

The American Model United Nations, Inc. (AMUN) is an organization for college and university students. Activities for high school students are also offered:

> 5005 West Winona
> Chicago, IL 60630
> Phone: 773-777-AMUN
> Fax: 773-777-1963
> E-mail: mail@amun.org
> www.amun.org

Thanks to the language skills you developed while you were abroad, you have access to research materials in the language of the country where you studied. Your language proficiency and your skillful use of materials that other students might not be able to use will add valuable insights to any topic you write on, as well as to any class discussion. Being able to see issues from the perspective of another culture adds dimensions to all your writing. In addition, you will enrich the discussion of many topics by encouraging your classmates to entertain a variety of interpretations of the material under discussion.

You might be able to use e-mail or the Internet to follow up on your readings by contacting people directly for additional information. The opportunity to discuss course topics with students who have just returned from different countries will enliven the classes you take on your home campus. You might take new pleasure in contact with professors who have done research in the country where you studied or who were raised or educated there.

Checking Up on Your Study Abroad Credit Status

You might find that it takes some time for all of your transfer credit to appear on your home college record. Be sure to monitor this process closely. Make sure that your transcript arrives on time and take responsibility for following up if an instructor has not submitted a grade. Double-check with the program sponsor to be sure you have taken care of all your obligations, paid all bills, and turned in all paper work.

Check with your home institution and make sure that you have arranged for the program to send the transcript of your study abroad grades to the right office.

If you took any courses that were not evaluated before you went abroad, make arrangements to take all the materials to the professor or advisor who will review the material for you and decide what credit you should receive. Make sure that you follow up and get the approvals to the right office.

Sometimes, your status for course registration, housing, and your class rank as it appears in the campus directory depend on getting all the transfer credit processed before the start of the semester. Don't pressure the study abroad office to process all

Bright Idea
My first day on campus after arriving from Australia, I met two students who were members of the campus Model UN group and invited me to join. We did so well that the college paid our way to the international competition.

your transfer credit at the last minute. Plan ahead and make sure that you take care of your part of the paperwork as far in advance as possible.

Double-check all the credit you receive with your concentration advisor, major advisor or academic advising office to make sure you have fulfilled all the degree requirements you expected to complete through study abroad. Don't wait until just before graduation to find out if there are any remaining requirements to fill.

When you apply for jobs, for graduation, and for graduate school, you want the record of transfer credit to appear on your transcript.

Maintaining Contact with Study Abroad Friends and Associates

The friendships you made overseas will appear increasingly precious as time goes by. Don't lose them. Collect e-mail addresses, parents' addresses, or other permanent addresses before you leave. Follow up with letters when you get home. Write at New Year's. Underscore any academic or professional interests you have in common. Discuss ways of staying in touch by Internet or by meeting again. These contacts will become increasingly valuable and meaningful as time goes on.

When the time comes to apply for jobs or for graduate school, a reference from an instructor from another country is very useful. Your contacts might also be useful if you plan another trip abroad. They might have advice about places to stay or know how to get access to people and organizations you need to contact. Your friends might be able to help you set up opportunities for other students. Some of your professors might appreciate having the opportunity to follow up on the contacts you made. Some

Moneysaver
Sign up for E-savers at www.usairways.com/travel/fares/esavers.htm. US Airways often announces super-saver extended weekend fares. During the winter months on "quickie," they include great deals on quick trips to Europe. This might be one way to stay in touch with friends, refresh those memories before they fade, or even to pick up books and materials you need.

of the business people you met may have ideas about ways to create internships for you or for other students from your institution.

Best of all, it is very rewarding just to keep in touch with your friends as the years go by.

Just the Facts

- Expect reverse culture shock when you return to the United States.

- Share your experiences with students interested in study abroad.

- Maintain your contacts abroad.

- Take the lead in activities with an international focus.

66

When I studied in France, I met a Hungarian student who invited me to visit her home in Budapest. The following Christmas, I went to Budapest to visit her. Thanks to the contacts I made through her, I am an intern in the American embassy in Budapest helping other students from my institution to arrange study abroad opportunities in Budapest.

99

GET THE SCOOP ON...
Making your experience work for you on campus
▪ Building on your experience in your job
search ▪ Designing a career with international
dimensions ▪ Making study abroad work for you
in the U.S. job market

Marketing Your Study Abroad Experience

Chapter 21

Even before graduation approaches, you can reap benefits on campus from effective use of your study abroad experience. The experience will also benefit you as you seek special opportunities for continued study. When you enter the job market, a world of possibilities will open to you because of your experience and the contacts and knowledge you have acquired. Whether you take advantage of them might depend on your skill in marketing the experience effectively.

Marketing Your Experience on Campus

Chapter 20, "The Unofficial Guide to Re-Entry," discussed some creative ways of using your study abroad experience on the campus to promote study abroad and to give you some ways of building on your experience in your academic work. There are many more ways to maximize what you have gained from study in another country to benefit you while you complete your studies.

A Student Speaks Up

After my experience studying at the Glasgow School of Art, I am much more focussed on my professional goals. Besides ideas, lectures by visiting artists showed me valuable practical techniques that I put into practice immediately. My work improved greatly.

Jobs, Scholarships, Internships, and Teaching Opportunities on Your Campus

After a semester or year of international training, many students return to campus with a range of immediately marketable skills that serve them well in the job market. In fact, they often provide direct access to jobs on campus.

Students who participated in professional training programs in fields such as healthcare, business, and international law come back with knowledge and skills that can go to work for them at once. Beyond these immediately marketable skills are a whole range of strengths that all students bring back to campus, regardless of their field of study.

Your international experience can be valuable to a number of offices on your campus. The international studies office might be able to use your familiarity with international travel to help advise students as they plan their travel. Because you are familiar with one or more countries outside the United States, your advice will be helpful to students in putting together their study abroad itineraries and budgets. You have learned the logistics of traveling from one country to another, solving visa problems, coping with exchange rates, and the like.

Because you understand the components of international programs, you will be able to process paperwork and files related to international student visas, sort study abroad publicity materials, and write newsletters for students abroad.

Your improved language skills are immediately helpful in the language department. As an undergraduate, you might be able to work as a drill instructor in language classes and labs, and graduate students can immediately begin teaching language classes. The study abroad office will welcome you if you can read other languages because you can interpret course descriptions and transcripts, as well as orientation materials. Therefore, you can assist outgoing students and the study abroad office staff. Many other offices on campus might take advantage of your ability to read communications in a second language and to proofread text. The registrar's office might be able to use your skills at reading transfer credit information from study abroad transcripts, and the library can use you to read book titles and help with circulation and shelving.

Having been an international student yourself, you understand the issues that face an international student adjusting to university life in a new environment. You might be able to use your language skills and experience to help arriving international students find their way around campus. Spouses and children of international students might welcome an opportunity to speak their language with you. Volunteer programs to help international visitors, students, and their families might welcome your new language proficiency and give you a chance to develop it further. Child care for non-native speakers of English could provide other opportunities to earn money. The families of international students and visiting scholars will enjoy conversing with you and will further improve your language skills.

Because you are accustomed to dealing with international travelers, you have experience talking with many people who are not native speakers of English or of the language you studied abroad. You can probably understand and communicate with non-native speakers better than people who have not traveled. Whether your campus job calls for welcoming international VIPs or teaching English to

Unofficially...
A student who served as a corporate intern in Japan served as the newsletter editor and coordinator of re-entry events for the study abroad office because of her experience with living abroad, Asian languages, and corporate procedures.

children, you will move comfortably in a multinational setting on campus and later in your career.

Counseling trainees with international experience can understand the difficulties faced by people of all ages when they arrive in a new culture. Your increased empathy might prove valuable in an internship in the international students office or in the counseling center.

Unofficially...
As a Spanish teacher, I worked extensively with healthcare services for Spanish speakers in our community and got jobs for students at local hospitals. I obtained a grant to take a Spanish concentrator to Honduras for one month of practical experience in a hospital to enhance her skills.

Hospitals in many communities need assistants to help interpret for native speakers of Spanish and, in some large cities, a number of other languages, including Chinese. Programs have been set up in some communities to provide Spanish language support for healthcare and other public services. Investigate some of these ways of using your language skill and developing it even further.

If you went abroad to do research, you probably had to design and carry out a project on your own, learning to use new types of materials and gaining insights into new methodologies. You might return with a strong reputation as an innovative and knowledgeable researcher with the potential to take on challenging new projects.

Beyond the specific skills related to the training you received while you were abroad, you have acquired a whole range of strengths that will undoubtedly position you for leadership roles on campus and beyond. You have learned to handle responsible decisions and have developed an above-average ability to function as an independent adult. As you adapted to unusual situations and found your way around strange campuses and cities, you learned how to be resourceful and to take responsibility for getting things done. Executive positions in campus organizations will lead to managerial opportunities in the world at large.

You have learned valuable communication skills because you had to see things from other perspectives and work with and learn from other peoples. In addition to citizens of the host country, you learned to get along with people from around the world whom you met and dealt with in a new learning environment. These skills will help you work with groups initially as a campus leader and later on as a professional, whether your career goals lead you toward management, education, journalism, counseling and advising, or marketing. Because you have gained a strong sense of your own abilities and have confidence in yourself, others will have confidence in your ability to handle responsibility and direct projects.

As a public speaker, classroom presenter, debater, or class officer on campus, you will take advantage of the fact that study abroad has improved your command of English and your ability to defend your point of view. In addition, you have learned how to see things from different perspectives and to set aside traditional solutions in order to find new, creative ways of dealing with problems. Not only will you show these skills in your academic performance, but you also will shine at working out problems in difficult situations.

In completing job applications, campaigning for office, proposing ambitious projects, and applying for grants and fellowships, you have a distinct advantage over many other candidates. To study abroad, you successfully completed an application in which you effectively organized and presented your capabilities, interests, and experience. Each successful application process prepares you for the next.

Each student returning from study abroad can identify many of these skills among the benefits of

Bright Idea
After I got back from study abroad, I was one of the founders and leaders of a conflict-resolution group on campus. We dealt with issues of international diplomacy and negotiation. Each week, we invited a speaker with direct experience in an area of conflict somewhere in the world.

Unofficially...
I make it a prac-
tice to apply for
fellowships,
grants, new posi-
tions, and offices
at least once a
year. It helps me
keep my experi-
ence in perspec-
tive—seeing
what I've learned
and where I'm
headed. The
more often I do
it, the more
effective I am.

study abroad. Being aware of your new strengths will serve you well as you look for campus jobs upon your return. Review the ones listed here, note some additional skills you have acquired that are directly related to the subject you studied abroad, and make a summary. Choose the skills that give you the greatest feeling of satisfaction and accomplishment. As you look for opportunities to display your achievements on campus, emphasize the capabilities that you most want to incorporate into your future career plans.

In addition to the suggestions here, you might find other positions on campus for which you could make a strong application. In fact, your increased maturity and initiative may qualify you for a responsible position in any campus office where you would be required to deal with confidential information, handle details, advise other students, or work independently. You might qualify for

- A position as a resident assistant in a residence hall
- Drill instructor in a language class or in a language laboratory
- Grader for a foreign language instructor or a professor in a related field
- Lab assistant in a field related to your research abroad
- Assistant in the office that serves international students, helping with visa matters, cultural orientation, and the like
- Assistant in the study abroad office, organizing materials, sending out program publicity, and answering questions for prospective study abroad students

- Talking about your institution and its strengths as an advertising representative for the campus newspaper or as an aide in the admissions office

- Intern in the international studies office

- English tutor for non-native speakers of English

- Assistant in the offices of career services, multicultural affairs, or modern languages

- Aide in a local public school foreign language, government, or world history class

If you went abroad as a graduate student, you will clearly return well qualified to conduct classes in your field, lead field research projects, and add a new dimension to your subject area because of the work you did overseas.

In addition to campus employment, you should consider scholarships for which you might qualify. You might earn a scholarship to return to the country where you studied or to carry out a project in a related region. Undergraduates should consider applying for prestigious study abroad scholarships for beginning graduate study. See the section on Rotary, Fulbright, Marshall, and other scholarships in Chapter 7, "Figuring Out the Cost of Programs and How to Finance Them."

The policies for awarding many of these fellowships discourage applicants from going back to the same country where they previously studied. However, your earlier experience probably qualifies you to carry out related work in a country that speaks the same language or to expand your experience by going to a different part of the world to continue your research. A student who studied in

A Student Speaks Up
When the students in our group became concerned about the way the institution was handling housing assignments, I was chosen as one of the program representatives to speak to the president and offer some diplomatic solutions to the problem. We persuaded him to reverse an unpopular decision.

Argentina, for example, might apply successfully for a grant to do research in Bolivia. An anthropology concentrator who studied in the U.K. might win an opportunity to begin graduate studies in New Zealand. By refreshing your language skills or beginning the study of a lesser-known language, you might improve your chances of going to a country where you could continue your study of that language, especially if it is gaining global importance. You might also go to a country where English is not the official language, but where it is widely used and where you can develop your skills in a language you studied previously.

Study abroad provides excellent qualifications for applications to graduate school and for grants and fellowships to support your professional studies. The same skills that help you apply for campus jobs, honors, and awards prior to graduation will strengthen your application for graduate study.

As you may already know, most American institutions do not factor transfer credit grades into your home university grade point average. Your transfer credit record will show only the home university course and the amount of credit you received. Therefore, many students ask how to document their grades in a manner acceptable to graduate schools and fellowship administrators.

If you studied abroad under the sponsorship of an American university, you can easily request additional transcripts as often as you require them. Many overseas universities accustomed to serving visiting American students are also willing to issue official transcripts as often as necessary. However, many universities in other countries still do not issue transcripts for their own students. They can issue only one official record of the credit and grades you

A Student Speaks Up
Describing disturbing experiences in the Czech Republic, I recognized my ability to move my readers without losing control of my material and to write persuasively about the importance of building cultural understanding. This is what persuaded me to become a journalist.

earned. In Germany and in some other countries, instructors give each visiting student a certificate. In Germany, this is called a *schein* (pl. *scheine*). It confirms that you attended the class. Some certificates indicate whether you performed satisfactorily or well. You receive no other official documentation of your attendance and performance from the university.

In some cases, the international affairs office can issue a transcript to record your performance in the special classes for foreigners, but you are instructed to obtain an individual certificate from the instructor of any regular university class in which you enrolled.

If you have no possibility of obtaining duplicate transcripts to send to graduate schools, employers, or foundations, ask your study abroad office to assist you. The study abroad office might be willing to issue an affidavit certifying the accuracy of its records showing the credit you earned and the grades you received. Graduate programs in many fields accept such an affidavit. If you study abroad on an official program of your home institution, the law school admission clearinghouse will accept confirmation from your home institution of the credit you earned and the grades you received.

Entering the Job Market

When it's time to enter the job market, you will have gained some practice in marketing your study abroad experience and in showing how you were able to build on it. This will benefit you in preparing your job applications. Employers will see that you have already taken advantage of the knowledge you've gained from study in another culture and have used it to make contributions through your academic work, your on-campus employment, and volunteer activities on the campus and in the community. This shows them that the experience will benefit them as well.

Building the Experience into Your Resume

Assess the aspects of your study abroad experience that gave you the most satisfaction and consider the skills that they reveal. Emphasize these skills in your summary statement. Mention your language skills, your ability to work with people from different cultures, your ability to handle the unexpected, and your ease with getting things done in challenging situations. Mention any special recognition or award, such as a merit scholarship or unique responsibility that you took on. Bear in mind that the program recognized your abilities when it accepted you to participate and give examples of any other ways in which you were singled out during your time abroad. Be sure to call the reader's attention to any world-recognized area you visited as part of your experience, any well-known figures that you met, and any features of the program which were noteworthy. If you cannot think of any prestigious aspect of the program, give it prestige in the way you describe it. Emphasize unique features of the site chosen, why it suited the program's educational goals, the strengths of the program, and what some of the students on the program were able to achieve. In your letter of application, discuss why you chose the study abroad experience and how you saw it fitting your academic goals. The strategies you used to select your destination and the critical thinking you used to build on that experience are more important than the distinguished name of the destination or program sponsor. Most employers and selection committees are interested in what you made of your experience and how they can benefit from what you accomplished. The fact that you studied at a famous institution does not necessarily signal real benefits to the organization unless you identify the skills you acquired and give examples of how your employer can use them.

In interviews, the employer will test your critical thinking skills by asking you to discuss the educational objectives of the program. You might point out factors influencing your home university to select that site as one of its approved programs. Above all, emphasize why you chose the program and how you benefited from it.

Be prepared for challenging questions. Recognize that employers might test your "center of gravity" and make sure that you can handle sensitive questions and challenges on the job. Employers want to make sure that you can work well with all the members of the organization. Be ready to answer difficult questions calmly and informatively. Demonstrate that you have the specific knowledge and training required to step into the position for which they are considering you and that challenging situations will not cause you to lose your temper or exercise poor judgment.

Remain positive and concentrate on the skills that you acquired while abroad. Emphasize the benefits the company will gain by hiring you. Do not be put off if an interviewer challenges you by asking about the program cost, implying that the money should have gone to other purposes. Someone might ask why you did not remain in the United States to address important social or economic issues. Some people might suggest that the content of study abroad courses is relatively "lightweight,"

Watch Out!
The doctor who gave me my physical examination said that my Fulbright fellowship was just a lot of money to go abroad and have a good time, and he supposed that I just wanted a rubber stamp on the form. I didn't think of a good answer until much later!

compared with the rigor of academic programs in the United States.

Remember when any of these themes come up that your objective is to demonstrate what you gained from your experience that will contribute to the organization. Emphasize the skills you acquired while abroad: the ability to see things from a broader perspective; ease in looking beyond the conventional approaches to find innovative solutions; comfort in working with people from many different nations, language groups, and cultures; confidence in your qualifications and your ability to get things done, even in difficult situations; improved command of English; fluency in one or more other languages; familiarity with issues of international travel, customs regulations, immigration requirements, planning itineraries, developing a budget, and managing it; ability to empathize with others who are crossing cultures; confidence in presenting your own point of view and comfort in responding to those with different views; and an awareness of your own capabilities and effectiveness in getting things done. The following sections cover some useful points to make as you point out your strengths.

Public Policy

All nations deal with the same issues of public policy that are important in the United States, whether they are most concerned with the management of scarce resources, transportation systems, mass transit, public health, medical care, early childhood education, food production and supply, low-income groups, unemployment, or immigration and race relations. Point out the perspectives and insights that you gain from observing different solutions to many of the problems American society faces. Be prepared to give some examples of your skills in this area.

Problem Solving

Develop some good examples of ways in which you learned to think "outside the box." Show that you can offer fresh approaches to your responsibilities because you have met people from widely different backgrounds and observed numerous solutions to life's problems. Give examples of leadership positions you held after returning from study abroad, and show how your improved skills benefited an organization.

Communications

While you were overseas, you had many opportunities to discuss and explain your culture, government, and educational background with people from other countries. You honed your communications skills at many levels. Mention situations in which you communicated effectively with people to get things done, solve problems, and earn academic credit. Show how you learned to deal with difficult people and deflect or respond to criticism of your country and its government. Point out any situations in which you were able to get people from diverse backgrounds to identify common goals and work together.

Creativity

Observing the contributions of other cultures to world civilization has contributed to your sense of design. Whether you hope to go into marketing or teaching, you can bring innovation and new energy to your work.

Unofficially...
I earned my degree as a language teacher and also taught English in a developing country. I persuaded job interviewers that my students would benefit from using French as a filter for gaining perspective on a third area of the world, as in fact they did.

Flexibility

You now have the ability to work with diverse groups. Working with people from many different cultures has taught you to respect different perspectives and to recognize the contributions of people from various backgrounds. Give examples of these skills in action.

Command of English

You studied one or more languages in addition to English, which enriched your vocabulary, improved your understanding of English grammar, and taught you how to use your own language more effectively.

Using Foreign Contacts as References

Before you go abroad, consider the value of using professors and other contacts from your year abroad as references. Remember how much your professors helped you by recommending you for this study abroad experience. Consider in advance the benefits of asking for references from professors or from other influential people you might meet while you are abroad.

Before the end of your year abroad, ask for letters of reference from one or two of the people in your field who knew you well and could comment on your effectiveness. Think about one or two references for graduate study, as well as some letters that might be useful in your job search. Provide them with forms and pre-addressed envelopes to send the letters to your college placement service file. Remember, it is never too early to build on your success in obtaining one opportunity to qualify for the next.

Throughout your year abroad, take advantage of your contact with people in many walks of life. Keep a journal in which you record interviews with many

Unofficially...
The professor wrote, simply, that he had complete confidence in my artistic qualities and musical abilities and that he was convinced I would succeed in my chosen career as a college music instructor. His letter helped me obtain an ideal teaching position.

different people, regardless of whether you consider them to be professional contacts or just interesting people. Write about your landlady, your program director, young professionals such as the program assistants or coordinators, and working people and professionals from the community. Write down their full names and addresses. You will easily forget those details when you get back to the United States. It is easy to misplace the address sheet that the program provides you, so keep your own record, either in your computer or in an address book prepared for the purpose.

Stay in touch with as many people as possible from your study abroad experience. This includes other students as well as people from the host country. After your return, as you begin to plan your career, you might be surprised at the usefulness of these contacts. If you create a network of contacts from your initial study abroad experience, you will find it useful in creating other opportunities.

Connecting Your Experience to Domestic Job Opportunities

If you don't want to go abroad again in the near future, you can use your international expertise in the domestic job market. Opportunities include providing a range of services to international students and immigrants. Some examples of these services follow:

- Immigration law
- Advocacy for disadvantaged groups
- Teaching English as a second language
- Counseling services
- Visitors' bureaus and related services
- Teaching languages

- Teaching global issues
- Teaching world history and civilization
- Teaching social sciences
- Academic advising
- Career services
- Study abroad advising
- Program marketing and administration
- Program services in the associations
- Administering academic programs

You might also consider teaching regional specialties at the college and university level such as Russian history or Russian studies. A great many teaching positions in anthropology, religion, film studies, literature, and even in the environmental sciences might relate closely to one region of the world in which you have a special academic interest.

Opportunities in international business are so important that many schools are developing ways to send more of their students abroad. One of the most important fields is exporting, which includes any services or products that are offered for use by citizens of other countries. This includes instructional workshops as well as products, services such as consulting, and manufacturing products for sale abroad. Expertise is required to deal with issues of taxes and import regulations as well as marketing and shipping products.

An important and rapidly developing export field embraces all aspects of computer software development, including design, installation, technical support, and a range of related services. Experts are frequently required to travel to install products and train staff. Skilled communication is required to ensure that the customers can use the product effectively. Importing gains importance when the dollar is strong. Many businesses flourish by identifying market trends and bringing needed products to American consumers at a reasonable price. Expert advising and research of international market trends are needed to help them avoid unnecessary charges and market effectively to keep their merchandise competitive.

Financial advising and investment counseling require an understanding of international financial markets, including the economic future of developing countries and the potential for developing sustainable industries in a rapidly changing global market.

In the field of publication, there is an urgent need for up-to-the-minute textbooks in many fields to explain and interpret the rapid pace of global change in a variety of fields from language study to business. Journalists are needed to analyze current events, identify crises, and help the average reader understand how world events affect his or her daily life. Their role in interpreting events is critical whenever an informed public must decide how national and regional policy makers should respond to events in the international sphere. Experts in graphics, design, and illustration travel abroad to get fresh inspiration from other cultures and to identify new trends in design that will make their work fresh and effective. Guidebooks need to be maintained and updated constantly to retain their usefulness to world travelers.

Although many people feel that it is more important to deal with social and public issues close at hand than to travel the world in search of information, international expertise can be a great asset to a policy maker. Washington leaders have expressed concern because they need quick, well-informed briefings on international events to make major decisions. Some leaders have expressed the wish for more international relations "think tanks" to help them make wise decisions on matters that affect the world. Scholars of international relations have the potential to influence the decisions made by policy makers in Washington. Skilled writers with a strong background in international relations work in the State Department, doing research on important areas of the world and preparing policy statements for public officials.

Regionally and even locally, public officials need to be aware of international trends when making decisions about developing resources, investing in industry, and providing transportation. Many of the problems facing the United States are not unique to this country, and officials would benefit from the opportunity to compare notes and learn from others.

Among the aspects of public policy where international experience is valuable are consumer advocacy (making the public aware of how things are produced and of their quality) and environmental advocacy (providing information about global environmental trends and the effect of local decisions on the whole earth's climate and resources). Candidates for public office must increasingly display their awareness of international affairs in expressing their vision for a community or region, and advisors with international expertise are needed to assist them with their duties.

Advice from Experts on International Careers

Samuel P. Huntington has said that the conflict between cultures will be "the latest phase in the evolution of conflict in the modern world." In response

A Student Speaks Up

After completing a summer internship in Asia, I got a position in the office of a Congressman [a representative from a large Eastern state]. I spend a lot of my time helping callers with immigration issues, international travel and commerce, and public relations efforts to attract multinational firms to the region. I will work in the office full time after I graduate.

to his statement, others have presented their views that the only solution to world conflict is to teach human beings how to take the best from all civilizations and build upon that (*Samuel P. Huntington's The Clash of Civilizations? The Debate,* pp. 1, 49).

Whatever position you prefer in this debate about the nature of conflict in tomorrow's world, it is clear to many students of international affairs that we need a better understanding of what constitutes a culture or a civilization. It is also clear that we cannot arrive at an understanding of the relations between peoples of different cultures without learning more about them.

Not long ago, a newly appointed dean of international affairs asked an expert in Washington what is the most important contribution that he could make at the center for international studies that he was going to oversee. The answer was to help Americans acquire a better understanding of the peoples of the Muslim world. Close upon this important task was helping Americans acquire a better understanding of each of the other cultural groups of the modern world.

In the 1996–97 edition of *Open Doors,* John Meyers emphasized the critical importance of creating a globally competent workforce and cited examples of academic institutions and corporations working together to offer work abroad experiences for students that would enable them to combine cross-cultural training with experience in the workforce of another country (*Open Doors* 1996–1997, pp. 142–143). In keeping with these findings, the recently appointed dean of a school of business announced that his most important task was to increase the number of graduate and undergraduate business students who studied abroad. He

Unofficially...
Contrary to what many believe, other nations deal with many of the same social problems that we consider unique to this country. Decision-makers would benefit from sending more students and scholars abroad to study the solutions found elsewhere. In doing so, we could avoid mistakes and identify the best examples.
—A professor of government

launched a systematic effort to develop appropriate study abroad programs for his students and to advise them on the selection of suitable study abroad opportunities.

Shimon Peres has said that "the great challenges of our era transcend national frameworks. Science knows no borders, technology has no flag, information has no passport." ("The End of the Hunting Season in History," *At Century's End: Great Minds Reflect Upon Our Times*, p. 303.)

Developing international expertise is essential not only to resolving world conflicts, but also to managing the global economy. Many have said that it is critical also in understanding what the sciences have to teach us about the state of the world in which we live, and in adapting to the international flow of information and technology. Your study abroad experience is one of the most important ways in which you can develop the competencies you need for the new century.

Just the Facts

- Identify your international skills and use them on campus and in your career.
- Explore the international dimensions of many careers.
- Capitalize on your international contacts.
- Emphasize how your experience will contribute to any organization.

Appendices: Other Information

PART VII

Glossary

Accommodation   The British term for rooms in a residence hall, hotel, or bed-and-breakfast.

Allocation familiale   A French term referring to a refund of the tax that all French citizens pay on their residences. Non-French citizens, including international students, can apply for a refund of the tax.

Apostille   Certification of the validity of a document under the terms of the Hague convention of 1961. With this certification, your degree or license to practice a profession is recognized by all countries who agree to the Hague convention so that you do not have to get further certification within other countries. If you need an apostille, the office of the secretary of state will certify your license or transcript in the state where you earned your degree or obtained your license. This is not required for study abroad but might be required to begin graduate study or to practice a profession in a country other than the one in which you received your previous training or license.

Buy rate   The amount of any currency that is exchanged for a specific foreign currency on any given day. For example, if you are in Spain, holding dollars, and you want to know how many pesetas you will get, you look at the "buy rate" for dollars on the chart. When you get back to the United States with pesetas in hand, you look at the "buy rate" for pesetas to see how many dollars you will get for them.

Class   In the U.K., an individual topic studied in any given academic term. In the U.S. and some other countries, class is synonymous with course.

College   *In France and some Spanish-speaking countries* A secondary institution or high school.

In Australia   A semi-independent residence hall with meal service. Much of the students' social life, including intramural sports and other extracurricular activities, centers on their residential college.

In England   One of the units in a larger university. In the cities of Cambridge, Oxford, and London, a number of independent colleges started during the Middle Ages, each with its own faculty and degree programs. In modern times, they have come together as universities to build libraries, laboratories, and other facilities, but each college continues to function independently.

Consolidator   An air-travel booking service which offers unsold seats that have been released by the airlines at a reduced price. Travelers can purchase the tickets at a discount. Consolidators do not provide any other travel services.

Consortial agreement   A financial aid term. This is an agreement between two institutions outlining the cost of a study abroad program and agreeing that only one of them will provide a participant with financial aid. A student who normally receives financial aid from his or her home institution, and who is planning to participate in a study abroad program offered by another institution, must arrange for both institutions to complete and sign the form in order to receive financial aid.

Consortium   An organization (usually nonprofit) formed by a group of institutions wanting to collaborate on initiatives of mutual interest, such as offering study abroad programs for the students attending the member institutions.

Consulate   A division or regional office of the embassy of a country. At the embassy, the consular officials grant visas to persons wanting to visit their country. The consulate might also assist citizens of its own country who have problems during their stay, such as severe illness, a lost passport, and so on.

Core course   An American term for an introductory course or class that takes a look at a country or a subject area through the perspective of several different disciplines. Examples are modern art, literature, and film of France or a socioeconomic study of modern Latin America.

Course   In the U.K., this term applies to your program of study (what Americans would call a major or field of concentration). What Americans think of as a course is a "class" or a lecture in the U.K.

Credential evaluation   The process of analyzing documentation from abroad about a person's training, degrees, and eligibility to fill a certain job or enroll in a graduate program in the United States.

Culture shock   Symptoms of anxiety and depression arising from adjusting to a new culture.

Degree examinations   The examinations administered by a British university at the end of the year. In the British system, there are few mid-term examinations or quizzes. The entire grade (mark) is usually based on a three-hour examination at the end of the academic year, plus one or more long papers.

Direct enrollment A type of study abroad experience in which the student can choose from a wide range of courses at a host university. The study abroad student attends the same classes as students from the host country, completes the same assignments, and takes the same examinations. An American institution might sponsor the program, in which case the study abroad student receives some special services. (See also *sponsoring institution.*)

Exchange rate The combined buy and sell rates for any two currencies on the world market.

Experiential learning Learning through practical experience as opposed to academic study of the theoretical foundations of a field. Examples of experiential learning include field studies, labs or workshops, internships, practical training programs, and volunteer or on-the-job experience.

Facilitators In an intensive language program, educational staff who work with small groups of students, organize activities, and provide constant reinforcement as students practice their language skills.

Flat British expression for an apartment.

Home stay A rooming arrangement in which one or more international students live in a private home and have some of their meals with the family.

Host country The country where a study abroad student goes to study for a summer, semester, or year.

Host country nationals   A term used in catalogs to refer to the citizens of the country where you are going to study.

Host country sponsor   An organization or institution in the country where you plan to study that manages a study abroad experience for you—coordinating the housing and payment arrangements and arranging for orientation, enrollment in courses, instruction, and awarding credit.

Host family   This term has two uses. Usually, it refers to a family that provides a room and meals to an international student. Sometimes, the term describes a family that provides social contact with the community, rather than lodging and meals. The second type of host family meets the arriving student, helps him or her settle in at the university, and arranges to spend time with the student periodically, but the student lives on campus in a university residence hall.

Host university   The university in another country where a study abroad student enrolls and takes classes.

Immersion   An intensive learning environment in which a student spends all of his or her time learning a new language or culture. The student might live with a host family that speaks no English, the instructors speak only in the language they are teaching, and the student devotes his or her free time to contact with native speakers to learn and practice as much as possible.

Island program   An educational program in another country especially to serve U.S. students or international students, with curriculum and instructors to fit their needs, academic schedule, and degree interests.

Language program   A program of study whose primary objective is to provide instruction in a second or third language for non-native speakers who want to begin study or to improve their proficiency in the language.

Lecture   A talk given by a professor as part of a course. In some countries, the lecture class is associated with a second class organized as a discussion group or seminar in which students do written work and participate in discussions.

Liaison   A person who serves as the main point of contact and communication between two institutions or organizations. For example, the study abroad advisor at an institution might be the main point of contact, or liaison, for communication with a university in another country.

Mark   British expression for a grade or score.

Mensa   A German word for a university restaurant. Depending on the size of the university, there may be several mensas at different locations around the city where the university is located.

Mutual associations   This expression can apply to many different types of cooperative associations, including credit unions for banking purposes or student organizations that own and operate services such as housing for the students of a given country.

Orientation   A formal process of familiarizing students with an environment different from the ones they know. Orientation might take place before students leave their home university or after they arrive at their host university. Orientation normally includes both practical information and an introduction to the culture the students will encounter.

Passport A document certifying your place and date of birth and citizenship and giving you the right to travel to other countries. To obtain a U.S. passport, you must submit to a designated official your application, a certified copy of your birth certificate, the required fee, and two photos of the required size and format and swear the truth of the information on the application. The application is sent to a central processing office, and you get your passport within six to eight weeks. At present, U.S. passports must be renewed every 10 years.

Pre-session A special course for visiting students that takes place before regular classes begin. The course introduces them to the university and the culture of the country, as well as intensive language training for students who are studying the language of instruction.

Proficiency In language teaching, a measurement of your combined skill levels in listening, speaking, reading, and writing and familiarity with the culture.

Program resident director Person in charge of a study abroad program who lives in the country with the students, oversees their academic progress and personal welfare, and takes care of administrative tasks. The resident director might be a faculty member from the sponsoring university who teaches a course.

Re-entry Returning to your home country. Some difficult adjustments might occur when you return to your original surroundings after study abroad.

Residency card   A legal document issued in many countries to confirm your right to remain in the country, and your legal address there, for a specific period of time. This may supercede the visa used to enter the country or replace it altogether.

Restaurants universitaires   The French term for student restaurants. Their nickname: resto-us. All the French university housing and restaurant services are operated by a single government agency.

Resto-us   See *Restaurants universitaires.*

Rolling admission policy   An admission policy in which applications are accepted on a continuous basis until the program is full. When a program has a rolling admission policy, students who apply and submit their deposits first have the best chance of being allowed to participate.

Self-catering   A British term sometimes used in other countries, which refers to a residence hall with kitchen facilities, where the residents prepare their own meals. This is in contrast to the typical British residence halls with a dining hall serving three meals a day that are included in the price of a room.

Sell rate   The rate at which one currency can be exchanged for another. If you hold Swiss francs and want to purchase Russian rubles, the "sell rate" is the number of rubles an exchange bureau will pay you for your francs.

Semester   A period of academic study, lasting 15 weeks or longer, which constitutes one-half of a full academic year at many educational institutions.

Sitting an examination   The British term for taking an examination.

Sponsor (sponsoring institution)   In study abroad, the institution or organization that manages or coordinates your program for you. Examples include your home institution, another American university, or the one to which you are going. The term sponsor might also refer to someone who promises to meet all your expenses so that you can obtain a visa for an extended stay in another country.

Statement of purpose (personal statement) In a study abroad application, a brief essay in which the applicant states why he or she wants to participate in the study abroad program and how the experience will contribute to his or her personal and academic goals.

Target language A language of which you are not a native speaker and which you desire to learn. If you go to a country where the language is spoken in order to develop your skills, you might take some courses in the target language and some that are taught in English.

Term An academic session of approximately 10 weeks, which constitutes one-third of the academic year at some educational institutions, particularly in English-speaking countries. Three terms of full-time study are the equivalent of two semesters of study. Normally, each credit a student earns in a term is considered the equivalent of two-thirds of a semester credit.

Transcript An official record of academic work completed, including the grades and amount of credit a student earns.

Transfer credit Credit you earn elsewhere that is accepted by your home institution, applied to your degree program, and recorded on the transcript of your home college or university. Grades for transfer credit often do not appear on your home institution's transcript.

Traveler's checks   Certificates of exchange that travelers can purchase from an agency, which guarantees their value and replaces them in case of loss or theft. They can be used in place of cash or deposited like checks and can be exchanged for the currency of the country in which you are traveling.

U.S. sponsor   An organization or institution in the United States that arranges study abroad programs for students. The sponsor might provide a variety of services—collecting program fees in U.S. dollars to pay for services provided in the host country; arranging international travel, orientation, housing, and meals; assisting students with class enrollments; overseeing their academic progress; and arranging for issuance of the transcript at the conclusion of the program.

VAT (Value Added Tax)   The English term for a sales tax assessed by all the EU nations and by many other nations on the sale of goods and services. To encourage export of products, non-citizens are allowed to get a refund of the VAT when they purchase a large amount from a single participating enterprise in a single day. In some countries, participating department stores can arrange to collect payment for all your purchases at once, after you have finished shopping, at which point they refund the tax in the form of a discount. In other countries, you must obtain a record of any large purchase at a participating store and present all eligible receipts to the customs officials when you leave the country. Your refund is issued later. Guidebooks for each country provide detailed instructions about obtaining refunds of the VAT.

Visa   A stamp, placed in your passport by a consular official of the country you want to visit, giving permission to enter that country for a specified period of time. After entry, a residency card is sometimes required to confirm your address for the period of your stay. Some countries might not require a visa for short visits or for students. Apply for the visa at the country's nearest consulate, and present the documents it requires. These usually include a letter of admission to a university and evidence that you have funds to support yourself while in the country. Sometimes, the results of a health examination are required.

Wire transfer   Electronic transfer of funds from your bank to a bank in another part of the country or the world. To arrange a wire transfer, your bank requires information about the account to which the money will be transferred as well as the name and telephone number of a bank official.

Directory of Online Resources

Information about Health, Safety, and Government Regulations

U.S. State Department Emergency Services
travel.state.gov/acs.html#emr

U.S. State Department Travel Information and Consular Information Sheets:
travel.state.gov/index.html,
travel.state.gov/foreignentryreqs.html,
travel.state.gov/travel_warnings.html

The Electronic Embassy—Information about all diplomatic missions to the United States and visa requirements for Americans traveling to those countries.
www.embassy.org

Centers for Disease Control
www.cdc.gov/travel/index.htm

Air Security International
www.airsecurity.com/hotspots/HotSpots.asp

Canadian Department of Foreign Affairs and Trade
www.dfait-maeci.gc.ca/travelreport/
menu_e.htm

British Foreign and Commonwealth Office
www.fco.gov.uk

Australian Foreign Affairs and Trade Office
www.dfat.gov.au/consular/advice/advices.
mnu.html

Sponsoring Institutions and Study Abroad Programs

The institutions listed here do not constitute a complete list of all the excellent programs that are available. Rather, they represent a sampling of institutions offering programs of various sizes and academic focus. Those chosen have Web sites and e-mail addresses at which you can get information about a number of programs in various locations. For a more complete list of URLs of sponsoring institutions, see *Academic Programs Abroad* Index I.

Arizona State University
E-mail: ipo@asu.edu
www.asu.edu/ipo/

Boston University
E-mail: abroad@bu.edu
www.bu.edu/abroad

St. Louis University Madrid campus
E-mail: Spain@sluvca.slu.edu
spain.slu.edu

Tufts in Madrid
E-mail: ghainswo@emeral.tufts.edu
www.ase.tufts.edu/studyabroad/tpa.geninfo.
html

Tulane University
> E-mail: Crystal@mailhost.tcs.tulane.edu
> www.tulane.edu/~intprog

Indiana University
> E-mail: Overseas@indiana.edu
> www.indiana.edu/~overseas

University of Kansas
> E-mail: osa@ukans.edu
> www.ukans.edu/~osa

Purdue University
> E-mail: Studyabroad@ipppu.purdue.edu
> www.ippu.purdue.edu/sa/
> welcome.cfm

Duke University
> www.aas.duke.edu/study_abroad

University of Pennsylvania
> E-mail: funaro@pobox.upenn.edu
> www.upenn.edu/oip

University of North Carolina at Chapel Hill
> www.unc.edu/depts/abroad

University of Minnesota
> E-mail: umabroad@tc.umn.edu
> www.umabroad.umn.edu

James Madison University
> www.jmu.edu/intl-ed

Middlebury College
> E-mail: Schoolsabroad@middlebury.edu
> E-mail: larock@middlebury.edu (M.A. in
> Spain)
> www.middlebury.edu

New York University
> E-mail: international.study@nyu.edu
> www.nyu.edu/studyabroad

University of Rochester
E-mail: csaip@cc.rochester.edu
www.rochester.edu/College/study-
abroad/europe.html

Syracuse University
E-mail: suabroad@syr,edu
sumweb.syr.edu/dipa

School for International Training, Center for
World Learning
E-mail: csa@sit.edu
www.sit.edu

Center for Global Education
www.augsburg.edu/global/studyabroad.html

University of Wisconsin-Madison
E-mail: abroad@macc.wisc.edu
www.wisc.edu/studyabroad

Beaver College Center for Education Abroad
E-mail: stern@beaver.edu
www.beaver.edu/cea

Butler University Institute for Study Abroad
E-mail: studyabroad@butler.edu
www.butler.edu/international

Direct Enrollment Programs

London School of Economics
E-mail: m.reddin@lse.ac.uk
www.lse.ac.uk/general_course

University of St. Andrews
E-mail: IntOff@st-andrews.ac.uk
www.st-andrews.ac.uk

University of Lancaster
E-mail (Ethel Sussman, North American
Officer): 74544.1273@compuserve.com
www.lancaster.ac.uk

University of East Anglia
    International Office
    The Registry UEA
    Norwich, Norfolk NR4 7TJ
    United Kingdom
    Phone: 011-44-1603-56161
    Fax: 011-44-1603-58553
    E-mail: julie.lane@uea.ac.uk
    www.uea.ac.uk

University College London
    Gower St.
    London WC1E 6BT
    United Kingdom
    Phone: 011-44-0-71-387-7050
    E-mail: sara.hibbert@ucl.ac.uk
    www.ucl.ac.uk/

Trinity College Dublin
    The Office of International Student Affairs
    Arts Building
    Trinity College
    Dublin 2
    Ireland
    Phone: 011-353-1-608 2011
    or 608 1396
    or 608 2331
    Fax: +353-1-677 1698
    E-mail: scoyle@tcd.ieDublin 2, Ireland
    www.tcd.ie/Senior.Lecturer/Admissions/
    isa_appl.html

Kanazawa University, Japan
    KUSEP program
    E-mail: Gak3531@kenroku.kanazawa-u.jp

University of Adelaide
    E-mail: lizzie.summerfield@adelaide.edu
    www.ipo.adelaide.edu.au/files/ipo_fr.html

American Colleges and Universities in Other Countries

Franklin College, Switzerland
E-mail: info@fc.edu
www.fc.edu

The Center for International Studies, Madrid
E-mail: mary.mccarthy@cis.edu

The American University in Cairo
E-mail: aucegypt@aucnyo.edu
www.aucegypt.edu

The American University in Paris,
E-mail: aup@interport.net
www.aup.fr/html/abroad.html

The Hebrew University of Jerusalem
E-mail: hebrew@compuserve.com
www.hujiac.il/

The American University in Bulgaria
E-mail: admissions@aubg.bg
www.AUBG.BG

Richmond College in London
c/o American Institute for Foreign Study
(AIFS)
www.aifs.org

Organizations Sponsoring Programs for a Consortium of Institutions

Council on International Educational Exchange
(CIEE)
E-mail: info@councilexchanges.org
www.ciee.org

American Institute for Foreign Study (AIFS)
www.aifs.org

Associated Colleges of the Midwest (ACM)
E-mail: acm@acm.edu
www.acm.edu

College Consortium for International Studies
(CCIS)
E-mail: ccis@intr.net

The Great Lakes College Association (GLCA)
www.glca.org

Institute for the International Education of
Students (IES)
in cooperation with the University of
Minnesota
E-mail: info@iesabroad.org
www.iesabroad.org

The Virginia Council for International Education
(VaCIE)
E-mail: Vacie@vt.edu

University Studies Abroad Consortium
E-mail: usac@admin.unr.edu
www.scs.unr.edu/~usac

The Oregon University System
International Programs
E-mail: amy.reardon@orst.edu
osu.orst.edu/internatioanl/oie

Danish International Studies
E-mail: dis@tc.umn.edu
www.disp.dk

Advanced Studies in England
E-mail: 100105.3531@compuserve.com
www.studyabroadbath.org/intro.html

Language Centers

Italian: With centers in Florence, Milan, and
Lignano
www.linguaviva.it/

French: Alliance Française—centers worldwide and
in France, by city on the Alliance Web page
www.best.com/~afsf/sites.html

German

www.goethe.de/p/depadr2.htm

Spanish in Mexico

E-mail: cmi@morelia.podernet.com.mx

www.spanish-language.com/

Programs Abroad for Older People and Families

Elderhostel

www.elderhostel.org

Eldertreks

E-mail: passages@inforamp.net

www.eldertreks.com

FAMILYHOSTEL

www.learn.unh.edu/INTERHOSTEL/IH_FH.
html

Friends in France

E-mail: stay@friends-in-france.com

Friendship Force

www.friendship-force.org

Programs for High School Students

The Experiment in International Living

A Program of World Learning

E-mail: eil@worldlearning.org

www.worldlearning.org/ip.index.html

StudyAbroad.com

Administered by Marc Landon

www.studyabroad.com

University of New Orleans

Division of International Education at
Metropolitan College

www.uno.edu~inst/Welcome.html

Pennsylvania State University Summer Study at the American University in Paris
www.summerstudy.com

Youth for Understanding
www.youthforunderstanding.com

AIFS College Summer Division
E-mail: bavitabi@acis.com
www.acis.com.

Transitions Abroad
www.transabroad.com/frames/trstudy.htm

EF Foundation for Foreign Study (known internationally as EF High School Year)
ef.com/default.asp

AmeriSpan Unlimited
E-mail: info@AmeriSpan.com,
www.AmeriSpan.com.

Online Information About Graduate Examinations

Graduate Record Exam
www.GRE.org

Law School Admissions Council (includes information about LSAT)
E-mail: LSACinfo@LSAC.org
www.LSAC.org

Graduate Management Admission Test (GMAT)
www.gmat.org/

Financial Aid and Loans

Federal financial aid Web sites:
www.ed.gov/offices/OPE/Students and
www.ed.gov/prog_info/SFA/StudentGuide

Citibank
> www.citibank.com/slcsite/

Chase
> www.chase.com/educationfirst

National Education
> www.nationaleducation.com

www.respfunding.com

Scholarships

NSEP
> E-mail: nsep@iie.org
> www.iie.org/nsep/

Rhodes
> www.rhodesscholar.org/

Marshall Scholarships
> E-mail: study.uk@bc-washingtondc.
>> bcouncil.org
> www.britishcouncil-usa.org/usabms1.htm

The Rotary Foundation
> www.rotary.org/foundation/index.htm

Fulbright Fellowships
> www.iie.org/fulbright/

Jobs, Internships, and Work Abroad

Directory of International Internships
> www.isp.msu.edu/InternationalInternships

BUNAC (British University North American Clubs)
> www.bunac.org/

Council on International Educational Exchange
> (CIEE)
> www.ciee.org

Institute of International Education (IIE)
> www.iie.org

Work Abroad: the University of Michigan Work
   Abroad Web Site Directory by William
   Nolting
   www.umich.edu/~icenter/overseas/work/
   workabroad1.html

UCI International Opportunities Program
   University of California, Irvine, Center for
   International Education
   www.cie.uci.edu/iop/

Transitions Abroad
   www.transabroad.com.

Careermosaic
   www.careermosaic.com.

Association of International Practical Training
   www.aipt.org/programs

IAESTE: Engineering and science placements for
   students
   www.aipt.org/prog_iae.html

Project Aspire: Assisting international students
   from Asia with re-entry and career planning
   www.aspireonline.org/

Career information: Database of overseas positions
   and links to other job databases for specific
   world regions
   www.overseasjobs.com

James Madison internships for students in the
   Commonwealth of Virginia
   www.jmu.edu/intl_ed/internships/

University of Pittsburg, International Affairs
   Network Web
   www.pitt.edu/~ian/index.html

NAFSA Regional and National Conferences (job
   registries and interviews)
   www.nafsa.org

The Chronicle of Higher Education
thisweek/chronicle.com

The Sunday *New York Times*
www.nytimes.com

Special Web Sites to Get Students Ready for Study Abroad

University of Wisconsin Steven's Point
www.uwsp.edu/acad/internat/boards/
announce.htm

Cornell University
www.einaudi.cornell.edu/cuabroad/
handbook/index.html

University of Wisconsin Milwaukee
www.uwm.edu/Dept/International/
StudyAbroad/forms.html

Queen's University, Kingston, Ontario
quic.queensu.ca/outgoing/index.html

University of Minnesota
Compiled by Angela DeGruccio
www.UMabroad.umn.edu

International Volunteer Organizations

Sierra Club
E-mail: information@sierraclub.org
www.sierraclub.org/

Rotary International
www.rotary.org/

Red Cross
www.redcross.org

Habitat for Humanity International
www.habitat.org/

Oxfam America (with links to Oxfam
    International)
    E-mail: Info@oxfamamerica.org
    www.oxfamamerica.org/

International Model UN Association (IMUNA)
    www.imuna.org/

The American Model United Nations, Inc.
    (AMUN)
    E-mail: mail@amun.org
    www.amun.org/amun_about.html

Travel Information

Pitkin Guides home page
    www.britguides.com/

Bridgham & Cook, Ltd.
    www.britishgoods.com/Pitkin_Books.htm

Editions Ouest-France
    E-mail: vacation@rextravel.com
    www.editions-ouest-france.com/

Travel Board of Ireland
    www.ireland.travel.ie/home/index.asp

Travel Board of Scotland
    www.holiday.scotland.net/

The Electronic Embassy
    www.embassy.org

The Australian Tourist Board
    www.tourism.gov.au

China National Tourism Association
    www.cnta.com

Tour India
    www.tourindia.com

Japanese National Tourist Office
www.jnto.go.jp

Korean National Tourist Office
www.knto.or.kr

Polish Tourist Information Center
www.travel-poland.pl/

Tour Egypt
touregypt.net/index.htm

Travel Time links for tourist boards of all the countries of Asia and the South Pacific, including Australia, New Zealand, and many more
www.pathfinder.com/time/asia/travel/links1.html

Audio Forum: a distribution center for language learning materials of all kinds, as well as audiovisual materials for travel and crossing cultures
www.audioforum.com

Publications on the World Wide Web

Havel, Vaclav. "The Need for Transcendence in the Postmodern World," speech made in Independence Hall, July 4, 1994.
www.globalideaasbank.org/worldtrans/whole/havelspeech.html

A review of various guides with reader comments. AOL August 18, 1999.
www.ricksteves.com/tips/letgo.htm

Studyabroad.com
www.studyabroad.com
Owned by EDU Liberty City Promotions, Inc., www.edudirectories.com

To subscribe to the studyabroad.com newsletter, send a message to:
listserv@studyabroad.com with "subscribesab_
newsletter" (without the quotes) in the
body of the message.
Message: subscribe sab_newsletter

Travel Services

Uniglobe
www.uniglobe.com/default.cfm

Expedia.com
www.Expedia.com

Airdeals.com
www.Airdeals.com

Travelco.com
www.Travelco.com

Airfare Busters
www.afbusters.com

Asia specialists
Hans World Travel
www.hanstravel.com

Australia
www.austravel.net

Discount Air Finders
A service of the Potomac Area Council of
Hosteling International
E-mail: baltimore.hostel@juno.com
E-mail: hostelling.travel@juno.com

Other Student Travel Services

Academic Travel Service
ats@mail.msen.com

Council Travel
www.counciltravel.com/

STA Travel
      (Offices in 15 cities)
      Phone: 800-925-4777
      www.sta-travel.com

Study Abroad Travel
      Kitt@mn.uswest.net

American Airlines
      www.americanair.com/

Northwest Airlines
      www.nwa.com

US Airways
      www.usairways.com/

US Airways Esavers
      www.usairways.com/travel/fares/esavers.htm.

Delta
      www.delta-air.com/

TWA
      www.twa.com/

United
      www.ual.com/home/default.asp

Japan Air
      www.japanair.com/

Air France
      www.airfrance.fr/

Air Courier Association
      www.aircourier.org

U.S. airports
      www.atlastravel.ca/map.htm.

Frankfurt
      www.frankfurt-airport.de/

Florence
      www.safnet.it/

Rome
> www.adr.it/en/fiumic/mappa-fco.html
> Train schedule for connections to the city,
> www.adr.it/en/fiumic/fiumic-treni.html

French railway system (SNCF)
> www.sncf.fr/voy/indexe.htm

Connections between the rail systems of different countries
> www.thetravelsite.com/Europe/
> RailCountries.htm

Book and pay in the U.S.
> www.raileurope.com

Rail Pass Express, Inc.
> www.railpass.com

BritRailLtd.
> www.britrail.co.uk/

Eurail Corporation
> www.eurail.on.ca/eurailhome.html

Eurostar (The Chunnel train)
> www.eurostar.com/eurostar/

Eurobus
> www.frugaltraveler.com

Eurolines Pass
> www.brtravelgear.com/euroline.html

The Cruise People Ltd.
> member.aol.com/CruiseAZ/freighters.htm

"Freighter Travel Review," Murphy Media Ltd.
> www.maxho.com/~frman/newsupdate.html

Cruise & Freighter Travel Association
> E-mail: info@travltips.com
> www.travltips.com/freighterdirectory.html

Around the World by Freighter
> www.atwtraveler.com/freightr.htm

Asia Budget tours
www.southeastasia.com

Asia Transpacific Journeys
E-mail: travel@southeastasia.com

Worldhotel
www.worldhotel.com

Americans with Disabilities Information

ADA Document Center
janweb.icdi.wvu.edu/kinder/

A Compliance Guide to the ADA
www.thompson.com/tpg/person/able/able.
html

Mid-Atlantic Region Guide
www.adainfo.org/

The U.S. Department of Justice
home page on the ADA
www.usdoj.gov/crt/ada/adahom1.htm

Disability Rights Activist, a publication for showing
people with disabilities how to obtain the services they should receive under the law
www.teleport.com/~abarhydt/

Other information about the law, activism, and
your rights
consumerlawpage.com/brochure/disab.shtml

Mobility International USA (MIUSA)
E-mail:miusa@igc.apc.org
www.miusa.org/

International Careers

International experience during your student years improves your chances of finding an internationally related career. The market is growing and changing rapidly in response to the needs of our increasingly global society. Your experience opens the door to many new types of international jobs that are only just emerging. To give you an idea of the new careers developing, a one-month survey of recent issues of college magazines and major newspapers produced the following array of people working in stimulating international jobs.

Law School Graduates

Attorney representing international clients before the Food and Drug Administration, Federal Trade Commission, and other federal agencies

Attorney specializing in international copyrights and intellectual property rights

Foreign Service officer

Immigration law attorney (several)

Judge advocates for U.S. Air Force in Korea (husband and wife team)

Law school administrator of international legal studies program

Lawyer practicing in England

President of an international telephone carrier

Business School Graduates

Head of treasury and marketing for London firm

Intern at Tokyo plant of international manufacturer of photo and photoduplication equipment

Manager of jewelry and watch-making business in Kenya

Software application consultant in London

Education Graduates

College study abroad program director

English teacher in China

High school teacher who received presidential recognition for having classes enact moral and legal debates from around the world

Intern in study abroad office

Intern and resident tutor in British secondary school

Intern/administrative assistant in study abroad program office in U.K.

Liberal Arts Graduates

Band leader starting an international rock-and-roll band in Taipei and Guam

Chemistry teacher at the American International School in Zurich, Switzerland

Coordinator of Japanese language program and exchanges for a Japanese university

Creative writing teacher in Canada

Designer of billing systems for U.S. firm on assignment in Tel Aviv

Employee of American International School in Vienna

Employee of center that provides legal aid and service to asylum seekers and serves as international defender of women's rights

Employee of General Electric in Brazil

Employee of the International Monetary Fund

English teacher in Hungary

English teacher in Finland

English teacher for the JET program in Japan

English teacher in China

French teacher

Fulbright scholars (several qualified by earlier experience abroad in other locations)

German teacher

International opera singers (three)

International relations expert at the World Bank

Interpreters, aides for international conferences

Leader of delegation from the American Jewish Congress to Cuba

Leader of garden history trips to Ireland

Marine Corps lieutenant doing NATO exercises in Norway

Member of international violin/piano duo (husband and wife team)

Movie reviewer for British journal

Peace Corps volunteer

Professors of British literature (two)

Professor of East Asian languages and civilizations

Professor of German history

Professor of Russian history

Professor of Russian politics

Relief services worker in Kosovo

Researcher of Mayan culture at archeology institute

Volunteer who ran Red Cross canteens in Cairo, Cyprus, and Tripoli during World War II

Rotary scholars in Japan and Italy (qualified by earlier experience abroad in other locations)

Software installer in Germany and France for Swedish financial software firm

Tour leader/activities coordinator on cruise ship

Editor of English subtitles for non-English feature films

The following job announcements appeared during June and July 1999. Many are professional positions with good salaries, requiring international experience, background, or training. Some require second language fluency, with a third language desirable. Several are internships or entry-level positions providing initial work experience abroad for students or recent college graduates:

Assistant university admissions director for international admissions

Community college international student recruiter, advisor, and program director

Business manager, international studies center

Director of education abroad

Director of overseas study center in Switzerland

Director of university center for multicultural programs

Director of university international programs office (study abroad, international student admissions and advising, international studies curriculum, and exchanges)

Director of university international student services

Director of university study abroad office

Engineering placements for students

English teacher at an international business school near Paris

English teacher at the University in Beijing

English language center directors in Tunisia, Kuwait, and the West Bank/Gaza

Evaluator of international credentials for American institutions

Group study exchange coordinator for an international scholarship association

Housing coordinator for a junior year in France program

Intern in information technology and Web design for a study abroad program in Bath, U.K.

Intern at the British embassy in Washington, D.C.

International student advisor

International student advisor at a medical institution

Manager of international admissions for a student placement service

Peace Corps teachers, managers, and trainers in many locations

Professor of Middle Eastern religion

Program associate arranging U.S.-based training programs sponsored by USIA

Science internships for students

Study abroad program administrator for Spain and Africa

Study abroad advisor at a major state university

English teachers in worldwide placements

Publications and Information Sources

Short-Term Work Abroad Visa Programs

BUNAC (British Universities North America Club)—A nonprofit, non-political student organization on British university campuses with its own travel company and work opportunities, including work in Britain, Canada, Ghana, New Zealand, Jamaica, South Africa, and Australia.
16 Bowling Green Lane
London
EC1R 0QH UK
Phone: 0171 251 3472
Fax: 0171 251 0215
E-mail: enquiries@bunac.org.uk
www.bunac.org

CIEE (Council for International Educational Exchange) Work Abroad Program—Short-term work permits for France, Germany, Ireland, Canada, Costa Rica, Australia, and New Zealand. Teach abroad program in China.
www.councilexchanges.org/work/index.htm

Web Sites

The University of Michigan Work Abroad Web site
directory—At 19 pages, it is by far the best
and most complete collection of organizations offering positions worldwide.
Continuously updated information sources
on work abroad for students, career opportunities for recent graduates, new resources for
parents, advisors, or job seekers with more
experience, and volunteer opportunities.
www.umich.edu/~icenter/overseas/work/
workabroad1.html

University of California, Irvine, Center for
International Education—Information about
short-term work, resources with international
opportunities, as well as study abroad.
www.cie.uci.edu/iop

Transitions Abroad—For students interested in
short-term or entry-level jobs abroad. Also
circulates e-mail newsletter and publishes
Transitions Abroad magazine.
www.transabroad.com

Careermosaic—Links to job databases for countries or regions. Lists mainly career positions,
not work abroad programs for U.S. students.
www.careermosaic.com

International Association for the Exchange of
Students for Technical Experience
(IASTE)—Engineering and science placements for students.
www.aipt.org/iaeste

Project Aspire—Nonprofit organization assisting
international students from Asia with re-entry
and career planning.
www.aspireonline.org/

Career information—Database of overseas positions and links to other job databases for specific world regions. www.overseasjobs.com/resources

University of Pittsburgh, International Affairs Network Web—Graduate programs in international relations and links to other resources. www.pitt.edu/~ian/index.html

Information Networks

Washington D.C.—For administrators already in the field, the Employment Roundtable in International Education meets to discuss the international job market once a month at NAFSA (Association of International Educators), IIE (Institute for Educational Exchange), or National Council for International Visitor offices. For information and an invitation to participate, call 202-737-3699.

NAFSA regional and national conferences—A job registry and job interviews take place at each conference. Students and recent graduates are welcome. For membership information, go to www.nafsa.org.

E-mail Newslists

The NAFSA Job Registry circulates announcements about all levels of jobs in international education via two e-mail lists: SECUSS-L and INTER-L. To join SECUSS-L, the Study Abroad Advisors' e-mail list, go to the NAFSA Web site, click on SECUSSA, and follow instructions for signing up. To join INTER-L, an e-mail list for persons in all aspects of international education, go to listserv@vtvm1.cc.vt.edu. Send the message subscribe inter-l yourname. Both listservs provide further instructions and some choice of discussion topics.

www.nafsa.org

Publications

Impact Publications—Extensive catalog of publications describing international careers with information on where to find jobs in specific fields or locations. Includes publications about short-term and summer jobs.

9104-N Manassas Dr.

Manassas Park, VA 20111-5211

Phone: 800-361-1055

The Chronicle of Higher Education—Job listings for administrators and educators in higher education. Job descriptions offer good "maps" for planning your career development strategy. Many libraries keep a copy of this publication. Most of the site is accessible only to subscribers. To subscribe to the Chronicle, write to the address or subscribe online.

The Chronicle of Higher Education

Circulation Department

1255 23rd St., NW

Washington, DC 20037

Phone: 800-728-2803.

thisweek/chronicle.com

Transitions Abroad—Regular issues on jobs abroad
with useful ads. Many opportunities for stu-
dents and recent graduates.
P.O. Box 1300
Amherst, MA 01004
Phone: 413-256-3414
Fax: 413-256-0373

The Sunday *New York Times* Job listings—
Traditionally, a location for professional job
listings from across the nation, although best
known on the East coast. Jobs do not appear
in the free Web edition (www.nytimes.com).
Circulation Office
229 W. 43rd St.
New York, NY 10036
Phone: 212-556-1234

Books

Arthur H. Bell, *Great Jobs Abroad.* McGraw-Hill, Inc.

Susan Griffith, *Teaching English Abroad.* Vacation
Work. (Order through Impact Publications.)

Eric Kocher, Nina Seyal, *International Jobs: Where
They Are and How to Get Them, 5th edition.*
Perseus Books.

Ronald L. and Caryl Krannich, *International Jobs
Directory: 1001 Employers and Great Tips for
Success!* 3rd ed. Feb 99

Ronald L. Krannich, *Complete Guide to International
Jobs and Careers.* Impact Publications.

Transitions Abroad, *Work Abroad: The Complete Guide
to Finding a Job Overseas.* Transitions Abroad
Publishing. (Order through Impact
Publications or Transitions Abroad.)

Bibliography

Choosing a Program

Association of International Education, Japan (AIEJ) and Monbusho (Ministry of Education, Science, Sports, and Culture). *Japanese Colleges and Universities, 1995–97.* Tokyo: AIEJ, 1995.

British Universities Transatlantic Exchange Association (BUTEX). *The BUTEX Guide to Undergraduate Study in the UK.* Plymouth: BUTEX, 1997.

Gateway Japan National Planning Association. *Japan: Exploring Your Options: a Guide to Work, Study, and Research in Japan.* College Park, Maryland: Gateway Japan, 1995.

Hoffa, William. *Study Abroad: A Parent's Guide.* Washington: NAFSA Association of International Educators, 1998.

Peterson's Study Abroad: A Guide to Semester and Yearlong Academic Programs. Princeton, NJ: Peterson's Guides, annual.

Steen, Sara J. Ed. *Academic Year Abroad: The Most Complete Guide to Planning Academic Year Study Abroad.* New York: Institute of International Education (IIE), annual.

Steen, Sara J. Ed. *Vacation Study Abroad.* New York: Institute of International Education (IIE), annual.

Transitions Abroad: The Magazine of International Travel and Life. Amherst: Transitions Abroad Publishing, bi-monthly.

White, Dawn. *Basic Facts on Study Abroad.* Rev. Ed. NAFSA, Council on International Educational Exchange (CIEE) and Institute of International Education (IIE), 1997.

Work Abroad: The Complete Guide to Finding a Job Overseas. Amherst: Transitions Abroad, 1999.

Understanding Other Cultures Through Literature

Achebe, Chinua. *Things Fall Apart.* London: Heineman, 1987.

Bird, Isabella. *The Yangtze Valley and Beyond.* Boston: Beacon Press, 1985.

Chang, Jung. *Wild Swans: Three Daughters of China.* New York: Doubleday, 1991.

Chan Khong, Thich Nu (Cao Ngoc Phuong). *Learning True Love: How I Learned and Practiced Social Change in Vietnam.* Berkeley: Parallax Press, 1993.

Davidson, Cathy N. *36 Views of Mt. Fuji: on Finding Myself in Japan.* New York: Plume, 1993.

Forster, E.M. *A Passage to India.* New York: Modern Library, 1940.

Forster, E.M. *A Room with a View.* New York: Dover, 1995.

Gide, André. *Voyage au Congo: Carnets de Route.* Paris: Gallimard, 1927.

Gide, André, Journal. Bibliothèque de la Pléiade, 54. Paris: Gallimard, 1951–1954.

Gu Hua. *A Small Town Called Hibiscus.* Beijing: Panda, 1985.

————. *Pagoda Ridge.* Trans. Gladys Yang. Beijing: Panda, 1985.

Havel, Vaclav. *Summer Meditations.* Trans. Paul Wilson. Reprint edition. New York: Vintage Books, 1993.

Havel, Vaclav. "A Grand Illusion? An Essay on Europe." Annual New York Review of Books and Hill and Wang Lecture Series. No. 3 Tony Judt, Ed. New York: Hill & Wang, 1996.

Holm, William. *Coming Home Crazy; An Alphabet of China Essays.* Minneapolis: Milkweed Editions, 1990.

Kingsley, Mary. *Travels in West Africa.* Everyman's Library. London: Dent, 1992.

Kundera, Milan. *The Unbearable Lightness of Being.* Perennial Classics. Trans. Michael Henry Heim. Harperperennial Library, repr. May 1999.

Montaigne, Michel de. *Essais.* Pierre Michel, Ed. Paris: Livre de Poche, 1965.

Montesquieu, Charles de Secondat, baron de. *Lettres Persanes.* Paris: Garnier, 1960.

Nhat Hanh, Thich. *The Stone Boy and Other Stories.* Berkeley: Parallax Press, 1996.

O'Hanlon, Redmond. *Into the Heart of Borneo.* New York: Random House, 1984.

Rushdie, Salman. *The Jaguar Smile: A Nicaraguan Journey.* Reprint. New York: Henry Holt, 1997.

Rushdie, Salman. *Midnight's Children.* Reprint. New York: Penguin, 1995.

Salzman, Mark. *Iron and Silk.* New York: Vintage, 1986.

Shostak, Marjorie. *Nisa: The Life and Words of a !Kung Woman.* New York: Vintage, 1983.

Zinsser, William, Ed. *They Went: The Art and Craft of Travel Writing.* Boston: Houghton Mifflin, 1991.

Getting the Most Out of Your Travels

Examples of useful guidebooks to buy before you go or while in-country:

Atkinson, R.J.C. *The Prehistoric Temples of Stonehenge and Avebury.* London: Pitkin Pictorials, Ltd., 1980.

Barber, Chips. *The Great Little Exeter Book: A General Guide.* Exeter: Obelisk Publications, 1994.

Bernhardson, Wayne. *Buenos Aires.* Oakland, CA: Lonely Planet, 1996.

Berry, Tom, Ed. *Mexico: A Country Guide.* Albuquerque: The Inter-Hemispheric Education Resource Center, 1992.

Booz, Patrick. *Yunnan: Southwest China's Little-Known Land of Eternal Spring.* Lincolnwood, IL: Passport Books, 1987.

Cant, R.G., Ed. *St. Andrews: The Preservation Trust Guide and Handbook.* St. Andrews: St. Andrews Preservation Trust, 1982.

Cunliffe, Barry. *The Roman Baths: A View over 2000 Years.* Bath: Bath Archeological Trust, 1993.

Decaens, Henry. *The City of Rouen.* Trans. Paul Williams, Angela Moyon. Rennes: Ouest-France, 1983.

Höfer, Hans, Ed. *Argentina.* Insight Guides, Boston: Houghton Mifflin, 1997.

McNeely, Scott, Ed. *Europe on a Shoestring.* Melbourne: Lonely Planet, 1999.

Routier-Le Diraison, Christine. *Frommer's Touring Guide to Thailand.* New York: Prentice Hall, 1988.

Scott, David. *Exploring Japan.* New York: Fodor's, 1998.

Tucker, Alan. *The Penguin Guide to Ireland.* New York: Penguin, 1990.

Zhewen, Luo and Shen Peng. *Through the Moon Gate: A Guide to China's Historic Monuments.* Hong Kong: Oxford University Press, 1986.

Building Language Skills

Examples of books that help you to learn useful phrases or brush up on a language you have studied:

Aria, Barbara. *The Nature of the Chinese Character.* New York: Simon and Schuster, 1991.

Berlitz. *Essential Spanish: The Practical Approach to Learning Spanish from Berlitz.* New York: Berlitz, 1992.

———. *Spanish/English Dictionary.* Oxford: Berlitz, 1995.

———. *Spanish Phrasebook and Dictionary.* Oxford: Berlitz, 1993.

Cummings, Joe. *Thai Phrasebook*. Victoria: Lonely Planet, 1984.

Levieux, Michel and Eleanor. *Cassell's Colloquial French: A Handbook of Idiomatic Usage*. Rev. London: Cassell, 1980.

Lübke, Diethard. *Survival Spanish*. New York: Langenscheidt, 1991.

Marshall, Terry. *The Whole World Guide to Language Learning*. Yarmouth: Intercultural Press, 1989.

Murray, D.M. and T.W. Wong. *Noodle Words: An Introduction to Chinese and Japanese Characters*. Rutland: Tuttle, 1987.

Nanyang Siang Pau. *Learner's Chinese-English Dictionary*. Singapore: Umum Publisher, 1984.

T'ung, P.C. and D. E. Pollard. *Colloquial Chinese*. London: Routledge and Kegan Paul, 1987.

Improving Intercultural Communications

Advisor's Guide. Greenwich: American Institute for Foreign Study, 1992.

Althen, Gary. *Learning Across Cultures*. Washington: NAFSA, 1994.

Bateson, Gregory. *Steps to an Ecology of Mind*. New York: Ballantine, 1972.

Berry, Howard A. and Linda A. Chisholm. *How to Serve and Learn Abroad Effectively: Students Tell Students*. New York: The Partnership for Service Learning, 1992.

Bryson, Bill. *The Lost Continent: Travels in Small Town America*. London: Abacus, 1989.

———. *Neither Here nor There: Travels in Europe*. London: Minerva, 1995.

Clayre, Alasdair. *The Heart of the Dragon.* Boston: Houghton Mifflin, 1986.

Condon, John C. *Buenos Vecinos.* Yarmouth: Intercultural Press, 1994.

————. *With Respect to the Japanese.* Yarmouth: Intercultural Press, 1984.

Fisher, Glen. *International Negotiation: A Cross-Cultural Perspective.* Yarmouth: Intercultural Press, 1980.

Flemons, Douglas G. *Completing Distinctions: Interweaving the Ideas of Gregory Bateson and Taoism into a Unique Approach to Therapy.* Boston: Shambala, 1991.

Hall, Edward T. and Mildred Reed Hall. *Understanding Cultural Differences: Germans, French and Americans.* Yarmouth: Intercultural Press, 1990.

Ladd, Jennifer. *Subject: India: A Semester Abroad.* Yarmouth: Intercultural Press, 1990.

Lewis, Tom J. and Robert E. Jungman, Ed. *On Being Foreign: Culture Shock in Short Fiction, an International Anthology.* Yarmouth: Intercultural Press, 1986.

Mann, A.T. *Sacred Architecture.* Rockport, MA.: Element, Inc., 1993.

Munsterberg, Hugo. *Zen and Oriental Art.* Rutland: Tuttle, 1993.

Platt, Polly. *French or Foe? Getting the Most out of Visiting, Living and Working in France.* Skokie: Culture Crossings, 1995.

Renwick, George W., rev. Reginald Smart, Don L. Henderson, *A Fair Go for All: Australian/American Interactions.* Yarmouth: Intercultural Press, 1991.

Samovar, Larry A. and Richard E Porter. *Intercultural Communication: a Reader.* 6 ed. Belmont, CA: Wadsworth, 1972.

Steele, Ross; St. Onge, Susan; and Ronald St. Onge. *La civilisation française en évolution; institutions et culture de la Ve république.* Boston: Heinle and Heinle, 1997.

Storti, Craig. *The Art of Crossing Cultures.* Yarmouth: Intercultural Press, 1990.

Summerfield, Ellen. *Crossing Cultures Through Film.* Yarmouth: Intercultural Press, 1993.

Uyeki, Eugene. *As Others See Us: A Comparison of Japanese and American Fulbrighters.* New York: Japan-United States Educational Commission and IIE, 1993.

International Affairs, International Business, and Economics

Barnaby, Frank, Ed. *The Gaia Peace Atlas.* New York: Doubleday, 1988.

Bill, James A. *George Ball: Behind the Scenes in U.S. Foreign Policy.* New Haven: Yale University Press, 1997.

Kidder, Rushworth M. *Reinventing the Future: Global Goals for the 21st Century.* Cambridge: MIT Press, 1989.

Moyers, Bill et al. *At Century's End: Great Minds Reflect On Our Times.* La Jolla: ALTI Publishing, 1995.

"Samuel P. Huntington's *The Clash of Civilizations?* The Debate." *Foreign Affairs.* New York: Foreign Affairs, 1996.

Zakaria, Fareed, Ed. "The New Shape of World Politics: Contending Paradigms in International Relations." *Foreign Affairs Agenda.* New York: Foreign Affairs, 1997.

International Studies

AACRAO/NAFSA Task Force on Study Abroad, *Study Abroad Programs: An Evaluation Guide.* Washington, May 1979.

An Assessment of the Interdisciplinary Concentrations in East Asian Studies, European Studies, International Relations, Latin American Studies, Middle Eastern Studies, Russian Studies, and Minors in African Studies, East Asian Studies, International Relations, Japanese Studies, Latin American Studies, Middle Eastern Studies, Russian Studies. Unpublished self study. Williamsburg: The College of William and Mary, 1994.

Byrd, Marquita L. *The Intracultural Communication Book.* The College Custom Series. New York: McGraw-Hill, 1993.

Davis, Todd M., Ed. *Open Doors: Report on International Educational Exchange.* New York: Institute for International Education, annual.

Day-Vines, Norma. "The Ghana Project: a Proposal Submitted to the International Studies Committee of the College of William and Mary." Unpublished proposal to the International Studies Committee. Williamsburg, 1998.

Goodwin, Craugurd D. and Michael Nacht. *Missing the Boat: The Failure to Internationalize American Higher Education.* Cambridge; Cambridge University Press, 1991.

Gore, Joan Elias et al. *Cost-Effective Techniques for Internationalizing the Campus and Curriculum.* New York: Council for International Educational Exchange (CIEE), 1995.

Herrin, Carl A., Ed. *Japan-U.S. Exchanges: Trends, Opportunities and Barriers.* Washington: Alliance for Intercultural Exchange, 1996.

Other Approaches: Comparative Religion, Philosophy, Comparative Culture, Art History, and Ecology

A variety of perspectives on international issues, to illustrate how international study can contribute to many different disciplines:

Bryant, Bunyan, Ed. *The Future: Images for the 21st Century.* Ann Arbor: University of Michigan Office of the Vice President for Minority Affairs and the Environmental Equity Institute, 1993.

Brown, Lester, Ed. et al. *State of the World 1999: A Worldwatch Report on Progress Toward a Sustainable Society.* New York: W.W. Norton, 1999.

Buck, William, trans. *Mahabharata.* Berkeley: University of California Press, 1973.

Burckhardt, Jacob. *The Civilization of the Renaissance in Italy.* trans. S.G.C. Middlemore. London: Phaidon Press, Ltd., 1950.

Forbath, Peter. *The River Congo: The Discovery, Exploration, and Exploitation of the World's Most Dramatic River.* Boston: Houghton Mifflin, 1977.

Guided Business Research (GBR). *Opportunity in Japan, Vol. II: The Kansai Region.* Osaka: GBR, 1996.

Kaptchuk, Ted J. *The Web That Has No Weaver: Understanding Chinese Medicine.* New York: Congdon and Weed, 1983.

Lamb, David. *The Africans.* New York: Vintage, 1987.

Manning, Patrick. *Francophone Sub-Saharan Africa 1880–1985.* Cambridge: Cambridge University Press, 1989.

Morris, Mary, Ed. *Maiden Voyages: Writings of Women Travelers,* New York: Vintage, 1993.

Nhat Hanh, Thich. *The Miracle of Mindfulness: A Manual on Meditation.* Trans. Mobi Ho. Boston: Beacon, 1987.

O'Neill, John. *Making Sense Together: An Introduction to Wild Sociology.* New York: Harper Torchbooks, 1974.

O'Sullivan, Jerry. *Teaching English in Japan.* Lincolnwood: Passport Books, 1996.

Prime, Ranchor. *Ramayana: A Journey.* London: Welcome Rain, 1988.

Steichen, Edward. *The Family of Man.* Catalog of photography exhibition, Museum of Modern Art. New York: Simon and Schuster, 1955.

Tregear, Mary. *Chinese Art.* London: Thames and Hudson, 1993.

A

Academic calendars
  island programs, 46
  universities, 43
Academic references,
  184–187, 438–439
Academic Travel Service,
  277
Academic Year Abroad, 22
Acceptance to programs,
  192–193
Addresses, forwarding, 396
Advanced Studies in
  England, 465
Advising, study abroad
  offices, 162–165,
  225–227, 411–412
  international programs,
  45
  island programs, 45
  universities, 41–42
AIFS College Summer
  Division, 90
Airlines
  airport maps, 280
  consolidators, 275–276
  cost, 136
  courier flights, 279–280
  discount fares, 277–279
  economy fares, 275
  frequent flyer miles, 282
  jet lag, 331–335
  lost tickets, 324
  luggage, 328
  reservations, 282–284,
  319–323
  safety, 284
  seat availability, 401–402
  strikes, 327–328
  Web sites, 422, 474–476
Alcohol consumption
  host countries, 360–363
  jet lag, 332
Alliance Francaise, 37, 465

Alliance for International
  Educational and
  Cultural Exchange
  (AIECE), 91
Allocation familiale, 447
American Airlines, 278
American colleges, 464
American Institute for
  Foreign Study (AIFS),
  464
American Model United
  Nations, Inc. (AMUN),
  420, 471
AmeriSpan Unlimited, 91
Apartment rentals, 207–209
Apostille, 447
Appliances, 305–306
Applications
  acceptance, 192–193
  financial aid, 148
  identification photos, 179
  mailing, 191–192
  non-traditional students,
  70–73
  passports, 180–183
  personal statements,
  189–191
  rejection letters, 193–195
  scholarships, 431, 432
  signatures, 187–188
  submission of, 188–189
  visas, 236
    preparation, 251
    requirements,
    239–240
    Web sites, 237–238
Approval process
  coursework, 218–220
  credits, 221–222
  graduation, 226
  honors projects, 226–228
  independent study,
  222–223
  internships, 224–225
  journal writing, 223–224
Argentina, 389

499